Control and Consolation in American Culture and Politics

RHETORIC AND SOCIETY

edited by Herbert W. Simons
Temple University

EDITORIAL BOARD

This series will publish a broad-based collection of advanced texts and innovative works encompassing rhetoric in the civic arena, in the arts and media, in the academic disciplines, and in everyday cultural practices.

Books in this series:

Control and Consolation in American Culture and Politics: Rhetorics of Therapy
Dana L. Cloud

Communication Criticism: Developing Your Critical Powers
Jodi Cohen

DANA L. CLOUD

Control and Consolation in American Culture and Politics

Rhetorics of Therapy

Rhetoric&Society

SAGE Publications
International Educational and Professional Publisher
Thousand Oaks   London   New Delhi

For information:

SAGE Publications, Inc.
2455 Teller Road
Thousand Oaks, California 91320
E-mail: order@sagepub.com

SAGE Publications Ltd.
6 Bonhill Street
London EC2A 4PU
United Kingdom

SAGE Publications India Pvt. Ltd.
M-32 Market
Greater Kailash I
New Delhi 110 048 India

Printed in the United States of America

Library of Congress Cataloging-in-Publication Data

Cloud, Dana L.
    Control and consolation in American culture and politics:
Rhetorics of therapy / by Dana L. Cloud.
        p. cm. — (Rhetoric & society; v. 1)
    Includes bibliographical references (p.) and index.
    ISBN 0-7619-0506-5 (cloth: acid-free paper) —
ISBN 0-7619-0507-3 (pbk.: acid-free paper)
    1. Social problems—United States—Psychological aspects.
2. Psychotherapy—Social aspects—United States. 3. Psychotherapy—
Political aspects—United States. 4. Psychoanalysis and culture—
United States. 5. Social control—United States. 6. Rhetoric and
psychology. I. Title. II. Series: Rhetoric & society (Thousand
Oaks, Calif.); v.1.
    HN59.2.C59 1997
    361.1'0973—dc21   97-21153

98 99 00 01 02 03 10 9 8 7 6 5 4 3 2 1

Acquiring Editor:	Margaret Seawell
Editorial Assistant:	Renée Piernot
Production Editor:	Michèle Lingre
Production Assistant:	Lynn Miyata
Typesetter/Designer:	Janelle LeMaster
Indexer:	Cristina Haley
Cover Designer:	Candice Harman
Print Buyer:	Anna Chin

Contents

Foreword

With the publication of Professor Cloud's bold offering, Sage launches its new series on "Rhetoric and Society." When Sage and I talked of starting a series encompassing rhetoric in the political arena, in the arts and mass media, in the academic disciplines, and in everyday interpersonal relations, little did we imagine that our first book would encompass all of these areas!

Operating from a materialist Marxism, as opposed to the culturalist academic neo-Marxisms that are fashionable these days, Cloud takes aim at "therapeutic rhetorics" of the right, left, and center in the United States, ranging from conservative family values discourse to popular feminine texts like Gloria Steinem's *Revolution from Within.* Says Cloud,

> This work defines what I call "the rhetoric of therapy," the discursive deployment of themes of consolation, waiting, coping, adaptation, and healing in response to economic, political or social crisis. The rhetoric of therapy dislocates political anger that might be directed toward structural social change onto the individual and family, framing responses to crisis in terms of private life.

Lest readers assume that she is opposed to visits to a psychotherapist for the usual run of problems, Professor Cloud sets the record straight. Go, she says, but preferably to a therapist who will contextualize your suffering in terms of social, political, and economic realities, and who won't discourage public, collective forms of protest against the broader conditions of human alienation, exploitation, and oppression.

More significantly, she argues, recognize that therapeutic orientations are "pervasive across popular and political realms, influential in and constitutive of both dominant culture and 'oppositional rhetorics.' " Contemporary American therapy has come, for example, in the form of support group news during the Persian Gulf War, the New Age movement, and the film *Thelma & Louise.*

In focusing on political and popular discourse, Cloud seeks to demonstrate that the decay of American civic life—manifested, for example, in the decline of public engagement and community responsibility—is partially an effect of persuasive therapeutic discourses, which are in turn a consequence of the growing interpretation of the public and private spheres of experience. Together with the introductory and concluding chapters, her case studies provide both a comprehensive and detailed examination of specific texts and a broad critique of political culture in the United States.

Trained in rhetoric and cultural studies, Professor Cloud currently teaches at the University of Texas in Austin. Her book is designed to reach a wide academic audience. Because of its close attention to texts, the book would make an excellent graduate level text providing model essays in rhetorical criticism and the rhetoric of popular culture. The book's intervention into current debates in communication studies about hegemony and popular culture will interest feminist critics and other cultural studies scholars. Potential audiences for this book also include political philosophers and social theorists, communitarians critical of individualism in America, American studies scholars, and postmodern critical scholars.

Acknowledgments

I have many people to thank for their support and advice during the process of writing this book. First, I owe a debt to *Rhetoric and Society* series editor Herbert W. Simons for his careful reading and exhortations to rhetorical moderation; what buffers against stridency there are herein are probably his suggestions. (The polemics are still all mine.) I also thank Stacey Connaughton, an extraordinary graduate student, editor, and research assistant, without whose tireless and meticulous work this book would not have seen publication.

I am also grateful to the many readers who have responded to and guided this project since its beginnings in 1992 as my doctoral dissertation, especially my dissertation committee at the University of Iowa: John Peters, Bruce Gronbeck, Michael McGee, Lauren Rabinovitz, and Paul Adams. Their advice on writing and the scholarly life still guides me.

At the University of Texas, my colleagues and students have provided an intellectual community in which the ideas herein have been tested, nourished, challenged, and revised. I am grateful to them for their rigor and support. In particular, Rod Hart provided support during the review and publication process, Naomi Warren provided a very helpful critical reading of the chapter on family values, and Kelly Fudge helped compile a mountain of Lexis-Nexis documents on "family values" during the summer of 1992.

In addition, I thank Susan Whalen for her insights about workplace therapies; and Jill Morawski and Ellen Herman, both scholars of psychology, whose correspondence and encouragement from afar meant a great deal to me as I sought a publisher for the manuscript.

This research was supported by the University of Texas Research Institute in the form of a Summer Research Award and a Special Research Grant for the study of the rhetoric of family values and by a College of Communication Jamail Grant for assistance in revisions, research assistance, and editing.

I reserve my deepest gratitude, however, for Keith Hutchinson and our daughter Samantha, who sustained me through this project and shaped this work and my life in immeasurable and uncounted ways.

For Rosa,
Proof that friendship is thicker than therapy.

Introduction

On Therapy and the Therapeutic

> Psychotherapy, generically understood, is more than a development
> of medicine or science; it is a phenomenon of culture, an aspect of
> the *zeitgeist* of twentieth-century America.
>
> —*Richard Weiss (1969, 195)*

In June 1996, the United States Census Bureau reported that this decade's disparities in wealth between the rich and the poor rival those of the pre-World War II era. Since 1979, the average American standard of living has declined by 20%; it declined by 7% between 1992 and 1994. By late 1994, 66.8% of the nation's wealth was held by the most prosperous 10% of the population (Bradsher 1996).[1] As Republican political analyst Kevin Phillips (1990) has warned, this kind of systematic, intensifying economic polarization has led, historically, to open class conflict and widespread social unrest.

In recent years, we have also seen an upsurge of other kinds of injustice, including racism. At the grassroots level, right-wing militias and hate groups such as the Ku Klux Klan have become more prominent, and the wave of black church arsons that swept the South during the spring of 1996 put the nation on alert: Racism is alive and well. Mainstream politicians, such as California Governor Pete Wilson and presidential candidate Pat Buchanan, have also participated in the scapegoating of immigrants and minorities for the nation's economic problems.

At the same time, women and gays and lesbians have been charged with contributing to the demise of the American family and of social order in general; the rhetoric of traditional "family values" has been concomitant with an accelerating erosion of women's rights, including the right to choose abortion and equal wages for equal work. We are, by many accounts, living during the "twilight of the American dream"—the era of a disaffected "Generation X," whose members will be the first in American history to be worse off than their parents, doomed to a series of McJobs and free only in virtual reality; material reality for young people today, as the 1994 film title suggests, "bites."[2]

What has been the popular and political response to this crisis of the American Dream? In this book, I argue that "therapeutic persuasions" have become the prevailing strategy of crisis management, offered by politicians, managers, and entertainers as ways of coping with the crisis. The following example illustrates the trend. A recent, best-selling handbook by Price Pritchett (1994), titled "New Work Habits for a Radically Changing World," was distributed in response to worker protests against unfair compensation and benefits practices at Texas state agencies. The text acknowledges worker discontent, anger, and fear in the current climate of downsizing, temporary work, and technological change as follows:

> Your organization will keep reshaping itself, shifting and flexing to fit our rapidly changing world. That's the *only* way it can hope to survive in this fiercely competitive environment. Look for it to restructure, outsource, downsize, subcontract, and form new alliances.
>
> You also can expect flexible ways of working. Duties will be constantly realigned. Short-lived assignments will be common. Maybe you'll work on a contract basis, or spend time on several project teams. You might even end up working for more than one "employer" at a time. You'll probably have a constantly new set of coworkers, more new bosses, even new careers. You're not going to like some of this.[3]

This passage, like many others in the pamphlet, euphemistically calls attention to some of the difficulties facing workers: "flexible ways of working" (shorter and inconsistent hours and temporary work for multiple employers); "realigned duties" (demotions for less pay); "outsourcing" (seeking out nonunion or private shops to do the work for less, shafting one's own workers and undercutting their wages); "downsizing" (hit the road, Jack); and "forming new alliances" (mergers, often resulting in downsizing).

Although refusing to blame owners or managers for these problems (even as profits skyrocket, as did AT&T's after layoffs of 40,000 employees in 1996), the pamphlet does acknowledge worker anxiety. What does it advise the worker to do? "Granted change can be painful. When it damages careers, emotions such as grief, anger, and depression come naturally. . . . Shoot for rapid recovery. Take personal responsibility for adapting to change." These phrases contain therapeutic buzzwords: "personal responsibility," "recovery," and "adapting." Such linguistic markers indicate that the text is working to personalize and privatize responses to crisis, turning workplace uncertainty and owners' ruthlessness into personal "grief, anger, and depression" that are, this rhetoric suggests, natural psychological phenomena rather than effects of decisions and actions made by business owners.

The "New Work Habits" pamphlet is emblematic of what I call therapeutic discourse. This pamphlet acknowledges and even accepts the existence of collective discontent and anger at systematic injustice. The text also recognizes that structural social conditions have produced the hardships that workers experience. Rather than offering systematic, collective redress or compensation for those hardships, however, the text's central rhetorical strategy involves utilizing words of consolation and advice for personal coping and survival. Like therapeutic discourse generally, the text substitutes symbolic consolation when material compensation has been demanded. Notably, such rhetoric is often recommended by management consultants to be a strategic intervention into a situation of conflict or crisis between management and workers—a situation that could escalate into a strike or other collective demonstration that would force the agency to compensate workers. *Control and Consolation in American Culture and Politics* is about how this rhetorical strategy of offering therapeutic consolation as a substitute for political and economic compensation has become a commonplace diversion from political engagement in contemporary American society.

At many points in U.S. history, social movements have risen to confront systematic economic and social injustice. The power of these movements stemmed both from the symbolic power of mass demonstration of collective cause and from the material threats posed to employers by workers willing to strike for economic justice. Across the decades, labor, civil rights, and women's and gay and lesbian movements all have challenged administrators, politicians, and employers to reform the capitalist system and ameliorate racism and sexism.

Currently, such movements continue to struggle for voice and power. Since 1968, however, therapy has become an increasingly persuasive alternative to political action from below. In response to the racialized urban crisis in Los Angeles in 1992, for instance, politicians blamed the unrest on a lack of family values, scapegoating people in their private lives for a problem with clear economic and political dimensions.

In response to what Susan Faludi has called an antifeminist backlash in popular culture and politics, feminist activist Gloria Steinem came out with a new plan for a "revolution from within" based on self-esteem. Family support groups were more prominent than antiwar activism during the Persian Gulf War, and former Marxists and feminists have, since the collapse of Stalinism, hailed a politics of self-expression, consciousness-raising, and social fragmentation as the new avenue for change.

Meanwhile, psychotherapists have taken to the airwaves, as talk show hosts, with the help of talk show psychologists, attempt to resolve their guests' conflicts in the space of minutes. Talk show producer Mary Duffy explained to a *New York Times* reporter that the therapists are there to "help the audience, too" (Berger 1995, 33).[4] To help the audience with what? Although popularized therapy claims to help individual people with their personal problems, the discourse of therapy serves a broader, cultural function for mass audiences: to offer psychological ministration for the ills of society. A common argument (Flacks 1988, Lasch 1979, Loeb 1994) suggests that since the Vietnam War, American culture and the American people have lost sight of political and social commitment and public responsibility in the narcissistic pursuit of individual interests. As Christopher Lasch wrote more than 15 years ago, "After the political turmoil of the sixties, Americans have retreated to purely personal preoccupations" (29). Scholars and activists on the Left should take warning: What were once political movements have become translated into personal quests for fulfillment.

My argument about this social transformation stands in contrast to other perspectives on the therapeutic. Unlike communitarians (Left and Right), who see the retreat into narcissism as a moral failure of our culture, I regard the therapeutic as a political strategy of contemporary capitalism, by which potential dissent is contained within a discourse of individual or family responsibility. Against postmodernists who celebrate the atomization of contemporary culture and proclaim the death of mass collective action for social change, I see a real need to repoliticize issues of power as a precondition for renewed oppositional social movement organizing. In contrast to scholars of liberalism who applaud therapy's near-exclusive emphasis on individual initiative and personal responsibility, my argument insists on acknowledging the collective and structural features of an unequal social reality in which individuals are embedded and out of which our personal experience, in large part, derives. Racism, sexism, and capitalism pose significant obstacles to individual mobility and well-being; their roles in structuring social reality, however, are obscured in therapeutic discourses that locate the ill not with the society but with the individual or private family. The goals of this book are to develop and argue for a materialist rhetoric of therapy that locates the emergence of therapeutic discourse at a particular historical moment, to link the rise of the therapeutic with particular political and economic interests, and to describe the specific mechanisms by which the therapeutic is a persuasive part of our culture.

Other therapy historians have located the emergence of psychotherapeutic practices and discourses with modern capitalism and its imperatives to privatize social responsibility, to stifle dissent, and to promote the elaboration of identity through consumption (e.g., Cushman 1995, Foucault 1973, Goffman 1961, Herman 1995, Lears 1983). In addition, the communitarian movement, emphasizing the importance of community belonging and responsibility over individual freedom and autonomy, has generated several key scholarly critiques of the ways in which therapeutic society exhorts citizens to abandon civic hope and responsibility in favor of the cultivation of lifestyle and self (Bellah et al. 1985, Etzioni 1993, Lasch 1984, Rieff 1966, Sandel 1982, Waltzer 1990). Finally, there has been among psychologists and psychiatrists a challenge to the individualist, apolitical limits of traditional psychotherapies (e.g., Agel 1972, Brown 1994, Cushman 1990, Hillman and Ventura 1992, Laing 1967).

I hope to contribute two things to this conversation: First, this book provides critical case studies that describe in detail not only what the therapeutic looks like but also how and why therapeutic discourses are persuasive. Second, although several scholars have noted the links between the therapeutic and modernity *writ* large, my argument is more specifically focused on how therapeutic rhetorics are situated at moments of social or political movement or crisis, delegitimating political outrage and collective activity in favor of more private endeavors. Thus, I am interested not only in "therapy" as a historical phenomenon and as a clinical practice but also in "the therapeutic" as a set of politically motivated instrumental discourses that can be described, explained in their political contexts, and evaluated.

In this book, the *therapeutic* refers to a set of political and cultural discourses that have adopted psychotherapy's lexicon—the conservative language of healing, coping, adaptation, and restoration of a previously existing order—but in contexts of sociopolitical conflict. The rhetorical function of therapeutic discourses in such contexts is to encourage audiences to focus on themselves and the elaboration of their private lives rather than to address and attempt to reform systems of social power in which they are embedded. Thus, we can view the therapeutic as having restorative and conservative effects in the face of conflict and change.

The agents of this discourse are everywhere and nowhere. It may seem somewhat abstract to suggest that capitalism itself deploys a therapeutic rhetorical strategy to respond to, acknowledge, and contain crisis. The very pervasiveness and proliferation of such rhetorics, however, make the therapeutic so influential in channeling individual responses to exploitation, alienation, isolation, oppression, and other socially pro-duced hardships. In Foucaultian terms, the therapeutic is an episteme, a discourse formation elaborated at many sites and spoken in diverse voices. I am calling it a rhetoric because, despite the scope of the therapeutic, in specific situations therapy serves clearly identifiable, strategic, and therefore rhetorical functions in public and private life.

Although this book focuses on the uses of therapeutic jingoism in political contexts—the Gulf War, the feminist movement, the New Age movement, and the rhetoric of family values—we cannot let psychother-apy, itself a body of theories and practices, entirely off the hook as part and parcel of the therapeutic society. Historians of therapy and of the therapeutic document the emergence of pychotherapeutic practices at the turn of the century, alongside the emergence of advertising and other consumerist cultural forms (see Chapter 2 for a full account of this history). Therapy is a historical product of modernity; more specifically, it is a product of industrial capitalist social imperatives and therefore cannot be separated from a critical assessment of the broader therapeutic society.

My own intellectual stance regarding psychotherapy is ambivalent. Psychotherapy is a politically contradictory phenomenon that sometimes helps suffering people even as it can reinscribe individuals into the very social relations that produced their "illnesses." This contradiction, however, also makes the therapeutic persuasive: It can admit to the existence of suffering in modern society without having to transform the society publicly or structurally. I think therapy is at times useful in generating insight and transformation among people who suffer from mental illness or who are disabled or maladjusted within their personal and social lives. Therapy is valuable for many individuals attempting to survive against the odds of unemployment, family stress, sexual and domestic violence, childhood abuse, and other traumas. These experiences are often rooted in widespread social structures, such as women's oppression, racism, and capitalism, but are felt at the level of the individual. Rarely have I known a person in a life crisis, suffering from depression or living with ongoing abuse, who is also a productive and engaged political activist. Sometimes, survival and coping, with the help of therapists and medication, are reasonably all that can be accomplished.

Furthermore, even when mental illness is explained in terms of social experience, it is experienced personally by individuals who require professional intervention and treatment. Psychosis, for example, generates a radical disconnection from the world that disables afflicted individuals. I do not want to romanticize schizophrenia as some social theorists do, mistaking severe mental disorientation for political activism (Deleuze and Guattari 1983). Even when psychotic responses to trauma are socially generated (e.g., within the nuclear family's contradictory set of expectations, as R. D. Laing suggests), these responses should not be heralded as emancipatory political expression, as if the sufferer had willful control over his or her interventions into political space.

I also grant that not all psychological problems have sociopolitical roots; recent research suggests that mental illness probably results from a mixture of organic features heavily influenced by the sociopolitical contexts and experiences of the individual. The efficacy of psychoactive drugs such as Prozac indicates that there may be some organic basis to psychological characteristics such as a tendency toward depression and shyness. Likewise, natural disaster or personal trauma, such as the illness or death of a loved one, can lead to distress requiring psychotherapeutic rather than political redress.

We ought not underestimate, however, the extent to which many psychological problems do, in fact, have social and political origins. The very categories we have available to us for naming and diagnosing mental illnesses have been constructed within social and political contexts. The availability of certain diagnostic categories themselves creates the possibility of labeling a sociopolitical condition as an "illness" to be cured. In a sense, psychiatry and psychology have "invented" mental illnesses through the elaboration of diagnostic schemata. This process of invention and construction always occurs in a historical context, influenced by the prevailing social climate. A cursory look at the evolution of the American Psychological Association's (APA) *Diagnostic and Statistical Manual of Mental Disorders* (DSM) over four massive editions shows that what "counts" as a mental illness changes over time given historical circumstances.

For example, homosexuality was once defined as a diagnostic category and disorder that therapists were to "cure" or treat as an illness. In the *DSM-IV,* however, homosexuality no longer appears on the list of mental illnesses. Ongoing battles in the APA over the diagnostic categories to be included in future versions of the DSM persist; feminists, for example, have had to fight not to have characteristics associated with femininity itself (menstruation and reproduction, the effects on women of domestic isolation, social training to nurture and empathize, and so on) defined as diseases. Clearly, diagnosis and treatment are influenced by social and political factors, resulting sometimes in treatments that oppress some groups, such as women or gays and lesbians.[5]

Psychoactive medication, like diagnostic categorization, can itself become a kind of social discipline. This possibility worries psychiatrist Peter Kramer (1993). As Kramer explains in his controversial book, *Listening to Prozac,* one function of psychiatry, and psychiatric medication, is to adjust people to their society and to enable them to adapt and cope with difficult situations. Those situations—including economic hardship, violence, lack of control over one's daily life, racism, and sexism— are often products of a society that is unequal and unjust rather than originating as intrapsychic illnesses. Kramer questions (but ultimately approves) the use of "thymoleptics," or drugs that stimulate neurotransmitters to produce a self who is dynamic, cheerful, and assertive:

> The argument can be made that, in "curing" women of traditional, passive feminine traits and instilling in good responders the attributes of a more robust feminine ideal, Prozac reinforces the cultural expectations of a particularly exigent form of social organization. . . . On the one hand, Prozac supports social stasis by allowing people to move toward a cultural ideal—the flexible, contented, energetic, pleasure-driven consumer. (271)

Kramer's concern is that even though Prozac and other antidepressants "help" people afflicted with depression, they exert a kind of social influence too, encouraging people to become "flexible, contented, energetic, and pleasure-driven" rather than active in their local community politics or social movement. Implied in his provocative writing about Prozac is the assumption that allowing people to adapt to their society can rid them of discomfort or anger they may legitimately feel against the social system itself.

The important point is, however, that many traumas associated with modern industrial life can be ascribed in part to the social, economic, and political conditions of life in such a society. For this reason, psychotherapy boomed in response to industrialization in the United States and around the globe. The stresses of assembly line or low-wage service economy work, the experiences of racism and sexism, the lack of control over technology or over the material conditions of one's daily life (wages, health care, housing, etc.), oppressions and isolation felt within the modern nuclear family (e.g., child sexual abuse and women's "double shift"), and the pressures of competition and consumption can generate a need for apparatuses and discourses to adjust people, psychologically, to function under such conditions.

When there are social causes, in whole or in part, of psychological distress (one thinks of the aftermath of sexual assault, posttraumatic stress associated with participating in warfare or working for the post office, or anorexia and bulimia), radical and feminist therapists take care to contextualize the experience of suffering in social and political terms, deflect blame away from the individual patient, and hold responsible structures of power generative of psychological distress.

Although psychotherapies do not always enable such contextualization, I do not mean to imply that they do no good. Mental illness is political in the sense that it can represent an encrypted expression of individual frustration with, anger at, and disclosure of a person's situation, which is of necessity socially embedded. Consequently, therapy may be a central way in which the conditions of life under modern capitalism are made bearable and through which the signs of mental distress can be decoded as a critical comment on how we live. In the best of circumstances—that is, with a radical or feminist therapist or in politicized consciousness-raising—therapy can generate the understanding necessary for political critique and action.

When the motifs of therapy, presuming intrapsychic rather than—and to the exclusion of attention to—social illness, are elaborated and deployed in political contexts, however, the effect is ultimately disabling to our collective political life. Therapeutic motifs at the level of cultural persuasion work against the formulation of a collective political project in the public sphere. This book does not deny that therapy can do good work for individuals. My question is not about what therapy does for us privately. Rather, this book asks, What are the consequences of a therapeutic rhetoric for politics, activism, and social change? Since the turn of the century, therapy has been with us as a hegemonic alternative to reacting to sociopolitical trouble in a sociopolitical way. As psychology historian Philip Cushman (1995) has suggested, American psychotherapy from its inception has allowed for new ways of talking about social and political life that are privatizing, but today are taken for granted (see Weiss 1969, for a condensed version of this history). Cushman writes,

> When social artifacts or institutions are taken for granted it usually means that they have developed functions in the society that are so integral to the culture that they are indispensable, unacknowledged, and finally, invisible. . . . Vast historical changes in the last 500 years in the West have slowly created a world in which the individual is commonly understood to be a container of "mind" and more recently a "self" that needs to be "therapied," rather than, say, a carrier of a divine soul that needs to be saved, or simply an element of the communal unit that must cooperate for the common good. There were, of course, sociopolitical reasons for these changes, and there must be groups and institutions that currently profit from the changes. (1-2)[6]

The aim of this book is to develop a set of critical case studies of taken-for-granted therapeutic discourses to reveal their integral rhetorical functions in contemporary capitalist society. My argument is that the therapeutic, as a situated, strategic discourse (or rhetoric), dislocates social and political conflicts onto individuals or families, privatizes both the experience of oppression and possible modes of resistance to it, and translates political questions into psychological issues to be resolved through personal, psychological change.

The diversion of political outrage into personal misery and consolation via the therapeutic is an old theme in American culture (Lears 1983, see also Cushman 1995), dating back at least 100 years to the rise of mass culture and the welfare state, which culminated in the New Deal. Philip Cushman (1995) begins his story about the emergence of psychotherapy alongside advertising as emblematic of American liberal capitalism at the turn of the century—developments indicating "a trend toward ignoring sociopolitical causes of personal suffering" (67).[7] As I argue, the therapeutic is an ideological mechanism of the liberal ideology deployed in response to social crisis at different times in U.S. history. My project, in particular, focuses on the post-Vietnam War period in the United States as one instance of such crisis—a time during which one clearly can perceive the workings of the therapeutic in response to the social upheavals and oppositional agitation of the late 1960s and early 1970s. I suggest that the crises in capitalism generating the political upheavals of the 1960s and 1970s led to a need for the system to recuperate challenges to itself. The themes and motifs of therapy, when articulated in the context of political opposition, have worked historically to blunt radical politics in the United States. In the pseudopolitics of the therapeutic, in the individualism of the self-help explosion, and in the translation of outrage over political or economic roots of crisis (e.g., unemployment, poverty, war, and overwork) into interpersonal rage and of collective structural problems into personal work, this recovery was partially accomplished and is ongoing in society today.

After I lay the theoretical foundations for a critique of the therapeutic in Chapter 1 and the historical trajectory of the therapeutic in Chapter 2, the greater part of the book traces the characteristics of therapy as a rhetoric and an ideology through several popular and political discourse formations. Chapter 3 unpacks the rhetoric of family values in popular culture, exposing the therapeutic strategy of blaming the family for social ills. Although communitarians sometimes hold up the family as the antidote to therapeutic individualism, I argue that familism is a form of the therapeutic. Chapter 4, a study of "support group" news during the Persian Gulf War, documents the news media's narrative process of acknowledging social problems; assigning blame; instilling guilt, shame, or anxiety; and offering redemption or consolation in personal terms. Support group news during the Persian Gulf War depended on a particular gendered mapping of the "home front" that created consolatory rather than political space for discussing the war.

Chapter 5 analyzes Gloria Steinem's *Revolution From Within* and the 1991 film *Thelma & Louise* as popular feminist texts that, unfortunately, participate in the therapeutic dislocation of political (feminist) anger. Each chapter describes and analyzes discourse employing the language of therapy to talk about political issues to determine if and how those discourses function to label oppositional ideas and encourage identification with the therapeutic ethos. Similarly, Chapter 6 lays out the therapeutic assumptions of the still-popular New Age "movement" and posits an analogy between New Age thinking and postmodernist social theory. I argue that in the post-Marxist rejection of economistic, class-based analyses of social reality, the Left enacts its own therapeutic retreat from political agency. The conclusion uniting these case studies, laid out in the last section of the book, is that the rhetoric of therapy is an ideological frame that bounds conceptions of political action and that works as a discourse of social control. The final chapter, then, constitutes a warning against political therapies and a challenge to envision and enact a public antitherapeutic politics in the postmodern age.

As a conservative ideological strategy of contemporary capitalism in the United States, therapy is clearly a political discourse, with political motives and political effects. Ironically, however, the political effect of the therapeutic is to shut down the possibility of public deliberation and collective engagement in politics. For this reason, throughout this book I clearly distinguish between the therapeutic and the engaged project of oppositional political activity. Even though therapy and politics, private and public, are ends of a spectrum rather than stark opposites, I believe it is important to emphasize the debilitating consequences of therapeutic discourse for those working for social change. Furthermore, I pose collective, public challenges to systems of exploitation and oppression as a clear alternative to therapeutic responses. Since the Vietnam era, the therapeutic imperative has ascended in the popular representations and framings of political issues, even within discourses posed as oppositional to established economic interests.

Certainly, therapy has its place: as an enabler of individual healing after personal trauma and as a prepolitical precursor to public engagement. It is inadequate, however, as a stand-in for public politics. In mass culture, therapeutic narratives neutralize anger and obscure the structures of power in which we must come to see our location and our work.

Let us move, then, to Chapter 1, which explores the various critiques of therapy and the therapeutic from communitarian to poststructuralist arguments. In Chapter 1, I hope to lay the foundation for a materialist rhetoric of therapy or an understanding of the therapeutic as a modern ideological, strategic discourse that has as its ultimate effects the privatization of social experience and the disciplining of private subjects into a regime of self-blame and personal responsibility.

Notes

1. © 1996 New York Times. Reproduced with permission.
2. *Reality Bites* features Winona Ryder as a college graduate who cannot find a job. Shortly after the film's release, *Money* magazine (Fenner 1994, 90ff) noted that fiction reflects fact: "From 1989 to 1993, anticipated hiring of first-year college grads by medium-size and large U.S. companies was off a full 35%." Similarly, the *Economist* ("Generation X-Onomics," 1994 27: © 1994 The Economist Newspaper Group, Inc. Reprinted with permission) reported that college graduates in the United States start off in debt, often take part-time or temporary work in a market in which 22% of Americans are employed part-time or temporarily, and work for low (and declining) wages.
3. © 1994 Price Pritchett and Associates. Reprinted with permission.
4. © 1995 New York Times. Reprinted with permission.
5. For a feminist critique of the DSM, see Brown and Ballou (1992). They note that although the DSM does call attention to the prevalence of certain diagnoses among women, it does not explain gender differentials in a way that "asks such questions about gender and about how the privileging of male experience leads inexorably to the pathologizing of female experiences in any sexist society" (115). Nor does it include categories of race, sexual orientation, or class status in its statistical analysis. Thus, the major diagnostic resource of practicing therapists fails to note that "disorders" may be products of structural, collective rather than merely individual experience.
6. © 1995 Addison-Wesley. Reproduced with permission.
7. © 1995 Addison-Wesley. Reproduced with permission.

1 Perspectives on the Therapeutic

If we psychologize and medicalize every human action by ridding it of any significant political cause, we condemn ourselves to denying the effects of the macro structures of our society. Therefore we will leave those structures intact while we blame the only positions in our cultural clearing that show up as responsible, culpable entities: the individual and the dyad. If we cannot entertain the realistic possibility that political structures can be the cause of personal, psychological distress, then we cannot notice their impact, we cannot study them, we cannot face their consequences, we cannot mobilize to make structural changes, as we will have few ideas about what changes to make. We will become politically incompetent.

—*Phillip Cushman (1995, 337)*[1]

The discursive pattern of translating social and political problems into the language of individual responsibility and healing is a rhetoric because of its powerful persuasive force; it constitutes therapy because of its focus on the personal life of the individual as locus of both problem and responsibility for change. This discursive pattern is ubiquitous in U.S. popular culture, especially in artifacts taking social crisis as their subject. Therapeutic discourse, a powerful rhetorical strategy

1

within liberal capitalist society, works to recover political challenges to the established social order and mitigates against collective social action for change.

The therapeutic persuades us to adopt private-sphere coping strategies in the wake of post-1960s social conflict and fragmentation and to translate challenges to an unjust political and economic system into personal survival or growth. Anthony Giddens states it well when he suggests that in the therapeutic, outrage is converted to rage and political energy is converted to life planning (Giddens 1991, 209-231).[2] As such, the therapeutic is the rhetorical response of an entire system under strain. It has no single rhetor or author but rather pervades American popular and political culture.

The Rhetoric of Therapy

For Kenneth Burke (1950/1969b), religion was once the primary cultural rhetoric that produced cycles of guilt, scapegoating, and redemption. As John Makay (1980) has argued, however, in contemporary American culture a more common enactment of this process occurs in therapy as "secular grace." Makay argues that narratives of sickness and healing are used to label those who transgress against the dominant moral code and to offer redemption in the form of therapies that reintegrate the transgressor into the culture—so long as the "sufferer" agrees to take responsibility for the "sickness." Thus, psychotherapy is a rhetoric that exhorts conformity with the prevailing social order. Even though mental illness and psychotherapy are discursive historical categories, the experience of mental illness can still be profoundly disorienting and disabling in real life for those who are afflicted. For this reason, I think Makay's indictment of therapy is more appropriate to a critique of the therapeutic than to all private psychotherapies.

Sometimes, however, psychotherapy has been used in repressive ways. Phyllis Chesler (1972) has documented the ways in which even literal, clinical therapies can marginalize and discredit challenges to existing power relations by labeling oppositional figures, especially women, insane or deluded and then committing them to mental institutions.

A second function of the rhetoric of therapy, more persuasive than repressive, is to encourage identification with therapeutic values: individualism, familism, self-help, and self-absorption. As Cushman (1995) argues, American psychotherapeutic traditions, including mesmerism, the American importation of Freudian analysis, object relations theory, and ego psychology, offer a "depoliticized" vision that valorizes consumption, elevates the ego and the family to primary epistemological status—in other words, as the isolated sites of human knowledge and agency—and obscures political and moral contexts of therapy.

David Payne (1989) has suggested that most, if not all, of the rhetorical enterprise is directed at offering consolation to those experiencing failure. For Payne, perceived failure "evokes a particular kind of thought and expression basic to a form of rhetoric that responds to and is a familiar part of human experience" (4). Payne argues that failure creates a rhetorical situation that in turn calls for the strategic deployment of themes of consolation and compensation and the renegotiation of the person's relationship with society at large (44). Payne (1989), however, provides neither a critique of this process nor a discussion of the ways in which therapy can function as a rhetoric that exhorts conformity with the prevailing social order. A further problem with Payne's analysis is that, potentially, any and every rhetorical act can serve therapeutic or consolatory functions for rhetors. In contrast, I believe that the therapeutic is a distinct rhetorical genre identifiable by linguistic markers: language of healing, consolation, and adaptation or adjustment. The most important rhetorical feature of the therapeutic is its tendency to encourage citizens to perceive political issues, conflicts, and inequities as personal failures subject to personal amelioration. Therapy offers consolation rather than compensation, individual adaptation rather than social change, and an experience of politics that is impoverished in its isolation from structural critique and collective action.

One caveat is in order regarding therapy and the therapeutic: Although many recent critics of the therapeutic lambaste the entire society as "the therapeutic society," not every individualist, personalizing discourse in contemporary political life is an exemplar of the therapeutic. The therapeutic is a more specific rhetorical permutation of the personalization of political life, distinct in several ways from the broader category. First, therapeutic discourse specifically deploys the language and themes of self-care, consolation, coping, self-esteem, family psychology, and ministration. These metaphors so saturate U.S. culture that the therapeutic is a prominent and perhaps paradigmatic personalizing strategy of the system.

A second defining feature of therapeutic discourse is that it often is deployed as a response to social conflict with regard to issues of race, class, and gender. At moments of political anger or disaffection, rebellion is possible, but therapeutic discourse effectively translates resistance into "dis-ease" and locates blame and responsibility for solutions in the private sphere. In these instances, medical or psychiatric metaphors used in a political context (e.g., inoculation, prescriptions, healing, and the social body) signal the presence of therapeutic discourse. For example, when Vice President Dan Quayle exhorted black families to take responsibility for healing the rift in the wake of the Los Angeles rebellion, he deployed a privatizing therapeutic discourse as a way of deflecting attention to the sociopolitical roots of the unrest.

Similarly, in the wake of a 1996 federal court decision (*Texas et al. v. Cheryl J. Hopwood*) annulling affirmative action programs at the University of Texas, students whose financial aid was at stake and who were, in effect, being told they had been unqualified for admission, were encouraged to attend self-esteem workshops and other therapy sessions. Meanwhile, outside the campus buildings, a social movement demanding the reinstatement of affirmative action in admissions and financial aid galvanized those students who chose to work for political redress instead of—or at least in addition to—therapy. University administrators attempted to minimize public protest and their own accountability by encouraging students to cope with the new situation as it existed rather than working to change it. In counseling sessions, advisory meetings, and press conferences, university representatives offered solace in the form of comforting words in the absence of the ability to produce material redress in the form of renewed attention to minority admissions and scholarships.

In a similar manner, the therapeutic can be a response to class as well as racial conflict. Susan Whalen (1996) has suggested that worker-management initiatives such as Total Quality Management (TQM), in which workers are encouraged to become self-actualized in the workplace by identifying with their bosses' interests, are exemplars of the therapeutic motive at work. Therapeutic discourses ask workers to take personal responsibility for coping with downsizing, decreasing wages, and other hardships. As consolation, discourses such as TQM offer psychological reassurance of worth in the form of team participation and nominal decision-making power. In addition to the deployment of themes of self-care and consolation in situations of social crisis, a third hallmark of this discourse is that it is significantly gendered because, as Julia Wood (1993) explains, the burden of private ministration and caring in our society falls predominantly on women. Therapeutic discourses, insofar as they are personalizing and domesticating, often are coded as feminine discourses, and women are ascribed particular agency in implementing therapeutic solutions to crises.

Gender and the Therapeutic

Women's oppression is linked to the therapeutic in three significant ways. First, women's anger at, rebelliousness against, or victimization by an oppressive gender system is often translated in the dominant culture into terms of madness. For example, women who rebelled against the Victorian Cult of True Womanhood were often marginalized as insane. Furthermore, women are the primary audience (e.g., of self-help literature) for messages exhorting them to cope, adapt, and heal themselves and others, especially in domestic space. Second, therapeutic rhetoric forces social issues into the private sphere, where attention to the emotional and social needs of the family are typically met by women. Finally, in American popular culture, national identity is often tied quite closely to the image and ideal of the traditional family.

Feminist cultural critics have commented on the extent to which therapeutic forms of popular culture are significantly gendered (Livingstone and Liebes 1995, White 1992). In a study of soap opera narratives, Sonia Livingstone and Tamar Liebes argue that the structure of daytime television is analogous to the therapeutic: Both are temporally limited and serial in form. More important, soap operas and therapy both offer women advice in the context of traditional narratives of male dominance: "Soaps and therapies can be seen as expressions of hegemonic popular culture, both of which socialize women to their dependency on men. Both constitute a daily fix, administered to women by therapists and producers" (161). In this way, daytime television dramas, like popular self-help literature and romance novels, exemplify a specifically gendered therapeutic culture. Although some feminist scholars are optimistic about the enabling potential of such texts for women and about women's capacity to decode self-help books and romance novels in counter-ideological and perhaps emancipatory ways (e.g., Grodin 1991, Leto deFrancisco 1995). I am more skeptical. Feminist celebrations of self-help texts themselves accept the limits of the therapeutic ethos, as if legitimating therapy as the limit of resistance to suffering in systems of exploitation and oppression. Indeed, feminism itself exhibits therapeutic variations. In Chapter 5, I establish that consciousness-raising and the tenet "the personal is political" constitute the core assumptions of feminist politics, despite variations across feminisms. The goals of therapy—to encourage personal expression and insight but not necessarily instrumental public action—parallel those of the feminist movement. Therapy and feminism both privilege psychological, consciousness, or identity change as their goals. Therapy also constitutes a kind of retreat from public engagement to achieve private healing; this aim very much resembles separatist radical feminist strategies.

Radical and feminist therapists constitute a middle ground between social movement activism and an insular therapeutic practice. In clinical counseling and academic and popular publishing that politicizes therapy, radical therapy calls attention to inequities of race, class, and gender as foundational to human suffering in the twentieth century. Laura Brown (1996), a prominent feminist therapist, has suggested that the role of the therapist is to "subvert the oppressive fabric of society" in two ways: by critiquing the role of the normative nuclear family in enforcing women's oppression (and thus encouraging clients to reenvision their social life) and by enacting an egalitarian relationship between therapist and client. When therapy is politicized, the once-privatizing encounter in therapy becomes a "subversive dialogue." When the process of subversion is framed as a dialogue rather than in terms of the structural transformation of society, however, I believe that even in radical therapy practices, which correspond quite directly to some social movement practices, especially in feminism, there are limits to what can be achieved. Because I support the project of women's liberation, I think it is crucially important to reflect on the potentially disabling and conservative metaphors that guide feminist political work.

Therapy as Ideology

First and foremost, therapy is a medical concept. In the context of physical healing, medicine rarely blames sufferers for their plight (with the possible exception today of long-term smokers). In the context of social problems, however, therapeutic discourses give the medical metaphor a conservative twist. It is only in the modern era that the language of ministration and healing have become applicable to the psyche, itself understood as a self-contained unit autonomous from social-, economic-, divine-, or political-determining contexts. In psychotherapy, to attend is to watch, to guard, to survey, and to control. To heal is to restore a previously realized order to the body and mind. Thus, the meaning of therapy, in a sociopolitical context, is inherently conservative and private. To receive therapy is to be reconciled to your situation, reintegrated, and restored. Reconciliation and integration are not always bad. When the therapeutic is invoked in racist, sexist, class society by politicians and others bent on winning mass acceptance to existing social conditions, however, reconciliation is not necessarily the best strategy. By the definitions I have sketched, the conservative, privatizing, normalizing, and marginalizing discourses of the therapeutic are incompatible with a public-, policy-, and change-oriented definition of politics.

From various perspectives, recent critics of therapy stress the need for social contextualization of individual experience and suffering. In the remainder of this chapter, I survey several variants on this critique: the radical therapy movement's critique of traditional psychotherapy practice, libertarian and poststructuralist critiques of the therapeutic as a "disciplinary" practice oppressive and constitutive of the modern self, and the communitarian indictment of therapeutic society. Taken together, these critics of both the literal enterprise of psychotherapy and of a culture informed by the therapeutic imperative suggest ways of opposing a dominant therapeutic discourse and contextualizing notions of self and suffering in political terms. I distinguish my own Marxist-informed materialist approach from these critiques as I go.

The Radical Psychiatry Movement: Feminist and Left Critics of Therapy

I use representatives of the radical psychiatry movement (which advocates politicizing therapy and including social activism as a component of therapy) and feminist therapy not because I wholly share their indictment of clinical psychotherapeutic practice. Rather, I am reading their critique of therapy metaphorically as a set of terms and critiques that can be applied to the therapeutic as I have defined it. Both Marxist and feminist "radical" therapists and antitherapists stress several themes in their critique of the prevailing modes of psychotherapy: (a) The traditional therapeutic relationship is marked by unequal power between therapist and client; (b) mental illness is a social construct leading to involuntary incarceration and other abuses of the therapist's and the broader society's power; (c) femininity itself is defined as madness according to the normative criteria of the mental health establishment, and women are disproportionately represented among targets of psychotherapeutic interventions that tend to reinforce oppressive gender roles; (d) therapists often fail to place mental health and illness in their political and social contexts, for example, acknowledging the role of poverty or abuse in producing mental distress; and (e) the tendency toward self-absorption and expression as a substitute for social change pervades traditional therapy (Agel 1972, Brodsky and Hare-Mustin 1980, Brown and Ballou 1992, Chesler 1972, Cushman 1995, Ehrenreich and English 1978, Foucault 1973, Goffman 1961, Hillman and Ventura 1992, Leonard 1984, Makay 1980, Masson 1988). Jeffrey Masson (1988) is the most recent in a series of outspoken critics of therapy, particularly of the power relations of Freudian psychiatry. He argues that "the unquestioning application of the medical model of mental illness to the multifarious problems of life creates more problems than it solves" (11). Masson indicts clinical therapy's fostering of unequal power between patients by therapists. In addition, he charges therapy with attempting or pretending to solve social problems at the level of the individual psyche. Leroy Frank (1988), a leader of the radical therapy movement of the late 1960s and early 1970s, summarizes the radical critique of mental illness as a depoliticizing myth and psychotherapy as a form of social control:

> Psychiatry has been able to disguise its real function in society which is to serve as an instrument of social control. Through use of labels such as "mentally ill," "psychotic," "schizophrenic," and the like, psychiatry attacks people's credibility and invalidates their anger, bitterness, and despair, which are reactions to real oppression and powerlessness. Mental illness is a pejorative label used to justify the social control of selected individuals through involuntary psychiatric interventions. Those affected—generally the most oppressed members of society—are people . . . whose ideas, actions, values, and life-styles disrupt or threaten to disrupt established power relationships. (60-1)

Perhaps Frank overstates his bleak assessment of therapy as social control, especially in light of recent developments in feminist therapy that have attempted to politicize therapy and encourage women to think about their "dis-ease" in ways that generate critical insight and impetus for social action after treatment. In 1972, Phyllis Chesler's *Women and Madness* described existing mental health professions as an apparatus that wittingly or not functioned to keep women in their place. Since then, a number of prominent feminist critiques have been published.[3] Because of these and other critiques, psychotherapy has changed to include, albeit partially, feminist perspectives in theory and practice. In 1994, feminist therapist Laura Brown wrote,

> Unlike other approaches to psychotherapy, feminist therapy concerns itself not simply with individual suffering but with the social and political meanings of both pain and healing. It has as its goals the creation of feminist consciousness and a movement toward feminist action. The first and most important "client" of feminist therapy is the culture in which it takes place; the first and foremost commitment of feminist therapists is to radical social transformation. (17)

Feminist and other radical critiques of therapy have generated new practices. Brown's project of social transformation and feminist political contextualization of suffering, on a politics-therapy spectrum, falls somewhere between the privatizing encounter of traditional psychotherapies and, for example, a mass strike for social justice. A gray area exists between public and private and political and therapeutic. Even so, I wish for readers of my book to consider how salient Frank's indictment of psychotherapy still is, if one reads it metaphorically, in terms of the way that therapeutic themes and motifs work as rhetorics in political culture. Historians of psychotherapy provide a bridge for this metaphorical link; they have documented the close connection between the rise of therapy and the rise of a therapeutic culture.

For example, Cushman's (1995) critique of psychoanalysis focuses on the particular ways in which Freudian psychotherapy was aligned with procapitalist and individualistic values when it was imported into the United States. Although Freud's understanding of the self locates that self in family relationships and in a broader social context, Cushman suggests that in the United States, psychologists latched primarily onto the notion of a realm of the private interior. In turn, they established a trained group of experts relative to advertising, entertainment, and politics who used sexual desire and Oedipal rivalry to sell products and sway voters (148). On this critique, the therapeutic in the United States fails to attend to the sociopolitical context of the individual and encourages adaptation to given social circumstances rather than social change. This presumption of intrapsychic as opposed to sociopolitical causation of disturbance is the source of therapy's ideological power. Therapy subverts potential opposition to the social order by blaming sufferers for their own sociopolitical victimization (predominantly, in our society, under capitalism and in systems of racial and gender oppression) and by encouraging people to adjust to life as it is rather than to attempt to change the structure of society.

What happens when rhetors, publicists, journalists, politicians, and other authorities discuss political issues in terms of psychological disturbance? The radical critics of therapy offer us a way of seeing the therapeutic as a hegemonic discourse. By *hegemony,* I refer to the process by which a social order remains stable by generating consent through persuasion to its parameters in part through the production and distribution of ideological texts that define commonsense social reality for most people (Gramsci 1936/1971). This notion of persuasion and social stability has come under fire from audience-centered cultural studies advocates (who call attention to the ways in which audiences can "misread" and resist hegemonic encodings) and from scholars who believe that the process of cultural negotiation is not as seamless as hegemony theory might imply (Condit 1994, Fiske 1986, Garnham 1995, Grossberg 1995). These scholars generally fall into what I call the poststructuralist-libertarian critical camp, heavily influenced by the writings of Michel Foucault. Some argue that mental illness is a disciplinary discursive construct or fiction of the modern age.

Therapy as a Disciplinary Discourse

In his early writings on madness, the asylum, mental illness, and psychology, Foucault argued for the deconstruction of mental illness as a social myth that justifies the disciplining and incarceration of marginalized subjects, who become in effect political prisoners disguised as mental "patients." Foucault contends that beginning in the seventeenth century, the forming bourgeois society invented "mental illness" and its cure, "psychology," so as to enable society to intervene in the private lives of subjects, regulating their behavior and disciplining them for their transgressions.

This argument is quite clear in *Mental Illness and Psychology* (1954/1987), one of Foucault's earliest published works. Although prior to modernity madness was experienced in a range of ways Foucault noted a major shift in seventeenth-century Europe, during which the mad— along with the poor, disabled, the elderly, the indebted, and others who exhibited "derangement" in relation to the order of reason—were declared no longer to be members of society and were incarcerated in the asylum. Alongside liberal revolutions (e.g., 1789 in France), however, reformers freed the poor and so forth, reserving confinement for the mad alone. The key shift during this period was toward a more philanthropic, medical model of treating the insane. Under the regimes created by Pinel and contemporaries, the mad person was subjected to uninterrupted social and moral surveillance and exhorted to feel guilt, humility, and gratitude before returning to civilized life (60-71). Similarly in *Madness and Civilization* (1973) (of which Part II of *Mental Illness* is a précis), Foucault explores the social conditions for the creation of a category of experience called "madness," which itself constitutes and legitimates the boundaries of reason, truth, and normalcy. Here, he argues that during the transition from repressive feudal state power to modern society, the mad became "the mentally ill," subject to a regime of normalizing therapeutic intervention. Foucault links the nineteenth-century movement against the criminalization and confinement of the insane to the emerging industrial society's need for an impoverished working class that consumes little but labors much on behalf of the new society. Prior to this period, those ravaged by poverty were labeled insane, criminalized, and incarcerated. Modern power, according to Foucault, operates on a somewhat different premises: normalization through therapy instead of criminalization (229-30). Foucault warns, however, not to mistake the modern philanthropic attempts to "cure" the insane as liberation. In *Madness and Civilization* (1973), Foucault notes that a key dimension of therapies for the insane, even before the invention of psychotherapy per se, is discursive: "How else explain the importance attached to exhortation, to persuasion, to reasoning, to that whole dialogue in which the classical physician engages with his patient . . . ? Language, the formulations of truth or morality, are in direct contact with the body"

(183). In addition to noting the rhetorical significance of early therapies for mental illness—in other words, that therapy is a rhetorical, exhortative form—this passage suggests what will become Foucault's emphasis on discourses as the sites and agents of power rather than serving the interests of extradiscursive agents. Foucault's stance in *Mental Illness* is more materialist because he situates discourses in the context of class interest and struggle rather than posing discursive constructs as autonomous, free-floating fictions.

Taken to an extreme, however, the idea of mental illness as a fiction inspires naive libertarian challenges to psychotherapy and institutionalization. Thomas Szasz (1970, 1984; see also Goffman 1961, and the work of R. D. Laing), for example, has argued that mental illness is simply a "myth" that punishes and scapegoats errant individuals, obscures the social origins of individual suffering in the family and society, and subjects citizens to regimes of social control in the form of incarceration, medication, and psychosurgery. In this view, the mentally ill are, in effect, political prisoners disguised as "mental patients." Although Szasz's critique of psychiatry as an ideological discourse serving the powerful resembles that of the radical psychiatry movement, his solution goes beyond the political contextualization of suffering. Instead, Szasz suggests that the mentally ill be liberated from institutions and allowed to self-define as autonomous subjects.

This policy prescription minimizes the real suffering felt by misfits, the traumatized, the victimized, and the oppressed. Even though mental illness and psychotherapeutic discourses are products of their historical contexts and are ideological constructs and discourses of behavioral and social control, this does not mean that people suffering from schizophrenia and other psychoses are self-conscious rebels against the system. To the contrary, they may be disabled by their inability to make sense of the world. Their suffering should not be valorized as political resistance. The libertarian romanticization of mental illness flows from a limited notion of resistance that recognizes only individual rather than collective political agency. Szasz recognizes therapy as an ideological discourse, but he perpetuates the illusion of the autonomous individual abstracted from collectivity, structure, and meaningful political agency.

In contrast to Szasz's dismissal of mental illness as a simple "lie," Foucault retheorized power as not only oppressive but also productive. This means that because (in this view, which I critique in Chapter 5) there is no "truth" outside of its discursive constitution, discourses create not only lies or fictions but also provide the only sources of identification, self-definition, and social reality that we have available to us. Recent theorists have applied this insight to the therapeutic, arguing that the discourses of mental illness and psychotherapy are not merely oppressive but also allow for the expression of a new kind of subject. In a book called *Governing the Soul* (1990), Nikolas Rose challenges traditional ideology criticism's approach to the therapeutic. Rose's overall argument is that since World War II, the language of psychotherapy in a vast range of contexts, including child discipline, interpersonal relationships, education, the family, and wartime morale, has created a new kind of subject in society: one that is, ironically, "obliged to be free." He describes therapeutic discourses not as dominating but as productive of a subject invested with an array of lifestyle and consumer choices (126). Throughout the book, Rose (1990) insists on the positive, productive effects of the therapeutic against the claims of ideology critics. His dismissal of ideology critics, however, relies on a straw person of ideology and hegemony theory, a caricature suggesting that ideology critics necessarily invoke the presence of a repressive state behind every therapeutic text. Although Rose notes the surveillance and social control functions of therapeutic discourses, he ends up celebrating the expansion of therapy into every aspect of modern life and the concomitant expansion of lifestyle and consumer "choice."[4] I hope for the case studies in this book challenge Rose's (1990) account in two ways. First, contrary to his stereotype of critical scholarship, I acknowledge that therapeutic discourses are not the product of an elite cabal set on controlling the minds of the duped masses. They are products of broad historical change and are complex and pervasive. Their complexity and historical situatedness, however, do not negate their hegemonic impact in some cases.

The period since the Vietnam War is of particular significance when discussing therapeutic rhetorics and their disabling political effects for two reasons. First, as social theorist David Harvey (1989) has suggested, the economic crisis of 1973 marked an end to the post-World War II economic boom, what Sharon Smith (1992) has labeled the "twilight of the American dream." With that crisis, American cultural and political unity and hopefulness were called into question, generating a culture marked by cynicism, narcissism, and the retrenchment of conservative social forces. Indeed, the social movements of the 1960s, peaking in 1968 around the world, also challenged the racism, sexism, and imperialism endemic to American capitalism. The waning of those movements saw the emergence of the "me generation," replacing collective movements for equality and justice with the therapeutic self-emancipation (Gitlin 1987, 1995).The year 1968 was also the hallmark year of a decade of massive grassroots involvement in social movements in the United States. The civil rights movement, feminism, and the New Left offer the last available examples of an antitherapeutic politics of resistance and struggle. For this reason, I examine post-1968 rhetorics of therapy as a set of persuasive ideas that have mitigated against collective movement for change in recent decades. In addition, I pose collective social movement politics as an antidote to therapy rather than celebrating the degeneration of collective self-identification and action into consumerist lifestyle or identity politics.

Of course, because therapeutic society is, as Giddens notes, the product of massive economic and political transformation, one cannot alter the society simply by talking in a nontherapeutic way. Part of the appeal of genealogical accounts such as Rose's (and Cushman's) is that they document the emergence and determination of discourses in massive historical processes that are beyond any individual's control. One cannot talk a new epoch into being. Even in the age of therapy, however, activists do strive for political engagement. Despite the pervasiveness of therapeutic discourse, alternative periodicals, community organizers, activist groups, citizen watchdog organizations, and others articulate themselves as meaningful collectives striving for public recognition and instrumentality. Many of these people and groups see through exhortations to cope, adapt, and heal, demanding compensation, social change, and a right to feel and express their anger. Although feminists and Marxists have indicted therapy, clinical psychotherapy can enable survivors of all kinds of trauma to become confident public persons.

My emphasis here, however, is on the saturation of rhetorical space with therapeutic themes and on their successful infiltration of even activist discourses. The prevalence of therapeutic motifs and antipolitical retreats in the rhetorics of post-1968 feminisms, post-Marxism, and antiracist identity politics shows that even public, oppositional social movements are vulnerable to the consolations of therapy. The interpretivist shift in cultural studies, in which critics look to audiences for some hope of resistance, seems to me to offer the pleasures of consuming popular culture texts as therapeutic consolation for the failure of larger political projects.

Viewing therapy as a historical product and as an ideological discourse allows us to understand modern society better. As Philip Rieff (1966) noted, psychotherapy was a product of modernity, developing alongside modern liberal constructions of selfhood and agency as properties inherent in individuals. The ideology of modern capitalist societies, liberalism, lays the groundwork for and is expressed in and through therapeutic culture.

 ## The Therapeutic Society Hypothesis and the Communitarian Critique of Liberalism

Liberalism is a philosophy of government based on the primacy of individual freedom from interference in matters of political or economic power. Obviously a contested terrain, liberalism is a complex political ideology, or framework of interpretation and meaning, born out of the political and philosophical revolutions of the seventeenth and eighteenth centuries and emerging as the ideological counterpart to modern capitalist economics. *Liberalism,* used in this way, does not refer to the commonplace opposition to "conservative" but rather to the ideological counterpart of modern capitalism, which encompasses both the "Liberals" and "Conservatives" of today's political usage. Liberalism's articulation varies between conservative, laissez-faire economic liberalism (such as Thatcherism or Reaganism) and a social democratic liberalism that favors state moderation of the effects of capitalism and tempers individualism with notions of social justice (e.g., the New Deal) (Hall 1986). Despite liberalism's historical variations, however, one can define the ideology's core concepts. Particularly important to my project are individualism and privacy as premises for liberal conceptions of the good society. Liberalism defines individuals as sovereign agents. The overriding goal of liberal society is the protection of the individual's private interests in the family and in the market. People, in this view, are not primarily social in nature but are figured as isolated, autonomous agents whose liberty depends on freedom from outside intervention or interference.

Insofar as liberalism constructs the political subject as an autonomous, knowledgeable social agent, liberalism acts as the political or ideological adjunct of the capitalist economy, which requires the illusion of "individual choice" in the buying and selling of commodities (including labor power) and individual responsibility for one's own well-being. Liberalism in the United States acts as a justification for and the naturalization of capitalist economic relations. Hall argues that despite the variance in the articulations of liberalism, the ideology is linked to the bourgeois class in the conditions of its emergence and as a set of naturalized arguments justifying modern capitalism (Hall 1986, 47-62). Liberalism is the ideological rationalization of capitalist relations insofar as it emphasizes individual freedom over the good of the collective community. In much liberal discourse, one finds the values of individualism and community participation in conflict with each other. The ideal community for liberalism is the aggregation of isolated and self-sufficient individuals participating in a mutual, temporary contract, an ideal forwarded by John Rawls (1971).[5] This morally empty public is what Sandel (1982, 147) condemns as "a universe empty of *telos*" inhabited by "deontological" subjects without commitment to purposive order or the common good—"a person incapable of constitutive attachments." Likewise, Cushman (1995) describes the self produced in therapeutic discourses as "the empty self." In the classical liberal universe, community relationships are ideally reciprocal and marked by a distance, as if each member leaves behind the baggage of personal life, conflict, and differences in power and status. (This is also the traditional model relationship between therapist and client.)

This review of the radical critique of therapy has targeted individualism and privatism as therapy's primary ideological components. Furthermore, because liberalism in the United States has so successfully thwarted attempts by alternative (collectivist and anticapitalist) political ideologies to take root, political anger in the United States necessarily has been articulated within and constrained by the assumptions of liberal individualism. Since the 1960s, the eruption of social conflict and clash of interests has begun to challenge the liberal ideology and the capitalist society it justifies. We have also witnessed, however, the intensification of the therapeutic motive, which serves as a liberal conduit channeling the oppositional political currents back into the mainstream.

It is my argument that therapeutic discourse becomes the locus of radical political energy because, within the framework of liberalism, opposition must be framed in individualist terms. "Dis-ease" is the major trope available for this impulse. In other words, the therapeutic provides a frame for complaints against the system but ultimately recuperates and neutralizes political opposition by rendering protest private.

The thesis that therapeutic sensibility leads to a decline of public political engagement is also central to the communitarian literature, the largest body of work critiquing the therapeutic. This critique views the therapeutic evidenced in all arenas of social life and interprets the therapeutic as a symptomatic cultural motif. The key representatives of this camp are Christopher Lasch, Alasdair MacIntyre, Philip Rieff, and Robert Bellah and associates, who label modern society the "society of the manager and the therapist."

Communitarians criticize liberalism and its commitment to individual rights over collective identification and community responsibilities (Mulhall and Swift 1992, Walzer 1990). These authors bemoan the expressive individualism of therapeutic culture, arguing that the individualism of our era and a shared cultural authority are at odds with one another. Variously, they are critical of capitalism, liberalism, modernity, or all three for generating expressive individualism and the decay of social bonds (Bellah et al. 1985, Lasch 1979, MacIntyre 1984, Rieff 1966). Nostalgic for shared cultural authority and collective identity, these authors offer images of various traditional communities—the Greek *polis,* the small town, the medieval church, the traditional family, and so on—as models for an integrated society.

Habits of the Heart (Bellah et al. 1985, 113) notes the "rise of the therapeutic as a major mode of thinking about the self and society" in the twentieth century. The authors argue that increasingly we create and perpetuate a culture that focuses on individual identity and individual gain. The rise of the therapeutic is part of the cultural emphasis on autonomous individuals that leads to an impoverishment of public life. Bellah and cohorts explicitly blame liberalism and modernity for the lack of community in America because they create a "culture of separation" (277). The group argues that liberal individualism is our "first language" (154) and that building a "culture of coherence" depends on the formulation of second languages of community commitment. The metaphor of first and second languages suggests an interesting parallel with the theory of ideology. The first language of individualism is a system of ideas that are historically perpetuated and constituted within and by capitalist economic relations, constraining our ability to think outside the parameters of individualism. Also, what is a second language if not an oppositional idea system or ideology that can be learned through individual effort and identification with an alternative community? Bellah (along with the other communitarians), however, fails to equate the need for alternatives with a program of radical opposition.

One exception to this rule is Christopher Lasch's *Culture of Narcissism* (1979), with its apocalyptic vision of a society dominated by a bureaucracy that fosters self-absorbed and apathetic individuals. This critique of capitalist society is featured in Lasch's other work, which argues that the forces of industrial capitalism near the turn of the century undermined the family as a consolidated, functional reproductive unit (Lasch 1977, 1984). At the same time, capitalism required the family to reproduce, nurture, and rejuvenate workers—in addition to constituting an ideological haven of personal freedom and responsibility. The bureaucratic welfare state and its agents (doctors, social workers, family psychologists, etc.) developed in response to the crisis of industrial capitalism, ministering to—and in the process controlling—families in their personal lives. Lasch condemns "politics of the psyche" represented by the New Age movement and other spiritualist programs and calls for a revitalization of public engagement.

Like Lasch, I argue that the therapeutic is a rhetorical response to material crisis. I also suggest, however, that the therapeutic response is not "natural" but ideologically constructed; the system offers consumption, self-care, and consolation as substitutes for meaningful social change. More than a moral cultural malaise, the therapeutic is a specific rhetorical-ideological mechanism in liberal capitalism—one that blunts the edge of potential opposition to the system (Lasch 1977, 1984).[6] Although Cushman aligns himself with the Left in passages describing the complicity of therapeutic discourses and American business interests,[7] he also, at times, seems nostalgic for a traditional moral order that is hardly democratic. He elevates religion and community over politics and economics as contexts for the therapeutic encounter. Historian Derek Phillips (1993) has suggested that communitarians in general are nostalgic for forms of collective life that are exclusive and oppressive. He sees the communitarian longing for a premodern gemeinschaft as a dangerous desire: "It is, in fact, a crucial weakness of the communitarians' celebration of the past that they almost totally ignore the extent to which the rhetoric of the common good has tended to benefit those with wealth, power, and privilege" (168). Phillips contrasts the myth of the ideal, harmonious premodern community with the realities of life in fragmented colonial America, the hierarchical Middle Ages, and the male-dominated Greek polis. Furthermore, the right wing in contemporary U.S. politics has appropriated the rhetoric of the strong family and moral community (Etzioni 1993).[8] For example, communitarian David Popenoe (1994), writing in the communitarian journal *Responsive Community*, argues that "The time is precisely right for the development of a new culture of familism in America." The Bush administration used the rhetoric of the traditional nuclear family to dislocate blame for urban crisis such as the Los Angeles rebellion away from structural conditions of poverty, lack of social support for poor urban families, and despair onto the family. Many communitarians fault the social movements of the 1960s for the fragmentation of American community. These theorists call for an end to division and strife in favor of unity and harmony. This move is itself an example of therapeutic rhetoric, as I argue in Chapter 3 on the rhetoric of family values.

The antidote to the therapeutic society is not a stronger family but a stronger sense of collective agency in the public project of social transformation. In contrast to the communitarians, each chapter of this book extends the claim that the therapeutic dislocation of political attention and energy, away from projects of collective social change and onto projects of privatized social stability, is an ideological strategy of the capitalist system—a strategy rooted in the assumptions of liberalism since its emergence as the ideological counterpart to modern capitalist society.

Materialism and the Ideology of Therapy

My critical approach to the discourses of therapy is rooted in the tradition of materialist ideology critique. In classical Marxist texts on language and culture, one can discover two meanings of the word *materialist*. The first suggests that social relations and concrete, sensuous human activity are the source of human consciousness, and that human beings derive identity and purpose from their social contexts. Marx (1843/1978a, 143) wrote that because "men" [sic] are products of their circumstances and upbringing, "changed men are products of other circumstances and changed upbringing." Thus, one aspect of materialism is its insistence that human nature is historically variable and that, as a consequence, the human subject is a historically situated product of discourses and relations. The second tenet of materialist discourse theories posits that the mode of production, or the way in which goods are made and distributed in society, determines the social relations and prevailing consciousness of any given epoch. In Engels's (1843/1978a, 701) words, "The final causes of all social changes and political revolutions are to be sought, not in men's brains, not in men's better insight into eternal truth and justice, but in changes in the modes of production and exchange." In this view, a critique of culture must unmask the shared illusions of a society as ideas promulgated by and serving the interests of those who control the production and distribution of material goods. Idealism, when defined in opposition to historical materialism, refers not to the commonsense notions of wishful thinking or hopefulness about the possibility of social change but rather to the tendency to overemphasize consciousness, idea, speech, and text as the determinants of such change.[9] From this vantage, the therapeutic, which assumes intrapsychic origins of change, is (like religion) an idealist discursive mode. Likewise, a communitarianism that seeks a revitalization of a unifying moral language rather than advocating practical struggle for material equity and political power is an idealist worldview that may itself be a therapeutic discourse. Also, although we may borrow from a Foucaultian poststructuralist description of the role of the therapeutic in the sweep of modern history, one must contest, from a materialist point of view, the sense in Foucault that discourses are themselves the site and the agency of power itself, abstract from material relations of class and race and gender oppression.

For a materialist ideology critic, the therapeutic comprises a set of discourses that are linked, albeit in complex ways, to a particular historical moment and to the interests of those who benefit from the perpetuation of a therapeutic society. Although communitarians have described the themes and parameters of this society, they have mistaken the motives undergirding the rhetoric of therapy. As sociologist Charles Derber (1995, 206-08) argues, it is important to distinguish a Left communitarianism from a conservative family-values communitarianism (promoted by Lasch, Etzioni, Popenoe, and the Clinton administration, among others) that sometimes "harkens back to the neoconservative politics of the 1970s" when sociologists complained about the dangers of "excess democracy" among groups struggling for political, economic, and social rights. Derber explains that rather than limiting claims on rights, a materialist or Left communitarianism would expand them to include income redistribution, integrating Marxist notions of economic democracy with a notion of community, or social solidarity. The project of radical, socialist democracy needs to challenge the reign of therapy, in which, according to the dictates of a capitalist consumer society, individuals are "obliged to be free" without reference to the social conditions of nonfreedom that constrain choice making and individual opportunity. This project must challenge the terms of therapeutic society and call attention to the many ways in which the language of helping disguises an antipolitics of privacy and privation.

Furthermore, this project needs history, to discover the preconditions of and the interests served by therapeutic rhetorics. Chapter 2 surveys modern recourses to the therapeutic, arguing that the rhetoric of therapy in history often has been a hegemonic ideological response to social crises posed by economic hardship, social movements, and other types of instability and unrest.

Notes

1. © 1995 Addison-Wesley. Reprinted with permission.

2. Giddens, however, celebrates consumer society and middle-class obsession with lifestyle.

3. See the journal *Women and Therapy* and the following books for an overview of this literature: Brown and Ballou (1992) and Brown (1994). These volumes contain summaries and bibliographic information about a wide range of feminist therapy texts and approaches. Some very interesting work is being done on diagnosis of "mental illness" and the sexist and otherwise biased assumptions in the making of the categories of the DSM.

4. See also Giddens (1991) for a similar celebratory account of lifestyle politics.

5. Mulhall and Swift (1992), summarizing Rawls's (1971) theory of contractual social obligation and justice, write, "The idea that society, and particularly its political arrangements, can be understood as the outcome of a contract between individuals has been a major theme in the history of liberal thought. . . . It would be foolish to deny that liberalism regards the individual as of ultimate importance, and the way in which justice as fairness involved the idea of people agreeing to a contract certainly reflects this strand" (14).

6. Sometimes Lasch is read as attacking "liberationist" elements of the Left and feminists for their pursuit of individual rights for going too far in dividing the American public along class, gender, and racial antagonisms.

7. For example, Cushman (1995, 72; © 1995 Addison-Wesley. Reprinted with permission) notes that during the 1920s and 1930s, therapy became an explicit tool for the control of workers. "By psychologizing the workplace, psychologists helped management reduce worker complaints to psychological symptoms, mystify class conflict, and develop psychological manipulations that controlled labor more effectively."

8. John Leo (1991a, 17) summarizes the conservative communitarian position as follows: "Defining and protecting rights is important in any political culture, but this culture has reached the point where the obsession with individual rights is making it hard for us to think socially, let alone restore the balance between individual and community rights. . . . Communitarianism will be to the '90s what neoconservatism was to the '80s" (© 1991 *U.S. News & World Report*. Reprinted with permission).

9. See Cloud (1994). I take up the defense of materialist ideology criticism in more depth in Chapter 6.

2 The Therapeutic in History

Inventing and Disciplining the Modern Self

> The general utility of a program such as personnel counseling can best be understood by specifying more clearly the general human problems to which this activity is addressed. Three major processes which result in human problems of administration are: (1) adjustment of the individual to the industrial structure; (2) communication and control; and (3) changes in the social structure. . . . [The counselor] can help to control and direct the evaluation the individual makes of himself and of his situation. Insofar as he can do this he is, of course, contributing directly to some of the major human problems of management.
>
> —*Fritz J. Roethlisberger and William Dickson (1939, 601-02)*

The shift to modernity from premodern social systems beginning in the seventeenth century generated a new sense of self for the modern subject, for whom therapy later helped to instill a sense of personal autonomy, responsibility, and psychic interiority. Although the constitution of this new sense of self is, in the broadest understanding of the concept, therapeutic, the history of psychotherapy and its widespread application per se begins with industrialization in the West during the eighteenth and nineteenth centuries. The forces of industrial capitalism and an emerging consumer society produced new kinds of people: one set of subjects who saw themselves as autonomous and free, possessed of such inherent human rights as property, privacy, and the right to manage their own affairs, and another set of subjects who worked for wages in squalid conditions, obliged to produce goods on a scale never before imagined.

For this class of subjects, the therapeutic ideologies of modernity are double-edged. The modern self was a product of liberal revolutions, thus affording at least the language of democratic self-determination of individuals conceived as autonomous, self-expressive, self-reliant subjects. This rhetoric of the "self-made man," however, masked the growing polarity between classes of owners and laborers. It also disguised the fact that for blacks, some immigrants, the working class, and, in large part, women, the right to self-determination has been a fiction. Thus, the therapeutic language of self-help, personal responsibility, adaptation, and healing serves not to liberate the working class, the poor, and the socially marginalized, but rather to persuade members of these classes that they are individually responsible for their plight.

The rhetoric of therapy represents an extreme of liberal individualism that calls not only for individual rights but also for the complete privatization of social responsibility (hence the etymological link between the words *privacy* and *privation*). Furthermore, implicit in the rhetoric of therapy is an unwillingness to acknowledge the validity of collective class identification, of the structural critique of existing social relations, and of the struggle to make the dream of democracy a reality.

In this chapter, I describe the two histories of the therapeutic, arguing that the rise of the therapeutic was an eventual outcome of the invention of the modern democratic self. In addition, I suggest that in the history of capitalist society, the therapeutic has a disciplinary edge that is, broadly speaking, a response to challenges to the legitimacy of capitalism and the oppressions it generates. Not coincidentally, the history of therapeutic public discourse corresponds to the disciplinary histories of psychology, psychiatry, and social work. At various points, specifically during the 1880s and 1890s, the 1910s, the 1930s, World War II, and the post-Vietnam period in the United States,[1] the importation of themes of therapy into the spheres of labor, social movements, and mainstream political life coded resistance as complaint or "dis-ease" and thus contained the threats to order posed by social movements and undermining radical transformative goals in favor of self-absorption and commiseration. In the big picture, however, the therapeutic was itself a product of radical social and cultural transformation, as various theorists, relying on the work of Michel Foucault, have documented.

Therapeutics of the Modern Self

In *History of Sexuality* (1980), Michel Foucault argues that the transition from feudal to modern world systems was matched by a reconceptualization of power. Anthony Giddens (1991) defines *modernity* as

> The institutions and modes of behaviour established first of all in post-feudal Europe, but which in the twentieth century increasingly have become world historical in their impact. "Modernity" can be understood as roughly equivalent to "the industrialized world," so long as it be recognized that industrialism is not its only institutional dimension. . . . A second dimension is capitalism, where this term means a system of commodity production involving both competitive product markets and the commodification of labour power. Each of these can be distinguished analytically from the institutions of surveillance, the basis of the massive increase in organizational power associated with the emergence of modern life. (14-5)[2]

Giddens goes on to explain that *surveillance* in modern society consists of "the use of information to coordinate social activities," or the discursive regulation of human behavior. Although the feudal lord legitimated his rule by the threat of repressive force, modern power is characterized by what Foucault (1980) calls "bio-power." Rather than relying exclusively on the threat of force (although, as Gramsci notes, the power of persuasion is, even in modern "democratic" capitalism, backed up by the military and police), modern power operates by producing webs of interconnected discourses that position subjects in regimes of normalcy (Foucault 1980).[3] These discourses provide sets of rules for the conduct of the most basic everyday life tasks: eating, sex, hygiene, education, spirituality, and family life. In other words, our identities are negotiated out of our location within discursive formations[4] that at the most mundane levels shape the prevailing consciousness of our epoch. Many authors have charted how formative and normative concepts through which we understand ourselves—such as "home," "privacy," "the family," "the self," "the public," gender identity, and so on—are historical products (Coontz 1988, Cott 1977, Habermas 1989, Rybcynski 1987; Sennett 1978). Each shift in the way these concepts are understood produces a new way of being in the world, a new morality, and a new set of subject positions.

The therapeutic is one such discourse formation whose function is to "normalize" and discipline citizens according to the prevailing "truth regimes." Although Foucault (1980) suggests that discourse formations themselves constitute and enact power, I argue that the therapeutic, like other normative discourses foundational to a modern sense of self, are linked to powerful, material economic interests that are real outside the discursive constructs legitimating those interests. In addition, contrary to Foucault, I argue that extradiscursive sites of material experience—of privation, harm, violation, and work—exist, sites that can enable subjects to articulate a class consciousness that runs counter to prevailing truth regimes. The weight of historical evidence, however, suggests that during approximately the past three centuries, a therapeutic sense of self has prevailed in capitalist societies. The history of capitalism is also the history of the elaboration and intensification of the therapeutic imperative.

Giddens (1991) calls the "reflexive mobilizing of self-identity"—in other words, the concern with the formation, expression, and continuity of the autonomous self—a "general feature of modern social activity." He continues:

> As academic disciplines, sociology and psychology are thus bound up in a direct way with the reflexivity of the self. Yet the most distinctive connection between abstract systems and the self is to be found in the rise of modes of therapy and counselling of all kinds. . . . Modernity, it might be said, breaks down the protective framework of the small community and of tradition, replacing these with much larger impersonal organizations. The individual feels bereft and alone in a world in which she or he lacks the psychological supports and the sense of security provided by more traditional settings. (33)[5]

Historians of psychology, psychiatry, and sociology confirm Giddens's remarks about the rise of therapy in conjunction with modern, industrial society (Cushman 1995, Grob 1985, Herman 1995, Howard 1981). Cushman writes, "Considering the fact that modern psychotherapy did not really emerge until the second half of the nineteenth century, psycho-therapy's rise to power has been rapid and pervasive" (5-6).[6] He dates the emergence of psychotherapy in America from the mesmerism move-ment of the 1830s, which was replaced at the turn of the century with a version of Freudian psychoanalysis and with advice manuals exhorting readers, for the first time, to develop their lifestyle and their "personal-ity" (64-6). Similarly, Grob begins his histories of American psychiatry from 1875, although signs of its emergence appeared earlier in that century. He offers some compelling statistics: Prior to 1820, only 1 state had a mental hospital. By 1875, more than 60 public institutions had been established in 32 states (2; see also Grob 1983).

This growth in institutional prominence was matched by a burgeoning of the fields of psychology and social work in the early twentieth century. These new disciplines were products of growing optimism and faith in science and rational progress. Founded in 1844, the Association of Medical Superintendents of American Institutions for the Insane trans-formed itself into the American Psychiatric Association in 1921, marking a shift away from mental institutions and toward a broader private role in American society for psychiatric therapies (Grob 1985, 6-7).

These facts of the institutional history of psychiatry and psychology are important to my project because they indicate a shift at the turn of the century toward the constitution of a new sense of self, exhorted to create one's own success and blamed personally for failure. Even when psychiatrists and psychologists acknowledged external sources of mental illness, they were more likely to attribute the causes of such illness to hereditary genetic factors. Therefore, "environmental" causes of mental distress were limited conceptually to biological theories. Especially to-ward the end of the nineteenth century, the ideas of the eugenics movement influenced psychiatry (Grob 1983, 145, 168-78). In addition, therapeutic discourses both inside and outside of the psychiatric profes-sion offered only personal consolations even when they did acknowledge the strains of industrial society.

This rhetorical pattern of simultaneous and contradictory blame and consolation is a hallmark of therapeutic discourses in politics and culture. Therapeutic rhetorics must acknowledge "dis-ease," but they also hold the individual or family responsible for the problem, thereby ignoring broader structures of power. As most historians of the mental health professions recognize, broader political and economic trends have influ-

enced the language of these professions, just as the emergence of psychology, psychiatry, and social work gave the larger culture a new
language in which to discuss and regulate the self. From the beginning,
psychiatric treatment was moralistic, emphasizing the personal defects
of the individual as the cause of psychic illness. Since then, the impulse
to examine, express, analyze, and improve one's "self" has intensified in
proportion to the expansion of industrial consumer society, although the
therapeutic project has taken different forms. For example, Grob (1983,
6-10) notes that after World War I, psychiatrists increasingly broke with
mental hospitals to practice outside of these institutions, forming more
liberal practices that did not rely on incarceration. After 1900, psychiatry
influenced and was influenced by the "mental hygiene movement,"
which posited a central role for psychology and psychiatry in creating
and sustaining a new industrial society. The social ills of the early
twentieth century were figured as "diseases" that could be cured through
the application of rational science to the individual. As a result, psychology and psychiatry became increasingly concerned with their legitimacy
as professions.

The terminology and practices of these new disciplines echoed across
American culture, for example, in the new advertising industry. Cushman
(1995) and Lears (1983) have described the therapeutic functions of
advertising since the turn of the century: Advertising offers lifestyle
solutions to the problems of modern life. For Giddens (1991), such
therapeutic discourses mediate between "abstract systems" of nation and
economy and the individual, who seeks moral guidance from therapeutic
texts. Because Giddens does not analyze the development of the modern
"reflexive self project" with regard to the capitalist maintenance and
legitimization of class relations, he tends to celebrate the therapeutic as
a source of solace in a posttraditional age and as an emancipatory site of
self-creation and self-expression without the rule of authoritarian tradition. For the working classes, the therapeutic has a more sinister disciplinary edge. A central tenet of the therapeutic ethos is, "We are not what
we are, but what we make of ourselves." Giddens himself acknowledges
(briefly) the following about the poor and disadvantaged:

> It might be assumed that such a person could only look on with bitter envy
> at the options available to the more privileged. For her there is only the
> drudgery of a daily round of activities carried on within strictly defined
> limits: She has no opportunities to follow a different lifestyle, and she could

hardly plan her life, since it is dominated by external constraints. . . . We should remember the point that lifestyle choices are often actively used to reinforce the distribution of life chances. (86)[7]

Giddens goes on to express faith, however, that even such a person has emancipatory lifestyle choices new to industrial capitalism. Giddens and Foucault offer an image in broad strokes of the large backdrop to therapy's emergence in modern society and an account of the constitutive functions of therapeutic rhetorics. By this, I mean that their histories describe how the modern subject is constituted differently than the premodern subject; how the agency of such constitution of self consists of discourses providing secular, posttraditional but still normative guidelines for the micromanagement of behavior; and how one very significant discourse for the constitution of the modern self is the therapeutic.

I believe, however, that such accounts are too broad for understanding how, at specific historical moments and in certain rhetorical situations, the therapeutic can have not only a constitutive but also an instrumental role. That is, we can map out the place of the therapeutic in modernity as being only broadly and indirectly connected to structures of power and to the motives of the producers of the discourse. From a materialist vantage, however, it is also important to understand that at specific times and places, we can also discover the specific, local material contexts and motives for therapeutic discourses. One significant genre in which the therapeutic transcends the private encounter of the therapist's office is the literature of "self-help," whose history reveals its particular instrumentality in United States history.

Self-Help, Meritocracy, and Therapy

The self-help movement has twice boomed in the United States—first in the early twentieth century and second since the late 1960s—and has so saturated popular culture in the United States that its texts and spokespersons are hard to avoid. Richard Weiss (1969, 195) stated, "The ideology of success through mind-power is intimately bound up with the growth of psychotherapy in the present century." Although not all self-help is therapeutic in tone or strategy (some of it takes the form of "success" advice tracts like those of Andrew Carnegie or today's business seminar gurus), its history is closely linked to the rise of the therapeutic at the turn of the century. A great deal of writing has appeared on this subject, some critical and some celebratory of self-help books, talk shows, videos, magazines, advice manuals, support groups, workshops, and so on. Because self-help texts can be regarded as occupying a middle ground between the private clinical psychotherapeutic encounter and the political and popular texts that are the objects of my case studies, however, a few words about self-help psychology and movements are in order here.

Therapeutic self-help is where the jargon and concepts of psychotherapies are translated for the masses and distributed well beyond the reach of clinical therapists' office practices. Hence, it is the most direct instantiation of psychotherapeutic themes in mass culture. The word *self-help* itself suggests the intensification of liberal discourses of self-reliance and personal responsibility since the turn of the century. Social work professor Alfred Katz (1993, 6) locates the origins of self-help in England's mutual-aid societies of the 1930s. Katz argues that such societies and their progeny (e.g., consciousness-raising groups, settlement houses, cooperatives, and immigrant aid groups), collectives geared to help their members through hard times in common cause, are examples of social movement organizations. As such, they possess ideological commitments, a sense of collective identity, a structure and organization, and action plans with the ultimate goal of social, not just personal, transformation (105-06). His analysis suggests that far from being isolating, depoliticizing discourses of ritual blame and individual responsibility, such groups were instances of collective organizing that influenced American social and political consciousness.

Oddly, the examples described by Katz (1993) may not fit the categories of self-help or the therapeutic at all. The collectives he describes are, on the whole, political organizations whose function is to diffuse blame and encourage political awareness and engagement. Although Katz and I may have diverging definitions of self-help, however, in Chapters 4 and 6 I argue that some collectives, such as support groups and consciousness-raising groups, do share some characteristics of a conservatizing therapeutic rhetoric that emphasizes personal rather than political transformation. The therapeutic motive exists in tension with the collective thrust and potential political consciousness and activity of groups united around a set of issues.

For my purposes at this point, self-help can be defined as a set of texts that, despite their presence across various mass media forms (e.g., talk shows, paperbacks, women's magazines, seminars, etc.), have generic ideological characteristics in common. Self-help exhorts its audiences to take exclusively personal (individual or familial) responsibility for solving their problems, often in psychological terms. Self-help literature is prescriptive and aimed at a mass audience. When self-help is invoked in the context of social, political, or economic crisis, it can be read as an ideological attempt to obscure the public, collective, political nature of such crisis and to demand that these crises, such as economic depression, racial antagonisms, and gender rebellion, be borne in privacy. Because the therapeutic translates unrest into "dis-ease," very often self-help employs the language of psychotherapy and thus participates in the therapeutic writ large.

Self-help books and other kinds of texts are personalistic in tone but ideologically uniform on the whole. They are produced for a mass readership and are designed to turn a profit for an enormous self-help industry. Oddly, there is a huge public relations industry devoted to publicizing thousands of texts that deal with some of the most intimate aspects of personal life. At the same time, self-help genres, by virtue of their ubiquity, personalize our experience of public life. They acknowledge a whole range of social problems, from domestic violence to racism to joblessness, but only in the context of personal advice and personal responsibility.

Philip Rieff (1966, 61-2), in his book *The Triumph of the Therapeutic,* describes the self-indulgence of industrial capitalist society as wholly therapeutic, a society in which "the self, improved, is the ultimate concern of moral culture." Steven Starker (1989, 16-26), however, makes a useful distinction between the broader category of self-help narratives and those that are specifically therapeutic. Although the eighteenth and nineteenth centuries witnessed the publication of a number of religious and moral treatises on personal improvement, at the turn of the century there emerged two new, secular kinds of self-help literature. The first is the familiar rags-to-riches success story of Horatio Alger. Starker cites the advice of the mid-nineteenth century *McGuffey Reader* to "try, try again" when success is elusive. Such texts served as primers for a new industrial world that valued individual persistence and disciplined hard work.

Another expression of this rapid change was the emergence, after the Civil War, of specifically therapeutic tracts stressing mental health and positive thinking in the face of new kinds of adversity. Starker (1989, 34) notes that by 1910 there were nearly 100 magazines and papers dealing with the therapeutics of "mind-cure." By 1934, along with the growing popularity of Freudian psychology in the United States, psychological themes and methods were being applied to every area of modern life in books with titles such as *Psychology of Buying, Psychology of Murder, Psychology and the Day's Work,* and even *Psychology of Group Insurance* (43). It seems clear from these titles that psychology attempted to explain and ameliorate at least one phenomenon, capitalism, and the new rules of laboring and buying associated with it.

For example, New York City neurologist Charles Beard commented in 1870 that a whole new crop of mental disorders requiring medical attention—fatigue, anxiety, tension, headache, alcohol abuse, and unhappiness, among others—accompanied the accelerated changes of modern civilization and its overload of information, technology, and sheer work. Beard acknowledged that modern life—society, politics, culture, and labor—caused these new problems. He advised addressing them not at the social level, however, but rather at the level of the individual (Starker, 1989, 33). Thus, Beard's work and writing may be regarded as an early example of the phenomenon I am attempting to describe: a strategic rhetoric in capitalist society that grants a hearing to complaints and even admits they have their origins in sociopolitical arrangements. These discourses, however, turn around and lay the responsibility for adaptation and coping on the shoulders of the individual in his or her private life.

Starker (1989) is mistaken, therefore, when he suggests that the new therapeutics were targeted toward only the affluent. Although only the affluent could afford to concern themselves directly with issues of personal expression and "self-actualization" through consumption, working classes and poor Americans were also among the audience for therapeutic rhetorics, exhorted to take responsibility for and cope with themselves and their station, no matter how mean or obviously unjust.

In summary, the rise of therapeutic self-help, concomitant with the professionalization of psychotherapy, was a response to modern capitalist society. Historian William Leuchtenburg (1958) wrote the following about the period between 1914 and 1932:

> The United States had to come to terms with a strong state, the dominance of the metropolis, secularization and the breakdown of religious sanctions,

the loss of authority of the family, industrial concentrations, international politics, and mass culture. The country . . . fell far short of working out viable solutions to the problems created by the painful transition from nineteenth century to modern America. (164-65)[8]

Wendy Simonds (1992) has suggested that if the period around the turn of the century (through the Depression) saw a first wave of self-help literature, the period since 1963 (when Betty Friedan published *The Feminine Mystique;* I concur that the social movements of the 1960s met a renewed emphasis on therapeutic self-help, with the result of producing amalgams of radical politics and therapeutic self-help) has seen another explosion of this genre. Bookstores now offer multiple self-help sections with thousands of titles in categories from business skills to sex and relationships.

In her study of best-selling self-help books published between 1963 and 1991, Simonds (1992, 143) notes that "unisex" exemplars of this genre (those not targeted specifically to women or men) rely on the turn-of-the-century success narrative, "I think, therefore I can." Most also employ the jargon of psychotherapy. Simonds criticizes the large number of self-help books oriented toward women, in particular, for portraying women as narcissistic, masochistic, needy, emotionally deter-mined, passive creatures. Often, men are the authors and the "experts" explaining to women why they themselves are the problem. Many of the best-sellers blame "bad" mothers for their children's unhappiness. In addition, Simonds's interviews with readers of self-help show that the readers are persuaded by messages in these texts encouraging them to take responsibility for their "illnesses" or negative behavior patterns without contextualizing these patterns in terms of structural commonal-ties with other women. (Ironically, however, we all know that millions of other people are reading the same book to solve the same problem, which each perceives as "personal," despite the mass experience of the problem.) The genre is powerful, according to womens' own accounts of why they read it, because it offers them sites for self-recognition during times when they are troubled by feelings of isolation and subordination in the family, of vulnerability, of inequity at work, of voicelessness, and of interpersonal conflict and unhappiness in relationships (Coyle and Grodin 1993).[9] As I argued in Chapter 1, the persuasive force of the therapeutic lies in its ability to acknowledge such problems while reduc-ing them to personal complaints, destined for personal rather than public attention.

Simonds's (1992) critique includes an awareness of the role that capitalism plays in establishing the normative values of self-help texts, including an economic "balance" or "give-and-take" in personal relationships. In addition, the books are marked by a tension between altruism, egalitarianism, and caring as appropriate values for women on the one hand, and the paramount importance of power, prestige, and individual success on the other hand (202). The books constitute the feminine subject as generous and caring even as they chastise readers for not having a strong enough sense of self-autonomy. Of course, as Simonds acknowledges, the reading of self-help has double-edged effects. At the same time that readers are persuaded to become a proper capitalist or feminine self, they are also seeking a way to express their current unhappiness and desire for change.

This double edge—between acknowledging crisis and "dis-ease" and accommodating complaint, on the one hand, and channeling responses into the therapeutic groove on the other hand—characterizes therapeutic discourses in general, beyond the genre of self-help. At this point, I turn to an examination of concrete instances in which the therapeutic rose to meet a set of political or social critiques with the language of personal healing. Usually, it is not simply a matter of an elite cabal manufacturing psychobabble propaganda in response to a direct threat. In each period identified by historians as key in the development of the therapeutic, however, we can identify a pattern in which the therapeutic emerges at a particular moment either as a consolation rhetoric during times of social change and cultural strain or (and these are not really separable) in response to the rise of mass movements demanding radical systemic reform. As movements peak, therapeutic discourses are introduced as a way of deflecting the energy and radicalism of activists toward personal concerns. As movements wane, the therapeutic becomes dominant in coding social critique as "dis-ease."

Of course, in the broad historical description that follows, absolute causal connection between the therapeutic and political disengagement cannot be established. The coincidence of the rise of therapy with the rise of industrialization and of protests against capitalism, however, suggests a significant interrelationship. Although one cannot argue that therapeutic discourses have been the sole cause of political quiescence, there is certainly evidence that the rhetoric of therapy has offered easy alternatives to political action and salvation in defeat to those suffering in contemporary society. Gitlin (1987) wrote the following about the waning of the social movement era in the early 1970s:

> If society was impenetrable and politics a simple reshuffling of elite creden-
> tials, the self could still be transformed at will. . . . In the early seventies,
> the journey to the interior preoccupied a good half of my old movement
> friends. . . . It was our Ghost Dance. Systems that some took up for the
> temporary licking of wounds, or anesthesia, for others became substitute
> faiths. . . . These [psychotherapeutic and New Age] sects not only stabilized
> shaky selves, they had the side value of channeling devotees back to
> conventional middle-class existence, giving them rationales for putting
> aside the travails of politics. (426)

The therapeutic, then, has competed against activism for the hearts, minds, and time of the dissatisfied, beginning with those dissatisfied with the contract of industrial labor.

Industrialization and Progressive Reform

As noted previously, therapeutic diversions away from attention to social ills emerged first, and not coincidentally, at the turn of the twentieth century (Lears 1983, see also Lears 1981). In his study of turn-of-the-century advertising, Lears (1983) found confirmation for the following claim:

> Something was different about the late-nineteenth-century United States.
> In earlier times and other places, the quest for health had occurred within
> larger communal, ethical, or religious frameworks of meaning. By the late
> nineteenth century those frameworks were eroding. The quest for health
> was becoming an entirely secular and self-referential project, rooted in
> peculiarly modern emotional needs—above all the need to renew a sense of
> selfhood. . . . The coming of the therapeutic ethos was a modern historical
> development. (4)

Lears, along with all the other historians whose work I have previously cited, links the rise of the therapeutic ethos to the technological and economic developments of industrial capitalism, in which people became enmeshed in a disorienting web of market and global social relations.

I do not mean, however, to romanticize the precapitalist past. As Derek Phillips (1993, 168) has noted, one fault of communitarian critiques of modernity is that these critiques tend to wax nostalgic for the traditional and exclusionary communities of ancient Greece, colonial America, feudal Europe, and so forth. Modernity, however, not only ushered in a new mode of wage labor but also raised public expectations regarding the potential of mass production, plentitude, and surplus, alongside a rhetoric of personal freedom and individual self-fulfillment. This transition required massive reorientation away from traditional (although not ideally egalitarian) communities and toward monumentally different social relations. Obsession with self-development represented desperate attempts on the part of the middle classes to reorient themselves during a time of massive social change (see Giddens 1991).

It was not only the affluent for whom the therapeutic imperative operated, however. The array of social changes made during the turn-of-the-century period situates the therapeutic in terms of the functions it served in a historical context. These functions included the invention of a modern self who identifies in terms of a life project of consumption, to reframe collective protest and class interest as individual pathology and responsibility, and thus to discipline women, minorities, and the working class. Industrialization began with the invention of the steam engine in Britain in 1769, accelerating into the nineteenth century, and making its way to the United States.

Industrial capitalism in the United States was plagued from its beginning with economic crisis and challenges from below on the part of workers, women, and blacks. In 1877 (during the Depression of 1873-1877), railroad workers held the first industrial strike in the United States, known as the Great Strike of 1877 or the Great Upheaval. Beginning in West Virginia, general strikes paralyzed Chicago and St. Louis, and rail service was halted across the country. These workers demanded an 8-hour workday, pre-Depression wages, an end to laws penalizing railroad vagrants or hoboes, and the nationalization of the railroads. The success of this strike, before it was crushed by the force of federal troops, shows how, during this time, mass movements were rising to challenge the legitimacy of industrial capitalism and the horrific work conditions and injustices it produced during the so-called Gilded Age from 1870-1920. Historian Jeremy Brecher (1974) writes,

The Great Upheaval was an expression of the new economic and social system in America, just as surely as the cities, railroads, and factories from which it had sprung. The enormous expansion of industry after the Civil War had transformed millions of people who had grown up as farmers and self-employed artisans . . . into employees, growing thousands of whom were concentrated within each of the new corporate empires. They were no longer part of village and town communities with their extended families and stable, unchallenged values, but concentrated in cities with all their anonymity and freedom; their work was no longer individual and competitive, but group and cooperative; they no longer directed their own work, but worked under control of a boss; they no longer controlled the property on which they worked or its fruits, and therefore could not find fruitful employment unless someone with property agreed to hire them. The Great Upheaval grew out of their intuitive sense that they needed each other, and together were powerful. (45-6)

The years 1884, 1892 to 1894, 1908 to 1909, 1919, and the Depression decade (1932, 1934, 1936, and 1937) all witnessed similarly massive strikes that threatened the viability of capital and showed what collective workers' solidarity could achieve.

In response, of course, the federal government, state governments, and corporations took up arms against these uprisings. Government reforms, however, such as those won by Progressivism and the New Deal, alongside ideological persuasion, became increasingly important to the maintenance of social order. With the advent of "Taylorism," or the scientific management of industrial work (1911), and "Fordism," the invention of the assembly line (1913), the industrial process became speedier and the conditions of work more hazardous. The era of the workhouse, the sweatshops, child labor, and the 16-hour workday witnessed massive unrest and protest against those conditions. In that context, the rhetoric of therapy consolidated the working-class family as the unit of social reproduction and responsibility and absolved the society at large of blame for the abhorrent and miserable conditions in which many people found themselves (Donzelot 1979).

I believe it is no coincidence that the establishment of psychotherapy as an institutional practice and its widespread penetration of social life coincided with these decades of the first major rebellions against industrial capitalism. Although there are, no doubt, other partial causes and precedents for the development of psychotherapeutic intervention into the workplace and into ordinary people's lives, evidence for this claim comes from the open acknowledgment in industrial psychology writings that psychotherapeutic intervention might stave off outright rebellion against the conditions of industrialized work. David Statt (1994, 3-22) explains how scientific psychology intervened to manage workers at around this time.

The best-known example of the rise of industrial psychology is the Hawthorne experiments of the 1920s and 1930s. A team led by Elton Mayo studied the effects of illumination, interview procedures, fatigue and monotony, handling of complaints, and employee social organization on industrial efficiency during a 4-year period at Western Electric Company's Hawthorne, Illinois, plant. As part of the human relations movement, Mayo and colleagues credited increased productivity to relaxed supervision, increased worker involvement in decision making, and a new focus on workers' values, relationships, and needs. According to Mayo (1933), managers should listen to workers, provide for a sense of community and participation in decisions, and strive to meet worker needs in a time of too-rapid social change (Daniels et al. 1997, Katzell and Austin 1992, Mayo 1933, Roethlisberger et al. 1954).[10]

In their emphasis on the well-being of workers, the Hawthorne experiments might be viewed as a prototype of today's experiments in Total Quality Management and workplace teams. The experiments and their outcomes, however, have a hegemonic, therapeutic edge. Although humanizing the workplace (in concert with other Progressive movement reforms as described below), they focused worker attention on psychological needs rather than on material grievances regarding wages, work hours, benefits, and pace of work. Furthermore, it is clear from the writings of some of the key Hawthorne researchers that the impetus of the experiments was to stave off worker rebellion and to increase worker productivity—and corporate profits.

Fritz Roethlisberger and William Dickson's (1939) account of worker complaints at Hawthorne is particularly revealing in this regard. The researchers are eager to attribute complaints about piecework rates, work conditions, and oppressive management behavior to psychological causes external to the material conditions of work. For example, they write,

> Suppose a worker, B, complains that the piece rates on his job are too low. In the interview it is also revealed that his wife is in the hospital and that

he is worried about the doctor's bills he has incurred. In this case the latent content of the complaint consists of the fact that B's present earnings, due to his wife's illness, are insufficient to meet his current financial obligations. (267)

The authors describe the complaint about wages as the "manifest" expression that obscures the "actual significance of the complaint," which is assumed to be psychological in nature. Therefore, the researchers advise interviewers and managers to encourage workers to talk freely: "The effect was not merely emotional relief but also, in many instances, the revelation to the critical listener of the significance of the complaint" (269). The emphasis on "emotional relief" and a talking cure in response to materialist grievances reveals that a "critical listener" in this context is one who plays the role of therapist rather than that of revolutionary or even reformer. Later in the book, the authors encourage interviewers to press workers during interviews until the worker offers a psychological motive for raising his material grievance (294-95). In this process, the interviewers find that a Mr. Brown, who complained about wages and treatment by supervisors, really was expressing unmet psychological needs:

> Brown's "unfair treatment by his supervisor" coincides with his "hard luck at home" and "feeling dumpy many a day." All the illustrations which Brown gives of unfair treatment . . . such as the supervisor's request that he work overtime and postpone his vacation, are suggestions which at any other period in Brown's life might have been welcomed. (310-11)

Likewise, the authors accuse a Mr. Green of "distortion" when he complains about his supervisor: "As the story is expanded, it looks as if Green's mental health has been somewhat shattered by the altercations he has had with his supervisor" (311). In the process of interviewing employees about grievances, material issues are turned into matters of "personal misfortune," and the solution is to offer "emotional relief."

The hegemonic intent of the managers and researchers is evident in the researchers' summary of the key goal of the Hawthorne study as being "to maintain equilibrium" by dealing with employees' emotional needs (even when they present with material complaints), thereby thwarting disturbance or unrest (Roethlisberger and Dickson 1939, 588).

The invention and widespread application of industrial psychology is testament to the significance of therapeutic salves for the industrial working class. Rather than protest against work conditions, they could see the plant psychologist for help in adjusting to the new social order. Cushman (1995) notes that during the 1920s and 1930s, therapy became an explicit tool for the control of workers: "By psychologizing the workplace, psychologists helped management reduce worker complaints to psychological symptoms, mystify class conflict, and develop psychological manipulations that controlled labor more effectively" (72).[11]

Social historian Stephanie Coontz (1988, 244-45) provides further examples of this strategy. The Depression of 1873 to 1877 ushered in an era of labor unrest and class conflict. At this time, 67% of Americans engaged in producing goods or services were employed by others as wage laborers, documenting the shift away from small-scale household production and toward modern, centralized production. At the same time as industrial capitalism imposed itself as an inevitable force for change, formerly radical reformers turned to rhetorics sentimentalizing the growing class divide and conflict and offering solace and consolation. At this same time, the division between public and private life, between politics and the family, was growing more definitive in response to the separation of labor and production from the household. The results of these trends were an overall privatization of political issues and an increasing disengagement from reform during the Gilded Age (1870-1890), locating the isolated family as the generator of success and the recipient of its fruits (252). In the wake of the growing polarization between classes, the middle class distanced itself from growing labor militancy, offering familial comforts and domestic instruction in the virtues of hard work, punctuality, self-development, and class mobility.

These lessons began to take explicitly therapeutic form during the early twentieth century. In the 1920s and 1930s, the field of industrial psychology took hold, advising corporate magnates how best to manage their workers while asking them to speed up the pace of their work and to perform for lower wages. For example, a 1919 volume titled *Psychology and the Day's Work* (Swift 1919) hailed the new field of industrial psychology as a tool managing the complete worker—from the science of rest and nutrition to learning, cognition, fatigue, and memory. The early industrial psychologist Charles Meyers (1925/1977, 11-12) stated in 1925 that industrial psychology is concerned with "the psychological relations between labor and management" and with researching ways to overcome worker complaints of industrial fatigue, overwork, stress, undercompensation, and so on through the sound application of psycho-logical principles. The book instructs managers on how best to adapt workers to the long industrial workday. Like today's initiatives in Total Quality Management (TQM), Meyers's book recommends the "feel-good" allowances for worker initiative and autonomy in the 1920s. Then, as now, workers were noticing an increasing polarization between rich and poor. Then, like today, workers faced pressures to speed up for less pay. The discourses of industrial psychology, like today's "new" management-worker initiatives, served the therapeutic function of con-taining unrest and deflecting it onto the psyche of the worker. They offered psychological consolation to workers for them to bear the material burdens of industrial society.

Steven Starker (1989, 63-4) notes that during the 1920s, psychology and psychiatry assumed a central place in American culture so that, as today, bookstores were filled with psychological advice about everything under the sun. For example, in response to growing unrest and workers' realizations that despite the promises of industry, their station in life remained constant, Andrew Carnegie (1936) offered a series of lectures and books establishing him as a self-help author. *How to Win Friends and Influence People,* a guide to public speaking and psychological confi-dence, was a best-seller in 1937 (it sold 700,000 copies in 6 months), during the height of the Depression.

A 1932 essay (Viteles 1932) on psychology and industry noted the following significant problems of "maladjustment" of workers in indus-trial jobs characterized by monotony and technological skill:

> Excessive fatigue, excessive irritation, a complete loss of emotional balance may result from an attempt on the part of the worker to continue on a job for which he is not adapted. These effects are displayed not only in the factory—in his production, in his contacts, with his fellow workers and supervisors—but they may be carried into the home. When carried into the home, they may result in conflict between husband and wife, and in misunderstanding between father and children. (145-46)

The author, a psychology professor and industry consultant, recom-mends a battery of tests and interventions for problem employees. The treatments emphasize the adjustment of the worker to the assembly line rather than acknowledging that the cause of the workers' ills is in the nature of industrial work itself: noise, monotony, distraction, speed, and physical danger. The article encourages business managers to seek out and train, with the help of the latest psychological science, individuals fit for the new kinds of work. We must not, however, underestimate the extent to which the "latest psychological science" itself constructed subjects fit for such work. The essay states that the objectives of psychology in the workplace are "to promote the adjustment of the worker—to insure a high degree of satisfaction from his work" and "to increase industrial efficiency—to decrease the cost of production, cost of accidents, and of other larger expense items in the budget of the industrial concern" (145).

It must be remembered, however, that tremendous social upheaval, protest, and change characterized the years surrounding the turn of the century. For example, the period between 1863 and 1867 witnessed the movement for radical Reconstruction, the second (after abolitionism) massive civil rights reform movement in U.S. history. Following the Civil War, freed blacks demanded suffrage and other political rights in addition to land and economic equality. The Knights of Labor began to organize blacks (in opposition to the American Federation of Labor's policy of racial exclusion) into industrial unions. Across the South, black and white sharecroppers and workers began to band together against a system of shared exploitation, forming the Union League and other organizations to forward interracial equality and black civil rights. Radical Reconstructionists proposed that the federal government overturn the plantation system and provide former slaves with homesteads. Thaddeus Stevens even called for the seizure of 400 million acres belonging to the wealthiest southerners for redistribution to former slaves (Foner 1990, 104-79).

Of course, such radical efforts were met by a backlash not only from the presidency of Andrew Johnson but also in the form of the rise of such groups as the Knights of the Ku Klux Klan, who took it upon themselves to keep blacks in their place after slavery lost its legal hold on them. In addition, moderate northern leaders put the brakes on the increasingly revolutionary tone of Reconstruction and were unwilling to embrace the proposal to redistribute land. The period of radical Reconstruction was followed in the years after 1867 by a time of factionalism, government corruption, and backsliding into denying freed blacks not only land, education, and economic rights, but also suffrage. Georgia in 1870 enacted the poll tax, for example, along with new residency and registration requirements (Foner 1990, 180-237).

I previously discussed how the thematics of self-help were part of a moderating response during this time period, encouraging individual effort rather than radical redistribution of property and expansion of civil rights. The turn-of-the-century period also saw a number of advice books written for women, even as women were mobilizing women's rights. Suffragist and reformer Charlotte Perkins Gilman was advised to seek psychiatric help in the late nineteenth century for "female nervous disorder." Gilman, however, documents in her autobiographical short story, "The Yellow Wallpaper" (1899), how her "illness" was the product of Victorian constraints on woman's self-development, public activity on behalf of women's rights, and subjugation and economic dependence in marriage. "The Yellow Wallpaper" charts Gilman's growing awareness that what she was battling was not psychic illness but her own oppression.

Barbara Ehrenreich and Dierdre English (1978) document the use of psychotherapeutic and self-help rhetorics in response to women's demands—since 1848 and the first women's rights convention—for greater economic autonomy, marital rights, and social and political rights such as the vote. The suffering that women felt as a result of being trapped in unequal marriages and denied any public role was real, but its origins were neither biological nor psychic. Ehrenreich and English write,

> In the mid- and late nineteenth century a curious epidemic seemed to be sweeping through the middle- and upper-class female population both in the United States and England. Diaries and journals from the time give us hundreds of examples of women slipping into hopeless invalidism. (105)

Ehrenreich and English argue that this invalidism was a response to the intensifying suffocation of domestic life for affluent and middle-class women, whose social role increasingly came to be defined in terms of sex and reproduction. The book describes how the medical and psychiatric professions "threw themselves with gusto on the languid figure of the female invalid" (109), prescribing the lengthy rest cure, which isolated the sufferer, and blaming women's sexual reproductive organs for her distress. Although women's suffering was materially real and disabling, the "new" female diseases of the turn of the century—"neurasthenia," "nervous prostration," "sick headache," and "hysteria," among others—represent the somatic expression of sociopolitical distress. Such limited expression was both necessitated by the strict Cult of True Womanhood, which limited women's public and collective work, and actively encouraged by medical professionals who stood to gain from "treating" wealthy women for such "disorders."

When women began using their sicknesses as reasons to refrain from reproduction, however, the therapeutic rhetorics took on a more sinister disciplinary tone. Ehrenreich and English (1978, 133-40) describe how women could use the labels of "hysteria" and so forth to resist, albeit in a passive and limited way, the cultural imperative to bear children and to fulfill the proper domestic role. At this point, late in the nineteenth century, a declining birthrate among white women led to eugenicist fears of racial decline. Doctors and psychiatrists found themselves in a power struggle with their unresponsive patients, to which the therapists responded with ever more disciplinary and intensive programs of "cure."

In addition to an explosion of therapies on a literal level, the political culture of the late nineteenth and early twentieth centuries was likewise infused with therapeutic thematics. The Progressive era of the early 1900s, like the later New Deal of the 1930s and Great Society of the 1960s, saw a number of modest reforms in American government and economic life, including improvements in food inspection, regulation of railroads and telephone and telegraph systems, the formation of the Federal Trade Commission, and, unevenly, the passage of laws limiting the workday and regulating wages and worker safety. Thus, the Progressive movement cannot be dismissed wholly as a therapeutic substitute for radical social change. One must not overlook, however, how often a therapeutic caretaking rhetoric accompanied such reforms. These reform movements were moderate, designed to ease the increasing pressure of unionizing labor on business, and accompanied by a strong rhetoric of self-help and moral uplift. As Ronald Howard (1981, 39) explains, the Progressive reform movement looked to the family to "solve the problems created by industrialization in America." Also, it is no accident that the fields of sociology and social work—fields whose concern was the interrelationship of private life and external social, political, and economic forces—were products of this period. This prototherapeutic discourse was an embattled system's ideological response to struggles from below. Even if it did not blame individuals and families alone for their failure to thrive, it provided moral solutions to political and economic ills, couched these prescriptions in psychological language, and looked to the domestic sphere to implement them.[12]

Cushman (1995) concurs with this interpretation of Progressivism as a therapeutic movement:

> The Progressive agenda, typified by the reforms of Teddy Roosevelt's presidency, should more accurately be seen as an attempt to face up to the evolving alliance between government and big business that would be more in keeping with the emerging needs of the new twentieth-century corporations. The alliance, we can now see, was necessary for the development of a new world of giant corporations and a fledgling consumerism. . . . It is true that the reforms restricted corporate management by placing limits on its behavior and by protecting labor, but the limits and protections were minimal; workers were only protected enough to ensure that they could live and toil the next day. . . . Progressive reforms ultimately opened up a new infinitely more effective way of controlling labor and manufacturing customers, one that fit much better with the emerging twentieth-century therapeutic ethos. (144-45)[13]

There has been some debate among historians over the consequences and motives of Progressivism. On the one hand, Richard Hofstadter (1955), in his Pulitzer Prize winning history of the turn of the century, calls the period from the 1890s through the New Deal—the era of the emergence and consolidation of therapy—"the age of reform." He defines Progressivism as not merely the Bull Moose or Progressive Party but also as:

> that broader impulse toward criticism and change that was everywhere so conspicuous after 1900, when the already forceful stream of agrarian discontent was enlarged and redirected by the growing enthusiasm of middle-class people for social and economic reform. . . . It was, to be sure, a rather vague and not altogether cohesive or consistent movement, but this was probably the secret of its considerable successes, as well as of its failures. . . . Its general theme was the effort to restore a type of economic individualism and political democracy that was widely believed to have existed earlier in America and to have been destroyed by the great corporation and the corrupt political machine; and with that restoration to bring back a kind of morality and civic purity that was also believed to have been lost. (5-6)

No doubt, reformers such as Jane Addams and muckrakers such as Ida Tarbell and Upton Sinclair tempered the excesses of industrial capitalism and offered a humanizing place for workers and immigrants to go to understand their situation. Hofstadter notes, however, that the limitations of Progressivism were often manifest in therapeutic terms:

> In time the muckraking and reform writers seem to have become half conscious of the important psychic function their work was performing for themselves and their public, quite apart from any legislative consequences or material gains. They began to say, in effect, that even when they were unable to do very much to change the exercise of political power, they liked the sense of effort and the feeling that the moral tone of political life had changed. "It is not the material aspect of this," they began to say, "but the moral aspect that interests us." (212)

Hofstadter's critique of Progressivism is that as an idealist moralistic program put forward by middle-class intellectuals, the reforms became increasingly detached from making a material difference in the real lives of ordinary people.

Similarly, historian Page Smith (1985, 1006-09) describes how Progressivism offered a range of therapies—"temperance, hot baths, exercise, rest cures, meditation," and, notably, psychiatry. Only the well-off could afford such indulgences as remedies to the feelings of powerlessness and confusion engendered by the industrial era. Also, although such measures could help people with their emotional ills, as the era progressed reformers paid less attention to actually challenging the conditions of work in industrial society. Other historians have stated this critique more harshly, suggesting that Progressivism was not progressive at all, but rather represented "the triumph of conservatism" or "the corporate reconstruction of American capitalism" (Kolko 1963, Sklar 1988). The basic thesis of these critics is that far from radicalizing American politics, Progressivism diverted attention away from the brutality of industrial capitalism and toward often psychological or moral explanations and solutions that left American capitalism intact.

In this way, the therapeutic is linked with reformist political programs, encouraging smooth adjustment over direct frontal systemic challenge. Does this mean that any political reforms short of wholesale revolution are by definition therapeutic? On the one hand, I suggest that therapeutic themes and interventions are rhetorically useful in encouraging people to "settle" for reforms that fall short of challenging capitalism. On the other hand, not all of those reforms—for women's suffrage, child labor laws, the shortening of the workday, and other material improvements—should be dismissed as mere therapy.

Of course, these same partial criticisms can be made of the New Deal, whose proponent Franklin Delano Roosevelt labeled himself "the best friend big business ever had." As Frances Fox Piven and Richard Cloward (1971/1993, 8) explain, "Western relief systems originated in the mass disturbances that erupted during the long transition from feudalism to capitalism." In their book *Regulating the Poor,* they argue that public welfare does provide relief for the poor, but only in the face of mass movements demanding such relief and only under the condition that the relief-granting agency be allowed to dictate that the poor work and to intervene in their private lives. Federal, state, and local relief for the unemployed came only after widespread unrest and riots during the 1930s. In Chicago and New York, public aid was forthcoming only after officials had had multiple contacts with disruptive social movement groups. By 1932, demonstrations of thousands of unemployed people were commonplace, including national days of protest that drew millions of participants nationwide. Socialists and Communists were central in organizing such protests, demanding that the capitalist system itself be overthrown. In the context of the threat of disorder turning to turmoil, the direct public relief of the New Deal and various state initiatives eased the pressure and consoled the people without fundamentally throwing the capitalist system into question.

The mobilization for and entry into the fighting during World War II meant the end of the Great Depression; the United States entered a period of unprecedented economic and social stability and conformity to patriotic, consumerist, and familial ideals. Despite the absence of an acute crisis, however, therapeutic persuasion still had a maintenance role to play in managing and normalizing private life in Cold War America.

After World War II: The Power of Positive Thinking

World War II marked another watershed in the credibility and influence of psychotherapy in the United States. Psychology historian Ellen Herman (1995) documents the ways in which therapeutic discourses and practices, already present, became technologies of routine and pervasive psychotherapeutic intervention into social problems from this time. She describes the ways in which psychological experts controlled and interred populations, tracked and adjusted wartime morale, and sought to induce personal psychological well-being during and after the war. The war, Herman argues, began a process of measuring Americans' psychological health and intervening on behalf of the collective psychological well-being of Americans, a trend that eventually influenced public health policy during the Cold War, domestic antipoverty programs, analysis of racial conflict, and feminist politics, in addition to the explosion of clinical psychotherapeutic practice.

In short, the government began to treat the nation itself as a "patient" during World War II. In a period of social stability and economic plenty, the therapeutic became entrenched, no longer needing to answer the complaints of radical and reformist movements. It was during this time that Norman Vincent Peale's book, *The Power of Positive Thinking* (1952), became a massive best-seller and an influence on American popular culture. This book was a symptom of the optimism and hope that characterized the period of economic boom and social stability.

Herman (1995), like Rose (1990), suggests that the therapeutic has exhibited both emancipatory and controlling dimensions; it has produced a kind of humanism in social policy but also has put citizens under the watchful caretaking eye of the state. In Chapter 3, I provide more detail about how nationalism and the therapeutic are connected; for now, suffice it to say that when there is a need for national unity and patriotism, the therapeutic metamorphoses into a discourse about the nation rather than about the atomized individual. Paradoxically, the rhetoric of therapy during wartime constructs the nation as a domestic, familial, private space with serious emotional needs. The emotional ministration of the state attempts to generate political quiescence.

Some postmodernist social theorists have celebrated the rise of the therapeutic as a vehicle of individual self-expression and freedom. For example, Anthony Giddens (1991) has argued that late modernity (post-World War II capitalist society) has ushered in an intensified emphasis on one's "life political agenda" rather than on collective, political engagement and social transformation. Despite the concomitant rejection of public politics in favor of a personalized "sequestration of experience," Giddens suggests that the new mode of self-elaboration through consumption and self-expression is emancipatory for ordinary people. Giddens writes,

In the post-traditional order of modernity, and against the backdrop of new forms of mediated experience, self-identity becomes a reflexively organized endeavour. The reflexive project of the self, which consists in the sustaining of coherent, yet continuously revised, biographical narratives, takes place in the context of multiple choice as filtered through abstract systems. In modern social life, the notion of lifestyle takes on a particular significance. (5)[14]

Of particular importance for Giddens, as a space for the articulation of the life project, is the therapeutic. In contrast to Rieff, who argues that the therapeutic has resulted in a moral and political crisis of public life, Giddens suggests that individuals use therapy in positive, self-emancipatory ways that are not ideologically governed by any single authoritative therapeutic doctrine. Although he acknowledges that some therapies are "oriented primarily towards control," overall "therapy should be understood and evaluated essentially as a methodology of life-planning" (179-80).[15]

Giddens (1991) acknowledges that the therapeutic is double-edged, but his stance is clearly one that sees more freedom than authority in therapeutic discourses. David Harvey (1989, 135-40, 353-55) offers a contrasting view. Although Harvey describes the same transformations in modern culture as Giddens, he emphasizes the potentially disabling consequences of late modernity's obsession with self-elaboration. For Harvey, the relative prosperity of the postwar decades allowed the therapeutic elaboration of selves through consumption to become a national preoccupation. Alongside the rise of suburbs came an intensification of the therapeutic imperative to become self-reliant and autonomous, resulting in an increasingly isolated—and politically disengaged— nuclear family.

Similarly, Cushman (1995, 186, 214-44) laments ego psychology's "depoliticized vision" and describes how in the post-World War II era psychology constituted the ideally functioning American as a psychological consumer and the purchase of goods as a moral and political virtue. Thus, the therapeutic exhortation to develop and express one's self serves the needs of consumer capitalism as it has developed over the course of this century. I suggest that although the therapeutic may be double-edged, one can most easily see its hegemonic, controlling dimensions when it surfaces in response to political challenge or conflict. For this reason, I mark the Vietnam War, and the protest movements against it, as another major watershed in the rise of the therapeutic in the United States.

▨ Posttraumatic Stress:
The Therapeutic Since Vietnam

The period since the Vietnam War is of particular significance when discussing therapeutic rhetorics and their disabling political effects. First, as social theorist David Harvey (1989) has suggested, the economic crisis of 1973 marked an end to the post-World War II economic boom, what Sharon Smith (1992) has labeled the "twilight of the American dream." With that crisis, American cultural and political unity and hopefulness were called into question, generating a culture marked by cynicism, narcissism, and the retrenchment of conservative social forces. Indeed, the social movements of the 1960s, peaking in 1968 around the world, also challenged the racism, sexism, and imperialism endemic to American capitalism. The waning of those movements saw the emergence of the "me generation," replacing collective movements for equality and justice with therapeutic self-emancipation (Gitlin 1987, 426; see also Gitlin 1995).

The year 1968 was the peak of a decade of massive grassroots involvement in social movements in the United States. The civil rights movement, feminism, and the New Left offer the last available examples of an antitherapeutic politics of resistance and struggle. In 1969, the publication of Thomas Harris's best-selling *I'm OK—You're OK* (1969) is emblematic of a shift away from activism toward personal healing and self-fulfillment—and, as the best-seller's title suggests, acceptance of the status quo: Everything is "OK."

Although the therapeutic imperative has been with us in the United States for more than a century, the period since the peak of student movement against the Vietnam War marks another key shift in the working of the therapeutic. The therapeutic imperative has never completely eclipsed the possibility of outward-looking collective solutions to America's social ills.

The post-Vietnam War decades have been marked by an exponential increase in personal help-seeking on the part of Americans and a corresponding decrease in social movement commitment. In 1976 compared to 1957, more people sought out mental health services, more people experienced anxiety about the future, and more people used personal rather than social or political criteria to assess their well-being (Veroff, Kulka, and Douvan 1981a, 1981b). Sociologists attribute this pattern of individual help-seeking to the social crisis engendered by the political upheavals of the late 1960s. In this way, the move to therapy is intensified in response and to and in recovery from political movements. Jack Whalen and Richard Flacks (1989, 247) conclude their study of antiwar activists from the 1960s as follows: "The story we have been telling depicts the gradual individuation and conventionalization of people who, in their youth, were wholeheartedly submerged in a collective effort to break free of collective identity."

Although Whalen and Flacks (1989) herald the growing individuation of activists once "submerged" in what the authors view as totalizing and irrational collective movements, Gitlin (1987) grieves over the depoliticization of American life after the 1960s. Gitlin notes that in the wake of fragmentation and disillusionment among sixties radicals, the struggle to articulate a collective politics became a journey to the interior in a "sea change from politics to personal salvation. . . . It was a holding action, a way of soothing wounds and greasing our withdrawal from politics. In truth our political will was sapped" (427).

Gitlin (1987) marks the end of protests against the Vietnam War as the beginning of "encounter culture" and political retreat, although of course protest movements did continue somewhat into the early 1970s. As noted previously, although therapeutic themes are not unique to the post-Vietnam War era, the last decades of the twentieth century are, perhaps in ways unprecedented in scope and persuasiveness, the age of therapy.

Both therapy as a practice housed in the disciplines of psychology, psychiatry, and social work and as the set of therapeutic imperatives attendant industrial capitalism are products of modernity. The degree of saturation of U.S. culture with the therapeutic has varied cyclically during this century, emerging with and peaking against social crises. I believe that 1968 was the year during which leftists, feminists, and other activists began to toll the death knell for bottom-up political engagement, substituting self-care justified in therapeutic terms for political transformation. In a sense, the displacement of public political protests by the lifestyle experimentation of the "counterculture" indicates the beginning of this transformation.

A *Nation* article (McGuire, 1992) stated that even mainstream politics has reflected a shift toward the therapeutic. Although John Kennedy exhorted Americans to "ask what you can do for your country," Clinton's key phrases were more personalizing: He asked us to find "the courage to change," told us he "felt our pain," and often spoke of how growing up in an abusive and later fatherless household affected his vision of the country as a "family coming together instead of apart."[16]

The remainder of this book focuses on the period since 1968, which is a period marked by recurrent, shallow recessions and a steady decline of the average American standard of living. In particular, this book analyzes the role of the therapeutic in contemporary American political and popular cultures. Many authors have argued that we are living during a second, postindustrial revolution characterized by a growing service economy, new information and production technologies, and new management techniques. The basic relation of labor to capital is unchanged, however, as the polarization between classes grows and labor organizations around the world show signs of stirring. Psychotherapeutic discourses still aid managers in maintaining worker participation and workplace stability. In recent years, these discourses have taken the form of worker-management "teams," TQM, or other programs that involve workers in feel-good aspects of decision making. Rarely, however, are U.S. workers asked to share in the making of decisions about their wages, duties, share in company profits, benefits, work hours, or hiring and layoffs. The therapeutics of TQM allow workers a release valve but leave the basic material inequities of work unchanged.

Likewise, therapeutic discourses are prominent with regard to crises of race and gender. Susan Faludi (1991) has argued that in response to the women's movement of the 1960s and 1970s, gender conservatives have retrenched in the 1980s and 1990s in a series of "backlash" cultural forms. Among the many examples analyzed by Faludi, the "men's liberation movement" (which employs Jungian psychology and group retreats) and the popular psychology movement count as explicitly therapeutic, antifeminist rhetorics. Faludi writes that the 1980s backlash therapists blamed women for falling wages, sexual harassment, abusive men, economic and emotional dependence, and their overwork in the family as well as in their professional lives:

> In the quietist '80s, the advice book and therapy couch may have been the only sources of relief left to women who were feeling demoralized. In an era that offered little hope of real social or political change, the possibility of changing oneself was the one remaining way held out to American

women to improve their lot. . . . Instead of assisting women to override the
backlash, the advice experts helped to lock it in female minds and hearts—
by urging women to interpret all of the backlash's pressures as simply
"their" problem. (337)

In recent years, racial inequality and tension have intensified in the wake
of the Rodney King police beating, the Los Angeles urban rebellion of
1992, the confirmation of Clarence Thomas to the Supreme Court, the
O. J. Simpson murder trial, the Nation of Islam-sponsored Million Man
March in 1995, and the wave of African American church arsons in the
summer of 1996.[17] In Chapter 3, I explore how one major therapeutic
response to social crises sparked by racism is the appeal to "family
values."

Chapter 3 is a historically contextualized study of the appeal to family
values in the 1990s. In the twilight of the American Dream, the popular
and political invocation of an idyllic family as a therapeutic norm is an
offering of consolation in an age of declining material expectations.
Furthermore, the image of this family is used as a therapeutic norm held
over the heads of black Americans who are encouraged to take private
responsibility for their failure to thrive.

Notes

1. Although psychotherapy has been present in U.S. culture since the
mid-nineteenth century, the use of therapeutic themes in political life has been
more cyclical, responding to periods of great social upheaval, economic recession,
war, or other crisis. The 1880s mark the beginning of the mass labor movement
in the United States, the 1930s witnessed the Great Depression, World War II
ushered in a period of political quiescence maintained, in part, by increasing
therapeutic intervention into daily life, and the period since 1968 has seen the
waning of the social movements of the 1960s in favor of therapeutic self-help.

2. © 1991 Stanford UP. Reprinted with permission.

3. Foucault (1980, 116) dates the "new technology of sex" as something
produced rather than repressed from the end of the eighteenth century.

4. Although I take issue with the excessive emphasis on discourse in
Foucaultian cultural studies, I use the phrase *discourse formations* and related
concepts because they aptly describe the major, paradigmatic shifts in socially
produced consciousness over time. I advise one caution: that the phrase *discourse
formation* not be taken to imply that discourses are all that comprise social reality.

5. © 1991 Stanford UP. Reprinted with permission.

6. © 1995 Addison-Wesley. Reprinted with permission.

7. © 1991 Stanford UP. Reprinted with permission.

8. Like many of the communitarians summarized in Chapter 1, Leuchtenburg seems nostalgic for premodern societies, which were, of course, characterized by agricultural scarcity and feudal social relations of serfdom—hardly a lost Eden. Capitalism, however, produces its own relations of exploitation and human hardship, requiring "new" technologies of personnel management. Whereas the feudal lord could rely on executions, physical violence, and the absolute subjugation of serfs to maintain his authority, modern power is more subtle; therapy is one of the discursive means by which people alleged to be "free" are convinced to participate in existing social relations.

9. Coyle and Grodin (1993) are more optimistic in this study of self-help readers and reading practices regarding the potential among women for oppositional readings that counter "the program" offered in self-help books (see also Grodin 1991, 404-20). I entail that the performance of oppositional readings on the part of some women with access to critical discourse communities and skills in no way materially subverts women's oppression or late capitalist society. Instead, these women's abilities to find pleasure in the margins of such books serves the ends of marketers who make a profit regardless of one's critical reading practices. Furthermore, attention to specific groups of readers cannot explain the overall impact of recovery culture on the American zeitgeist in general in terms of establishing an antipolitical response to political problems.

10. Notably, humanistic (person-centered) psychology pioneer Carl Rogers was closely involved with the Hawthorne studies.

11. © 1995 Addison-Wesley. Reprinted with permission.

12. Women played a central role in the Progressive movement, coding the family aid and advocacy for legislation protecting women and children workers in feminine, private terms (see Kelly 1987, 269-73).

13. © 1995 Addison-Wesley. Reprinted with permission.

14. © 1991 Stanford UP. Reprinted with permission.

15. © 1991 Stanford UP. Reprinted with permission.

16. Ellen McGuire, "I'm Dysfunctional, You're Dysfunctional," *The Nation* magazine. © 1992. The Nation Company, LP. Reprinted with permission.

17. The not-guilty verdict in the Simpson case revealed a sharp divergence in the ways in which black and white Americans view issues of race. Martin Gottlieb (1995, A1) writes, "The reactions to the verdict parallel the racial divide in every opinion poll taken since the trial began. Separated by a constant gap of about 40 percentage points, many whites seemed to hold fast to the belief that Mr. Simpson was guilty, while blacks believed as adamantly in his innocence. Several polls indicate that behind the response of many blacks is a deep suspicion of the police and the criminal justice system. A poll taken by CBS News immediately after the verdict found that about 6 in 10 whites believed the wrong verdict was reached, while 9 in 10 blacks said the jury had come to the right conclusion" © 1995 New York Times. Reprinted with permission).

3 Family Therapies

From the White House to the 'Hood

> I want to be able to cite the disastrous consequences that follow when the family supplies not just the only symbols of political agency we can find in the culture, but the only object upon which that agency can be seen to operate as well. Let's remind ourselves that there are other possibilities.
>
> —*Paul Gilroy (1992, 315)*

In the wake of the May 1992 urban rebellion in Los Angeles, then Vice President Dan Quayle gave a speech in California blaming the uprising on the rioters' lack of "family values." Quayle intended to impart a simple message: We can blame the racial and economic crises of our cities on the failures of families. To ensure media attention to an otherwise obscure speech, Quayle remarked that it did not help that prime-time television characters such as Murphy Brown (a journalist played by Candice Bergen on CBS) were having babies out of wedlock. Although Quayle's speech came under fire for targeting a wealthy, white feminist television character for her choice to bear a child out of wedlock (suggesting that career women were his primary target), family values rhetoric—by Democrats and Republicans alike—also constructs a certain stereotype of black men, blamed personally for their families' hardships (Cloud, 1995). Feminists and pundits, however, focused their attention on issues of gender roles in Quayle's attack, leaving debate about race and class behind. Carol Stabile (1994) notes,

> The erasure of the L.A. uprising in the "Murphy Brown" incident moved the debate away from issues of race, from the condition of inner cities, and from the deteriorating economic base in the United States to a much safer, symbolic ground. (48)

As in the "family support" news that saturated the coverage of the Persian Gulf War (see Chapter 4), explanations of social problems viewed through the lens of the family obscure the social, political, and economic roots of those problems and disable public response. In place of progressive change, a discourse of family therapy encourages families, particularly those in black America, to pull themselves together. The result is what Dizard and Gadlin (1990) call the "familial public"—a sphere of privatized response to public problems. In her introduction to the book, *The Social and Political Contexts of Family Therapy* (1990), Marsha Pravder Mirkin questions her role as a therapist to "help wounded people conform to the system." She writes, "When we work solely within the family context, are we simply changing the message from blaming the individual to blaming the family?" (xi; see also Solomon, 1980). The volume calls on therapists to consider performing family therapy in politicized contexts, with an understanding of how economic deprivation, racism and the legacy of slavery, cultural transition, fear of nuclear war, systematic sexism and abuse of women and children, and other political and social issues can generate family trouble. In these contexts, the contributors argue for viewing therapy as a kind of political intervention that takes awareness from the private family and expands it to a critique of the broader society.

The rhetoric of family values, however, offers a more traditional therapy, deploying a personalizing, depoliticizing strategy that combines scapegoating with moments of utopian yearning for a nurturing community and familial haven of a mythical bygone era. When they hail the traditional family, politicians and pundits also put forward a compelling social critique of a society stratified by race, gender, and class and fraying at the multicultural edges. The solution to the decline of public life, however, is not to reentrench a mythical nuclear family; rather, a rhetoric that builds on the utopian gesture of family values talk—one that acknowledges the need for public services and support enabling greater public activity and engagement—might reconstitute publics for argument instead of reinforcing familial isolation in the private sphere.

In this chapter, I analyze political speeches and subsequent books published by the disputants of the 1992 presidential campaign deploying the family values slogan alongside representatives from the genre of " 'hood" films popular in the 1990s, which provide therapeutic narratives analogous to the political rhetoric. My argument is that the political and popular texts work together in a kind of family therapy reaching from the White House to the 'hood. This analysis will support the argument that family values rhetoric works as a therapeutic discourse that is most conservative in its implications in racialized contexts. Furthermore, family values rhetoric displaces attention and resources that would otherwise go toward addressing the macrosocial problems of racism and poverty onto the family, which is constructed as an ideally self-reliant unit in isolation. The wave of family values talk since 1992 is only the most recent episode in a series of moral panics over the "decline" of the family in the industrial era.

History of Familialism as Family Therapy

The nuclear family as we know it is a relatively recent historical development, emerging as the family form of the rising bourgeoisie in the modern era. The modern family was a product of changes in early capitalism that over time separated work from the household, reinforced an oppressive, gendered division of labor, and placed an increasing domestic burden on the family as a private unit (Ariès 1962, Coontz 1988, 1992, Frazier 1951, Laslett 1972, Mintz and Kellogg 1988, Shorter 1975). The bourgeois nuclear family, however, was only ever a reality for its namesake: the bourgeoisie. Throughout American history, working-class, black, and immigrant families have struggled in the context of slavery, sweatshop labor, 14-hour days, child labor, multiple family wage earners, extended family living, and so on. Hence, it is important to view the nuclear family ideal as a potent and disciplinary ideological fiction that produces a normative gendered division of labor and discrimination as well as a notion of the family as the site of individual freedom and responsibility.

In this way, the debate over family values becomes fundamentally a contest over labor and social responsibility. The invention and vigorous ideological defense of the nuclear family supports capitalist social relations. Barrett and McIntosh make a useful distinction between the actual, unstable, and varying experience of diverse families at different moments in history and "the family" as an ideological construct that has been, in contrast, remarkably consistent and stable across more than a century, working as "a vigorous agency of class placement and blame." Although nineteenth-century familialism served as ideological justification for increasingly divergent and unequal gender roles in what Barbara Welter (1966) has labeled the "Cult of True Womanhood," Barrett and McIntosh (1982, 29) remind us that the "imagery of idealized family life" exhorts the oppressed, the exploited, and the poor to strive to better their private lives. Waves of familialist panic have occurred during periods of economic or social crisis and during class-based challenges to the rhetoric of personal responsibility and self-blame. This history suggests that we might read moral panics over the family as hegemonic rhetorical responses to crises of capitalism. Thus, the 1840s through the turn of the century were marked by a surge of family moralism in response to feminist, antiracist, and labor movements (Coontz, 1988). Much of the nineteenth-century familialist discourse constructed the middle-class family as a utopian sanctuary of affection removed from the clash of public life. Nikolas Rose (1990) argues that there has been an intensification of the themes of familialist discourses in the twentieth century since World War II, notably in the disciplines of child development, family sociology, and social work. Also, as with therapy in general, the field of family therapy originated during the nineteenth century in response to the private sphere pressures generated in a rapidly industrializing world. These fields developed discourses and regimens training families in their proper conduct—and surveying and blaming them when their personal lives fell short of the ideal. Since 1992, the impetus of much family values talk is therapeutic: to offer private consolation and personal advice to counter the implicit social critique posed by the Los Angeles riots of 1992, which occurred after the acquittal of police officers accused of beating black motorist Rodney King. The riots raised the specter of the late 1960s, during which riots erupted in major cities around the country out of anger at police brutality and frustration with the failure of civil rights reforms to address urban poverty. The urban rebellions of past and present have called attention to ongoing inequality and injustice and have modeled, albeit in unfocused ways, collective resistance to systemic problems.

These problems include segregation; police violence; racial discrimination in imprisonment, employment, housing, lending, and education; and poverty. Of 37 million poor Americans, 10 million—nearly a third— are black. The median net worth for white households in 1991 was $44,408. For black households, it was $4,604 (statistics cited in Bradley 1996).[1] The black infant mortality rate is double that for white children. Black unemployment has remained double that of whites during the past two decades, and for young blacks, the national unemployment rate is higher than 30 percent (Smith 1992). In this context, the rhetoric of family values, used by politicians including Quayle to contain the impact of the riots, suggests once again that the problem in the cities is not racism, poverty, or the police but rather the personal irresponsibility of families, particularly black families. The lesson is that getting one's family's act together can solve systemic problems.

Robert Staples and Leanor Boulin Johnson (1993, 35-6) argue against this therapeutic explanation of crisis, which they label the "pathologization" of the black family. They explain that "culture of poverty" approaches blame an alleged lack of appropriate family values for racial inequality in American society. They write, "In essence, this theory is simply an attempt to shift the responsibility for the conditions of racial and class inequality onto the victims themselves" (28).

Elsewhere, Staples (1987) has argued that previous accounts of black families in the American context have tended to "shift the burden of black deprivation onto the black family rather than the American social structure" (270). Similarly, noted psychiatrist Alvin Poussaint (1996) argues against the discursive demonization of single-parent families. Though a psychiatric professional, Poussaint contextualizes family crisis in terms of unemployment, racism, and poverty. Rather than suggesting psychotherapy for besieged black families, Poussaint recommends political organizing for increased material aid and public respect on the part of single parents and the poor. In contrast, therapeutic familialism serves as ground for arguments against welfare and other social programs: The caring family, in this rhetoric, is to replace social responsibility for poverty. Added to this privatization of social responsibility is an idealist causal argument: Rather than poverty and hardship producing disrupted families, a crisis in values produces poverty. The rhetoric of family values, however, continually, and persuasively, mistakes correlation for cause. In the family values debate, both conservatives and liberals work within a familialist frame that contains and constrains interpretation of statistics on poverty and race.[2] Coontz (1992) cites research findings that the higher the level of public assistance for poor women in advanced industrial democracies, the lower the teen pregnancy rate. In the United States in 1986, the General Accounting Office found that "research does not support the view that welfare encourages two-parent family breakup" or that it reduced incentive to work (83). Furthermore, Stacey (1994, 120) stated that "when other parental resources—like income, education, self-esteem and a supportive social environment—are roughly similar, signs of two-parent privilege largely disappear."[3] This comparative evidence refutes the conservative claim that welfare dependency causes family breakup or teen pregnancy; furthermore, it suggests that no single family form is more economically viable than any other. Rather, the evidence shows that what poor families—whatever their makeup— need is more, not less, material support.

If individual parents are not to blame for the failure of their families to thrive in contemporary capitalist society, then we must recognize in the racialized rhetoric of family values a strategy of racist scapegoating in political and popular culture. A critique of familialism must be placed in the context of sociopolitical and economic struggles in capitalist society. My goal is not to argue against conventional family life itself but rather to focus on the discourses about families as those discourses relate persuasively to political and economic relations of their historical moment. Our contemporary political climate—one marked by renewed attacks on the living standards of poor and working people, in which a rhetoric of family values legitimates the exposure of millions of women and children to desperation and poverty—warrants a renewed emphasis on the ideological functions of such discourses. Such an emphasis asks what ideological work is accomplished by talk about the family.

Family Values as Scapegoating Discourse

The rhetoric of family values vilifies feminists along with gays and lesbians for disrupting "traditional" family forms. What is often overlooked by critics of family values discourse, however, is the additional, and quite pronounced, element of racist scapegoating. The speeches of the 1992 campaign exhibited three important themes regarding race and class in the United States: the assumption of existing opportunity and prosperity for American blacks, the construction of a "good black"/"bad black" dichotomy, and consequently a vilification of unsuccessful or angry black men, who are accused in this rhetoric of personal moral failure. Although the news media ran with the story of Dan Quayle's attack on sitcom feminist Murphy Brown, most media commentators neglected to mention that the bulk of Quayle's (1992a) first family values salvo, delivered in San Francisco, addressed the Los Angeles rebellion of April and May 1992:

> When I have been asked during these last weeks who caused the riots and killings in L. A., my answer has been direct and simple: Who is to blame for the riots? The rioters are to blame. Who is to blame for the killings? The killers are to blame. . . . In a nutshell, I believe the lawless social anarchy which we saw is directly related to the breakdown of family structure, personal responsibility, and social order in too many areas of our society. For the poor the situation is compounded by a welfare ethos that impedes individual efforts to move ahead.

Here we see strong emphasis on the individual as an autonomous agent in this passage and a corresponding unwillingness to discuss the scenic context of urban problems such as rampant police racism and brutality and unemployment in Los Angeles. Quayle and Bush were under pressure to respond meaningfully to the Los Angeles rebellion of May 1992. Quayle told his speech writers (John McConnell and Lisa Schiffren) the following (Rosenthal 1992):

> He wanted a speech on urban problems to give in California. Quayle had been hearing a lot from Republicans around the country about how weak the administration had looked in its response to the Los Angeles riots. The speech seemed like the perfect time to put the conservative spin on the turmoil. (32)[4]

Quayle's remarks helped to set up an impending (and now realized) bipartisan assault on welfare, affirmative action, and other social programs. In this way, the battle over words must be understood in the context of erosion of material support for women, minorities, and the poor. The cuts in services depend rhetorically on racist stereotypes suggesting that the urban poor, figured as mostly black and Latino, are largely undeserving of public aid.

Conversely, Quayle attributes success among minorities or the poor to their demonstration of "positive" traditional family values. His book (notably, coauthored with psychologist Diane Medved), *The American Family* (1996), holds up "model" families, such as the De La Rosas of Los Angeles, who, despite their poverty and despite racial discrimination against them, manage to make ends meet and to instill traditional religious values and a procapitalist work ethic in their children. The lesson explicit in all five of the book's case studies is that regardless of material disadvantage or systematic oppression, those who work hard and keep their families together survive. It is no accident that Quayle chooses struggling families as emblems in this morality tale. The selection of only five stories, however, reveals a common persuasive strategy in family values arguments: the argument from anecdote, in which the cases are selected in such a way as to obscure the broader picture. In an editorial based on his 1992 speech, Quayle (1992b) presumes that the United States affords blacks and other minorities ample opportunity to succeed: "By any measure, the America of 1992 is more egalitarian, more integrated and offers more opportunities to black Americans and all other minority group members than the America of 1964" (3B).[5] Black Republican Gary Franks (of Connecticut) (1992) echoes this claim in his Horatio Alger-style family narrative, delivered to the 1992 Republican National Convention:

> I am here to tell you about an American success story. It's about a family where the father had only a sixth grade education and worked for 40 years in the brass mills of Waterbury, Connecticut. Where the mother worked full-time at a hospital while raising six children. . . . Today, I have three sisters who hold doctorates, a brother who is an Army colonel, and another brother who is a teacher. Black Americans need nothing more than an equal opportunity to succeed. Therefore I strongly oppose any affirmative action programs that would feature preferential treatment or set-asides for minorities.

In passages such as this one, the connection between a moral rhetoric of the family and policy issues such as affirmative action is clear. The moral claims of family values rhetoric, however, are rarely subjected to rational scrutiny. Franks, like Quayle, assumes based on his family's history that the "equal opportunity to succeed" already exists. Although a certain layer of black Americans have found places in the middle class, the

Milton S. Eisenhower Foundation (1993) reported on a study showing that the number of blacks living in poverty and the degree of de facto racial segregation in the United States have changed little or grown worse (contrary to Quayle's claim) since the 1960s. Today, half of all black children live in poverty, and well-paying jobs enabling the poor (regardless of race) to leave welfare rolls are scarce. The rhetoric of family values explicitly sets up a contrast between successful, middle-class blacks and the "culture of poverty—some call it an underclass" (Quayle 1992b):

> The underclass is a group whose members are dependent on welfare for very long stretches and whose men are often drawn into lives of crime. There is far too little upward mobility, because the underclass is disconnected from the rules of society. We are in large measure reaping the whirlwind of decades of changes in social mores. The intergenerational poverty that troubles us so much today is predominantly a poverty of values. (3B)[6]

As Herman Gray (1989) pointed out, middle-class success stories work as morality tales in conjunction with racist portrayals of the black criminal underclass ("disconnected from the rules of society") in a rhetoric that blames the poor for their own plight. This analysis in turn serves as grounds for arguments against welfare and other social programs. Despite its privatizing and scapegoating dimensions, however, the rhetoric of family values contains moments of utopian yearning for a nurturing community of a mythical bygone era. This mythic vision depends on the construction of women's identity as the keeper of the family utopia and guarantor of national unity and prosperity.

Back to the Future: Utopian Family Values

Stephanie Coontz (1992) has noted the mythic quality of nostalgia for an idyllic nuclear family. Coontz shows that today's "troubled," "declining" family closely resembles turn-of-the-century families in its incidence of single motherhood, poverty, and premarital sexual activity. A product of the 1950s, the traditional American family ideal was only approximated by some families. The stability of the family ideal depended on the postwar economic boom that produced cheap mortgages, loans for housing and education, and other "entitlements" for some middle-class households. In this light, today's crisis of family values can been seen as the product of the American Dream in disarray.

The mythic family, however, becomes a persuasive fiction in the rhetoric of family values. Fredric Jameson's (1979/1980) classic essay on utopian moments in popular culture argues that ideological conservatism in popular texts is often matched by a utopian moment. In other words, at moments of political crisis or upheaval, cultural texts acknowledge the limits of what exists and gesture toward what could be different. As a form of therapy, they acknowledge "dis-ease" but only within prescribed ideological limits. Jameson writes,

> The works of mass culture cannot be ideological without at one and the same time being implicitly or explicitly Utopian as well: They cannot manipulate unless they offer some genuine shred of content as a fantasy bribe to the public. . . . Such works cannot manage anxieties about the social order unless they have first revived them and given them some rudimentary expression. . . . Anxiety and hope are two faces of the same collective consciousness. (144)

If racist scapegoating in family values rhetoric expresses American anxieties about the social order, then a maternal domesticity offers the hope, or "fantasy bribe," that makes the rhetoric so compelling to both liberal and conservative rhetors. Familialist discourses explicitly acknowledge public discontent with political strife and social fragmentation. At the same time, however, they offer as a solution the reconstituted family as both haven from the turmoil and handmaiden to it. Jameson unpacks this contradiction in his analysis of *The Godfather* (1972) as a text that acknowledges public yearning for collective identification and community but offers, instead, the mob as Family—with a capital "F."

Similarly, the family values utopia in contemporary political rhetoric depends on an image of woman as the keeper of the domestic hearth, guarantor of stability and prosperity. In this way, 1990s familism resembles nineteenth-century rhetorics addressed to women instructing them to "carry out the work of domestic good cheer" in a sphere increasingly separated from the realms of politics and wage labor (Voss 1995, 4; see also Cott 1977). Then, as today, mythic familism justified the brutal exploitation of wage labor outside the home and the exclusion of women from political arenas by constructing the domestic realm as utopian space of freedom and authenticity. Even in this conservative vision lies an ember of social critique—suggesting that modern life lacks freedom and authenticity and that the American Dream has fallen short of expectations.

During the 1992 campaign, both First Lady Barbara Bush and Marilyn Quayle self-consciously enacted the role of domestic woman in support of the family values theme. Their performances, in television and radio interviews and in addresses to the Republican National Convention, posed a direct contrast to the persona of Hillary Clinton, wife of candidate Bill Clinton, who was cast as villain in a "good woman-bad woman" opposition. Described in the press as a "tough-minded," "impatient," and "brusque" woman with a severe image problem (Grove 1992),[7] Hillary Clinton spent the campaign attempting to remake herself according to a familial ideal. Even so, no one on the Democrat side could outperform Barbara Bush in a domestic bliss contest. Her popularity as the nation's grandmother figure was important to the Bush-Quayle campaign because she enacted the family values theme at every opportunity. Both she and Marilyn Quayle contrasted their traditional, Christian family histories with the alleged decadence of baby-boom rebels. They became icons of maternal care held up as the alternative to the "caretaking state." Because the image of domestic stability and harmony presented by the Republican women depended on a certain economic prosperity, however, their rhetoric was fraught with contradictions when the utopian vision encountered the reality of some families.

For example, in his remarks to the Republican National Convention, Pat Robertson (1992) extolled Barbara Bush as an exemplary family woman: "Ladies and gentlemen, we have a First Lady, Barbara Bush . . . she's a gracious lady, a devoted wife, a dedicated mother, and a caring grandmother." Robertson recounted a story about a trip with the Bushes to Sudan, during which Barbara Bush met a starving child: "I will never forget Barbara Bush in the midst of the dust, the flies, and the disease, taking a little boy like that in her arms and loving it as only a mother could." Robertson's account exaggerates the lesson implicit in every instance of family values rhetoric: The solution to poverty and suffering—even starvation—is not material aid but maternal love. Biographical narratives were central to crafting this message. Barbara Bush (1992), speaking before the Republican National Convention, told the story of her marriage as follows:

> As in our family, as in American families everywhere, the parents we've met are determined to teach their children integrity, strength, responsibility, courage, sharing, love of God, and pride in being an American. However you define family, that's what we mean by family values. You know, we know that parents have to cope with so much more in today's world; more drugs, more violence, more promiscuity. . . . You know, when George and I headed West after World War II, we already had our first child. . . . We eventually settled in Midland, a small, decent community where neighbors helped each other; a wonderful place to bring up a family and it still is. In many ways, these were the best years of our lives. George's days in the fields were dusty with long hours and hard work, but no matter when he got home, he always had time to throw a ball or listen to the kids. I car pooled, was a den mother, and went to more Little League games than I can count. We went to church, we cheered at Fourth of July picnics and fireworks, and we sang carols together at Christmas.

From the outset, Bush's biography teaches a lesson in determination aimed at "American families everywhere." Bush paints an idyllic portrait of small-town life—"a small, decent community where neighbors helped each other" and "a wonderful place to bring up a family"—during the postwar boom. Her role as den mother was to facilitate wonder and decency, just as her role in the campaign was to facilitate Republican victory on themes of the utopian family.

Even as she chronicles her wonder years, however, she makes it clear that such bliss is difficult to come by today. She notes that "parents have to cope with so much more in today's world" and grants to nontraditional families that "however you define family, that's what we mean by family values." At the same time, she insists that families are like hers in their attempt to instill integrity and responsibility and claims that small-town Texas remains "a wonderful place to bring up a family." As in the account of the Sudanese child's plight, difficult realities creep into the rhetoric of family values, revealing the rhetoric as pure, but persuasive, nostalgia for a utopia—etymologically, "no place."

This construction of 1950s family nostalgia serves as a direct contrast with the fractured public of the 1960s and 1970s. Marilyn Quayle's contributions to this discourse pose family values against feminism. Although Quayle worked as a lawyer outside the home, she insisted that "women do not want to be liberated from their essential natures as women. Most of us love being mothers and wives" (1992a). In her speech at the GOP convention, Quayle (1992b) exhorted her audience to "go back to the future" of restored family values. Like the 1980s film, *Back to the Future* (1985), Quayle's speech attempts to re-create the conditions of American prosperity by invoking the ideological products—traditional gender roles and the nuclear family ideal—in the context of contemporary economic and social crisis and fragmentation.

The Cold War family constituted, as Elaine Tyler May (1988) explains, an expression of both optimism and middle-class affluence on the one hand and Cold War anxieties over the possibility of nuclear war on the other hand. Undoubtedly, the vision of a prosperous suburban family living the dream of security and harmony amid new appliances and tricycles on the sidewalk depended on the relative economic stability of the period between 1945 and 1973. David Harvey (1989, 140) argues that despite the tensions of racism and the eruptions of social movements during the 1950s and 1960s, "material living standards rose for the mass of the population in the advanced capitalist countries," enabling the spread of the "benefits" of mass production and consumption to some layers of the working class, even as new assembly-line techniques also regimented and disciplined workers. Harvey argues that postwar Fordism—assembly-line mass production on an unprecedented scale—alongside the geopolitical hegemony of the United States "meant a whole new aesthetic and a whole new way of life" (135). American culture expressed this new way of life through the proliferation of consumer choices and the celebration of consumption. The family, then, became the site of mass consumption and the expression of the dream of eternal American prosperity. The recession of 1973 marked an end to that dream. To maintain profitability, capitalists introduced a new regime of what Harvey (1989, 149-50) calls "flexible accumulation," marked by increased internationalization of capital, innovations in production, flexibility with labor and resources, and rapid growth in the service sector. In recent decades, under the banner of flexible accumulation, employers have taken advantage of weak unions to push for overtime, speed-ups, wage and benefits reductions, and irregular work hours. Gone are the 8-hour day and the family wage, replaced by workers holding multiple part-time jobs, working split shifts, or working from home.

Harvard economist Juliet Schor (1991, 1) reports that "in the last twenty years the amount of time Americans have spent at their jobs has risen steadily. . . . Working hours are already longer than they were forty years ago." Schor goes on to explain that not only are women working longer hours at work and then coming home to the "second shift" but also that working people of both sexes are under tremendous pressure to put in longer hours. Many workers cannot make it on only one low-wage job; Schor reports interviews with four-job families (20-1). Investigators have discovered a resurgence in the number of urban sweatshops across the country along with widescale abuses of labor laws regulating allowable hours. Schor writes,

> My estimates . . . confirm not only that more people are working, but that they are working more. According to my estimates, the average employed person is now on the job an additional 163 hours, or the equivalent of an extra month a year. (28-9)[8]

In 1990, one fourth of all full-time workers spent 49 or more hours on the job each week. Of these, reports Schor, almost half were at work at least 60 hours per week (30). Schor concludes that capitalism has not reduced human toil but rather has increased workforce productivity through longer hours, mandatory overtime, split shifts, shorter vacations, and other measures that have cut into human leisure—and family—time. Thus, contrary to celebratory postmodernists who claim that capitalism is disorganizing itself without the need for political activism, social theorist Harvey (1989) maintains that the underlying logic of capitalism and its tendency toward crises that throw millions of people into poverty and joblessness are still present. In this context, conservative familialists offer a vision of the Cold War family as a utopian corrective. It is as if the rehabilitation of intimate life could restore the material conditions that generated the 1950s nuclear family ideal.

The stark contrast between this ideal of an orderly world of family, nation, church, and work, on the one hand, and the chaos of social strife, on the other hand, marks conservative family values speeches. Indeed, the appeal to order in the face of conflict and uncertainty is a significant feature of the utopian edge of family values rhetoric. I argue that this utopian resonance has allowed conservative political interests to appear universal and persuasive, isolating a progressive critique of spending cuts in the name of family values.

Gitlin (1995) has described how Americans face a "twilight of common dreams." He holds the therapeutic ethos partly responsible for the atomization and fragmentation of the Left, in particular, as we settle for the consolations of therapy instead of building coalitions and movements. Since the late 1960s, the Left has failed to articulate a unifying progressive vision in favor of a fragmented politics of identity and difference. In the process, Gitlin argues, the Left has ceded the rhetoric of moral order and unity of purpose to the Right, even though historically the Right has worked in defense of minority privilege. The rhetoric of family values demonstrates successful conservative universalism. Indeed, this privatizing, therapeutic rhetoric has found a voice even among independent, ostensibly oppositional black filmmakers.

Family Therapy in the 'Hood

In mainstream political rhetoric, maternal domesticity offers the "fantasy bribe" that makes the rhetoric of private blame persuasive. In the recent explosion of " 'hood" films, an image of responsible black fatherhood as a solution offers viewers a similar, but paternal, utopian antidote to blame and scapegoating. Familialist discourses, as a subset of therapeutic rhetoric, explicitly acknowledge public discontent with political strife and social fragmentation. At the same time, however, they offer as a remedy the reconstituted family as haven from the turmoil. The films *Menace II Society* (1993), *South Central* (1992), and *Boyz N the Hood* (1991) offer at once a critique of urban poverty and alienation (through discomfiting realist images of young people's lives) and a consolatory solution to those problems in the persona of the responsible black father whose presence—and appropriate demonstration of family values—solves the problems of alienated black youth. Michele Wallace (1992, 125) wrote the following about *Boyz N the Hood:* "Its formula is simple and straightforward. The boys who don't have fathers fail. The boys who do have fathers succeed. And the success of such a movie at the box office reflects its power to confirm hegemonic family values." In such films, as in *The Godfather,* gangs are tropes for family life gone awry. The films can be read as popular attempts to discipline black men and scapegoat them for the problems of a deeply racist society.

The Fatherhood Formula

John Singleton's *Boyz N the Hood* presents the story of Tre Styles (Cuba Gooding, Jr.), a youth in South Central Los Angeles. With his father's strong moral guidance, Tre avoids the fates that befall his friends, including gang membership, drug addiction, imprisonment, and violent injury and death. On the retail video, a public service announcement precedes the film with a warning from Singleton addressed to black youth not to blow their future but rather to get an education. He endorses the United Negro College Fund (UNCF). The film opens with the displayed words, "One out of every twenty-one Black American males will be murdered in their lifetime. Most will die at the hands of another black male." Then the film cuts to a centered, red stop sign. Despite these propositional and policy-oriented messages (support the UNCF and stop the violence), the film eventually proposes a different, more private solution to the problems depicted.

Early in the film, Tre's father, Furious Styles (Larry Fishburne), tells Tre to do what he says so he will not end up like his friends. The rest of the film proves Furious right, as Tre's friends Dough Boy (Darren; played by rapper Ice Cube), Chris, and Mark—all without strong father figures—cycle downward into gang activity, imprisonment, drinking, and drugs. The film's tragic ending—in which Ricky, Dough Boy's athletic brother who has hope of attending college, is killed by a gang rivaling Dough Boy's—underscores Furious's lesson to Tre. The film sets up a good black—bad black dichotomy in the figures of Ricky and Dough Boy, in which Ricky is the martyred role model. Ironically, despite its pacifist message, the film's opening provoked riots in urban theaters across the country.[9]

South Central did not even open in Los Angeles due to fears of renewed violence and reminders of the L.A. riots. The *Los Angeles Times* commented, remarkably, that this decision was unfortunate because "the movie has nothing to do with the riots" (Galbraith 1992, 25).[10] I argue that this film—along with the others in the genre—has everything to do with the riots insofar as it is linked to an ideology of family values that politicians and pundits deployed directly in response to the riots. *South Central* tells the family values story of Bobby Johnson (Glenn Plummer), a young man with a small child living in an apartment complex in South Central Los Angeles. Again, the scene includes rival gangs, including the Deuce gang, which Bobby helps to form with his friend RayRay (Byron Keith Minns). When a rival gang challenges Deuce, Bobby goes with other Deuce members to "smoke" members of the rival gang. Bobby hesitates to participate but ends up killing a man. The story shifts to a point later in time, when Bobby is in prison realizing his mistakes, while his son Jimmie (Christian Coleman) struggles in South Central. Even as a youth, Jimmie is a member of Deuce under the tutelage of Ray. Jimmie is shot while escaping a burglary scene by Willie, an older black man. He is taken to the hospital and nursed to health by a caring nurse, who is hyperbolically portrayed as the benevolent alternative to Jimmie's own crack-using mother, Carole (LaRita Shelby).

Meanwhile, Bobby hears about Jimmie's involvement in Deuce and begins to question his commitment to the gang. A black Muslim named Ali (Carl Lumbly) takes Bobby under his wing and guides his rehabilitation so he can get out on parole to save his son. Ali and the other Muslims in the prison defend Bobby against white supremacists. Because Ali's own son had been killed in a gang incident, Ali took revenge on the gang, ending up in prison for life. He stated, "I was some daddy. . . . That's the problem in our community man. Black man in prison and his kids suffer. It's the anger, the cycle of hate, you're in that cycle. . . . You still have time. Break the cycle." Ali educates Bobby in the history of civil rights, racial oppression, and black nationalism.

A chastened Bobby wins parole and goes out to find his son, who has been placed in a halfway house. Jimmie is still involved in Deuce and wants to kill Willie (the homeowner who shot Jimmie) in revenge. In the film's climactic scene, Bobby confronts Ray in a warehouse where Ray and Jimmie are holding Willie, pending execution. Ray and Bobby vie for Jimmie's trust and loyalty. During the confrontation, Bobby explains to Ray that he is through with the gang. Ray asks, "How can you be through with your family?" Indicating to Bobby that he (Ray) and the gang have been Jimmie's mother and father, Ray represents bad parental influence. As Bobby implores Jimmie to leave with him, Ray brings in Willie, blindfolded and tied. Jimmie holds the gun.

Bobby warns him about committing an irrevocable crime and asks Ray to let Jimmie go:

> That boy you're holding is my son. I told a man in prison I would save my son's life even if it took my life. I'm willing to die here today, Ray. For my boy. I love him. Do you love him? . . . All I want to give him is something you or I never had—a father.

This speech convinces Jimmie to leave with his father.

The opening scene of *Menace II Society,* set in the film's present, portrays its main character, Caine Lawson (Tyrin Turner), witnessing his friend commit an armed robbery and murder. The scene then flashes back to 1965 around the time of the Watts riot.[11] As Caine narrates the film, he tells of his childhood in the 1960s with a drug-dealer dad and an addicted mother. Scenes of parties and criminal life play out on the screen. For example, Caine's parents neglect to intervene as gang members introduce him to drinking, drugs, and guns. Caine also witnesses his father murder a person over a dispute during a card game. The action of the film then cuts to Watts in 1993, with an overhead camera shot paralleling the 1965 scene. Implicit here is a critique of racist society: Watts in 1993 suffers from the same systemic and structural problems that prompted urban rebellion three decades earlier. Caine is now a high-school graduate and drug dealer, living with his kind but out-of-touch grandparents. When gang members shoot and kill Caine's cousin Harold, Caine and O-Dog (Larenz Tate) plot revenge. With friends, they go to confront the killers at a drive-in fast-food place called Jungle of Chicken and kill the two rival gang members.

Meanwhile, Caine is falling in love with Ronnie (Jada Pinkett), the girlfriend of Pernell (Glenn Plummer), a friend of Caine's who is currently in prison. Ronnie has a son, Anthony, whom she is trying to protect from gang warfare. She prohibits Caine from inducting Anthony into gang life. Eventually, the police question Caine about an auto theft and connect him to the liquor store robbery that occurred at the beginning of the film. Scared, Caine starts to rethink his life. He continues to commit robberies and deal drugs, however. Sharif's teacher, Mr. Butler (Charles S. Dutton), advises Caine to go with Sharif (a Muslim) and Stacey (an aspiring college athlete), two friends who are planning a move to Kansas. After an unprovoked police beating, Caine ends up in the hospital. Ronnie visits him and confesses that she, too, has romantic feelings. Eventually, Caine reassesses his priorities and begins to think of himself as a potential family man.

He gets involved in a fight, however, with a former girlfriend's brother (who claims the girl is pregnant). Caine becomes the target of a drive-by shooting in Ronnie's yard. Gang members gun down Sharif and Caine, who has thrown his body over Anthony's to protect the child, who has witnessed the incident. As Caine dies in Stacey's arms, he reflects on how he could have lived his life differently. The closing montage, set to the sound of heartbeats, reviews Caine's mistakes, ending with Caine's insight that "it all catches up with you" and "now it's too late." Despite this film's tragic ending (Caine does not get rescued by a father figure), there are clear familialist lessons in Caine's assuming the role of family man with Ronnie and Anthony and in his realization—too late—that his life could have been different if he had adopted that role earlier.

Antitherapeutic Critical Moments in the Films

In its very setting, the " 'hood" genre cannot help but pose a critical comment on contemporary urban social reality.[12] Run-down housing projects and business districts, addict-populated parks, and the pervasive sound of sirens and police helicopters all evoke, in Kenneth Burke's (1945/1969a) terms, a literally scenic point of view that foregrounds context, system, and structures of oppression in contrast to a privatizing individualist or familialist rhetoric. David Denby (1993, 54-5) stated the following about *Menace* in *New York* magazine: "The Hugheses have shot the film in cramped tract houses and tawdry streets. . . . The filmmakers' point is that Caine lives in an enclosed world."[13] These images, however, sometimes work to subvert awareness of the broader political scene. All the films, by virtue of narrative convention, focus on a protagonist's individual, existential struggle, making it almost inevitable that social problems will be personalized in the stories of individual moral struggle. Indeed, it can be argued that this personalization of political issues is an unavoidable feature of modern narrative in general.

One or more characters, however, provide explicit political commentary in each film to keep audience attention on the sociopolitical issues at hand. In *Boyz,* children walk to school through a scene of urban decay, past posters promoting the reelection of Ronald Reagan: "Four More Years," as gunshots sound in the distance. The images suggest that Reagan's two terms in office and his economic policies are partly to blame for the situation in which these children find themselves.[14] At the film's end, Dough Boy comments that "they don't know, don't show, or don't care what's going on in the 'hood" in an explicit critique of news media. Each film also places a heavy emphasis on a critique of racist police violence. In *Boyz N the Hood,* the sounds of sirens and police helicopters are omnipresent, suggesting a hovering malevolent force. Each film features a scene in which police beat main characters without warrant or provocation, emphasizing the oppressive actions of the police and building sympathy for the plight of the urban youth whose own violence becomes less exceptional in this context. In addition, *Boyz N the Hood* is the only one of these films that does not feature a "good" police officer whose presence serves to legitimate the police, implying that "only a few bad apples" contribute to the cycle of violence.

Perhaps the most significant source of scenic critique in these films comes from the ways in which the films encourage identification with their protagonists, regardless of their criminal or violent actions. *Menace II Society* goes the farthest in this regard, offering absolute narrative identification with Caine through his voice-over commentary that guides viewer interpretation. To sympathize with criminals while politicians outside the film's frame call for more police and more prisons automatically calls into question the crimewave hype and encourages viewers to understand the boys' actions in their contexts of despair and lack of opportunity. Because the characters are allegorical stand-ins for a whole class of people, the boys represent a collective of sympathetically portrayed black urban youth, whereas the police represent the institutions of criminal justice, indicted for racist violence. Thus, the generic formula contains a moment of collectivist critique.

In an ideologically problematic way, however, the protagonists of *Boyz, Menace,* and especially *South Central* all undergo conventional transformations, winning audience sympathy only to the extent that they learn their lesson and repudiate both their anger and their criminal pasts. They are all formally punished for their actions by imprisonment, injury, death, or a combination of these.

Family Therapy and the Recuperation of Critique

In this way, critical moments that encourage scenic, sociopolitical critique are counterbalanced with a more conservative, therapeutic narrative that replaces political action with family responsibility. *Menace II Society* is preceded on the retail rental video by a public service announcement for the Institute for Black Parenting, described as a private company that is "concerned about our future." The segment, featuring actor Charles Dutton, exhorts viewers to take personal responsibility as parents and offers a toll-free number to call. In this advertisement, the film is explicitly connected with therapeutic intervention, whose goal is to remake the black family as the way to make a better future.

South Central's narrative of a repentant man atoning for his past and taking on the burden of saving his son's life offers an obvious example of a family therapy morality play. Similarly, in *Menace,* Caine narrates his childhood in terms of his parents' failure: "I learned a lot, saw a lot.

I caught on to the criminal life real quick. Instead of keeping me outta trouble, they turned me on to it." The rhetoric of family values in this film blames parents for the drugs, gangs, and violence rather than enabling a critique of a desperate social and economic scene in which the parents' behavior might seem tragic but understandable. This lesson is reinforced by the direct visual and narrative contrast between the party scene at the beginning of the film, in which Caine is exposed to beer and guns, and the later one, in which Ronnie protects Anthony from such exposure. Later, Pernell (in prison) tells Caine, "Take care of my son. I can't do shit for him in here. Teach him better than I taught you. Teach him the way we grew up was bullshit. All right?" Again, parental education is suggested as the only possible solution to the problems of city youth.

In *Boyz N the Hood*, Furious Styles matches his conventional parental responsibility with a radical-sounding black nationalist politics and prevents his son's demise from the film's beginning. His role is referred to in the film in explicitly therapeutic terms when a teacher calls Tre's mother to tell her about Tre's disruptive behavior. Significantly, the teacher recommends therapy for Tre and implies that Reva's career-woman status has put Tre at risk. Reva Styles, implicitly conceding this last point, responds that Tre will live with his father, who becomes the therapeutic remedy for Tre's problems.

Furious's intervention is framed in terms of traditional gender roles. When Reva drops Tre off, she tells Furious, "You wanted him, you got him. I can't teach him to be a man. That's *your* job." The education in manliness includes lessons in hard work and personal responsibility, as Furious asks Tre to rake the yard, do dishes, clean the bathroom, and so forth. Tre confronts him: "What do you have to do around here?" Furious replies, "Pay the bills, put the food on the table, put clothes on your back. . . . You may think I'm being hard on you but I'm teaching you how to be responsible." Therefore, black fatherhood is not only the solution to urban problems but also a particular, traditional, masculine kind of black fatherhood—one that fits neatly with the American success myth of individual hard work resulting in individual rewards, regardless of structural obstacles to success.

In a key scene after Tre and Ricky take their SAT tests in the hopes of going to college, Furious takes the boys to see a billboard in the neighborhood reading, "Cash for Your Home." To a crowd of gathered onlookers, Furious (himself a mortgage lender) lectures about the lessons of the sign. He explains the process of gentrification, saying, "We need to keep everything black owned, black dollars, just like Jews, Mexicans, Koreans." He implies that whites have imported drugs into the ghetto to get young black men to kill themselves.[15] Furious is clearly speaking for Singleton here (later, Ricky comments, "My brother should have heard that"), laying out an ideology of black capitalism reminiscent of the movement led by Marcus Garvey. This position of nationalist self-help is a retreat from demanding systemic redress of injustice. In other words, rather than holding racist society accountable for racial inequality, black capitalism puts the burden of self-help on black individuals.[16] Singleton's film, however, may be read as an enabling response to the demeaning caricatures of black manhood propagated in the mainstream media. Naomi Warren (personal communication, October 1996) asks, "If Singleton is responding to hegemonic discourse which 'disses' Black males, how can Black males ever 'redeem' themselves without being subjected to some other type of critique wherein their redemptive strategies are deemed problematic?" In the pseudo-autobiographical narrative of Boyz, however, Singleton offers a conservative self-help morality play that, ironically, blames black men who fail to model appropriate familial responsibility. Critics of this film have also commented on its' and the other films' ambivalent gender politics (Wallace 1992). The failures of black sons are blamed on bad mothers, whereas "good girls" such as Brandi and Ronnie, who are virginal or piously maternal, are sympathetically portrayed. Women—and men who do not live up to the gang code—are labeled "bitches" and are punished by the male protagonists. A review of Menace in Cineaste (Massood 1993) noted,

> Shot in soft focus and with soft lighting, in contrast to the harsher realities of Caine's world, Ronnie and her house become Caine's only refuge. Within this space, Ronnie's subdued dress and practical manner sustain Caine in a way his own mother never could. Ronnie's role as nurturer and protector emerges through her strong desire to shield her son and Caine from the very same things. (45)[17]

As in political family values rhetoric and as in familialist discourses since the mid-nineteenth century, the good woman is figured as the nurturer and guarantor of domestic serenity, keeper of a haven or refuge in a heartless world. Furthermore, the films counterpoise "good" women to drug addicts and prostitutes, structuring a similar moral lesson to the one that blames poor black men for failure. In *Boyz,* Dough Boy's "bad" mother, whose image resonates with political invocations of a mythical welfare queen, is implicitly blamed for her sons' downfall. In one scene, she is unsympathetically portrayed in robe and curlers haranguing Dough Boy: "You're just like your father. You don't do shit. You ain't got no job." The scene reminds viewers that the mother has no job either. In addition, the film implicitly suggests that Dough Boy's problems stem from his father's absence. Tre's mother Reva, a professional woman, is depicted as too busy with her career to care properly for her son.

In the end, the film upholds a kind of masculine heroic individualism as the way forward. Critic Michael Dyson (1992) writes,

> The film's focus on Furious's heroic individualism fails, moreover, to fully account for the social and cultural forces that prevent more black men from being present in the home in the first place. Singleton's powerful message, that more black men must be responsible and present in the home to teach their sons how to become men, must not be reduced to the notion that those families devoid of black men are necessarily deficient and ineffective. Neither should Singleton's critical insights into the way that many black men are denied the privilege to rear their sons be collapsed into the notion that all black men who are present in their families will produce healthy, well-adjusted black men. So many clarifications and conditions must be added to the premise that *only* black men can rear healthy black men, that it dies the death of a thousand qualifications. (133)

Dyson's comments apply equally to the other films of this genre. Richard Merelman (1995, 97-128) points out that it is important to ask not only that blacks be represented in film but also to ask "What themes or stories about the black experience do these media projections contain?" He concludes that films such as *Boyz N the Hood* and *New Jack City* do not coherently develop a counterhegemonic perspective to white racism. In *Menace to Society,* the familialist lesson is constructed through the contrast between the bad gang family and the good nuclear family that might have been. Likewise, in *South Central,* the gang is a trope for a family life distorted by social pressures. The solution posed by the films, however, does not address these distorting social pressures but asks the family to conform to an orthodox ideal despite those circumstances. This solution is analogous to the one posed by family therapists, whose interventions cannot address the scope of racism and injustice, instead trying to mold the family, as family therapists must, against the circumstances shaping their lives.

Ultimately, this genre serves the broader, conservative political movement to cut social services and deny the continuing reality of racism in favor of disciplining and scapegoating black men (and others) for these problems. The rhetoric of family values is conveniently aligned with the bipartisan assaults on welfare, immigrant rights, and affirmative action across the country.

All in the Family: Family Therapies in Contemporary Politics

For the most part, the Democratic Party's references to family values during the 1992 campaign were brief and pragmatic. Never did the Democrats challenge the implicit racism of family values discourse nor challenge the familialist terms in which policy debates have been encoded. Indeed, Bill Clinton (1992) said (in a speech to the National Association for the Advancement of Colored People during the campaign), "We want to be the family values ticket." He added the following: "You know, most people in Los Angeles did not riot. Most people's children stayed home. They didn't steal, they didn't loot. They did the right thing. Why? Because they believe in the Ten Commandments and the teachings of family values." This passage is notable not for its difference but for its similarity to Republican rhetoric, indicating that Quayle was allowed to frame a bipartisan discussion of racism and poverty in familialist terms. In his nomination acceptance address, Clinton condemned parents who renege on child support (stigmatizing so-called deadbeat dads, who are often as impoverished as the women they abandon). Also, in a speech peppered with references to family values, he promised, like the Republicans, to end welfare as we know it, to enforce personal responsibility even among those with few personal opportunities. In July 1996, Clinton signed into law such a bill. The consequences of that legislation will be discussed later in the chapter.

Similarly, Hillary Clinton's (1996) recent book about the family, hailed as a progressive response to Republican family traditionalists, itself reproduces the logic of familism. On the one hand, she disparages the Republican "nostalgia merchants" who "sell an appealing Norman Rockwell-like picture of American life" (28). On the other hand, she writes, "our challenge is to arrive at a consensus of values and a common vision of what we can do today to build strong families" (21). She also states, "The American Dream is within reach of anyone willing to work hard and take responsibility" (15). She exhorts parents to teach children religious faith, self-discipline, and character as the way out of hardship (147). Although Clinton acknowledges that the kind of responsibility she means must be supplemented with support from the broader community and social networks (plus a minimum of government help), she does not take issue with the causal reasoning of familialists that obscures structure and system in favor of personalistic explanations for family crisis. For example, she attributes child poverty to divorce rather than some divorces to the stress of family poverty. She approvingly cites remarks by conservative William Bennett to the effect that "divorce is hard on children" and is responsible for "damage to the children of America" (39-41). On this rhetoric, one wonders whether parents have a right to escape the "damage" (both physical and emotional) of obligatory and oppressive marital relationships. In addition, Mrs. Clinton (1996) glowingly recounts anecdotes of poor children who made good as a result of growing up in strong families and about more affluent children who suffered because of growing up in a "broken" or untraditional family. Like her Republican counterparts, Clinton disavows materialist explanations—such as unemployment, poverty, parents working multiple jobs on split shifts, and so forth—for family stress and breakup. Democratic complicity in the privatizing and conservative rhetoric of family values is clear when Clinton states, "As always, the solution [to racism, poverty, and other structural crises] begins at home" (188). An important implication of this critique is that the Republican loss in the presidential election of 1992 did not mean that a conservative familialist rhetoric was unsuccessful. Quayle and Medved (1996, 2) write, "Bill Clinton, then a candidate for President, attacked the [family values] speech. . . . Today, as president, he frequently punctuates his speeches and comments with the term *family values.*" Indeed, the Republican sweep in the Congressional elections in 1994 suggests that the family values slogan—and its associations with traditional gender roles, racist scapegoating, and exhortations to personal responsibility—was infused with meaning in ways that were compelling for large numbers of Americans across partisan lines.

The extent to which the rhetoric of family values has come to inform political consciousness about issues of race and class is demonstrated by Louis Farrakhan's "Million Man March," which took place on October 16, 1995. Drawing approximately 800,000 people, the march and rally exhorted its black participants to atone for their family failures and to take personal responsibility for their families and communities.[18] The march excluded women, encouraging them to stay home and to play peripheral support roles. Thus, the themes of private responsibility and traditional gender roles go together in Farrakhan's rhetoric as they do in right-wing family values talk. On the one hand, the march represented a crying need for a movement demanding racial and economic justice. Michael Dawson (as quoted in Terry 1995a, 24), an associate professor of political science at the University of Chicago, told the *New York Times,* "In the black community, there is a unified unhappiness with the state of racial progress and a wide level of unity about seeing something done." In contrast, George Mason University professor Roger Wilkins, a critic of the march, stated "I don't think black men have to atone to the nation at large. What black men need is not atonement, they need jobs. You need jobs to make strong families" (Terry 1995a, 24).[19]

Chicago writer Salim Muwakkil notes, likewise, that "The atonement talk certainly has the whiff of blame the victim" (Terry 1995b, 1).[20] In this interview, Muwakkil compares the march to the men's conservative Christian movement, "the Promise Keepers, flavored with black nationalism." Tellingly, the Religion News Service (1995) hailed the march as proving that "the rhetoric of morality is rapidly becoming a cornerstone of American public discourse." The article reports that Farrakhan's remarks "echoed similar exhortations from Pope John Paul II, President Clinton, religious broadcaster Pat Robertson, and the speakers at mass rallies for men staged by the Promise Keepers Christian Organization." Robertson applauded Farrakhan for "embracing initiatives that we all applaud: law and order, discipline in children, family, unity." After the march, Farrakhan acknowledged the common ground between his, the Pope's, and Robertson's messages: "If there are similarities in our speaking, it's because we're coming from the same frame of reference."

This "frame of reference" is conservative familism, a discourse whose primary rhetorical function is the exoneration of capitalism and racism in favor of personalized explanations for social crisis. The rhetoric of therapy dislocates political anger that might be directed toward structural social change onto the individual and family, framing responses to the crisis in terms of private life. To the extent that the rhetoric of family values implies that family therapies can solve the problems of racism, sexism, and poverty, it is a therapeutic discourse.

▓▓ The Familial Public as Oxymoron

At the time of this writing, President Clinton had signed a draconian welfare "reform" bill into law. The bill will, according to the *New York Times* ("Mr. Clinton's Duty on Welfare" 1996),

> Hurl more than a million children into poverty. It will slice food stamps by an average of $600 for families earning less than $6,300 a year. It will strip legal immigrants, including some elderly, of health insurance. It will, for the first time ever, tell workers who lose their jobs after years of steady work that they cannot collect food stamps for their children. (A22)[21]

Although welfare programs comprise only 1 percent of the federal budget and those most likely to be hit hardest by such reform will be poor children (Pear 1996, A21),[22] Democrats and Republicans alike justify such draconian measures in terms of a persistent rhetoric of personal familial responsibility. The claim of these politicians that they "value families" is contradicted outright by the threatened institution of such harsh material cutbacks in aid to poor and working-class families.

I do not claim that family life is never a proper subject for policy discourse. Nor do I suggest that therapy is valueless for troubled families. Although this chapter, like this book, sets up activism and therapy as opposites alongside the binaries private versus public, agent versus scene, and atonement versus redress, the comments by Mirkin (1990) about the possibility of political contextualization of therapy stand as evidence of a spectrum of therapy and politics. What I do suggest, however, is that a problem arises when all policy matters are rhetorically and ideologically transformed into issues of family life and when the talk of the family begins to code and constrain discussion of issues broader than the side of a home. During and since the 1992 presidential campaign, all sides in the limited argument over the family have focused attention on private life, replicating long-standing patterns of surveillance and discipline; consequently, family values rhetoric discredits critiques of the systematic injustices of late capitalist society. In a society marked by a fundamental class divide, in which gendered and racialized sets of "shared values" are used to justify the perpetuation of that divide, contest of those values and their rhetorical functions becomes more appropriate than building community around them.

The rhetoric of family therapy, in the White House and in the 'hood films, privatizes our experience of political life and thus participates in the destruction of public political understanding, space, and activity in the United States. This rhetoric backgrounds or effaces the role of political and economic systems and interests in generating and perpetuating inequality and injustice, and it ritually scapegoats the individual and the family. Specifically, the rhetoric of family values is a rhetorical weapon against the development of class consciousness because although the realities of a society divided by class and the poverty, hunger, and profits made from exploitation exist outside the discourse, class consciousness is a rhetorical product.

In Marx's terms, a class in itself is not automatically a class for itself. To generate collective political consciousness and action, we need not only the making of antitherapeutic narratives that sustain sociopolitical critique but also the rebuilding of movements for social justice. To the extent that familism saturates political discourse, it works against class solidarity and collective social action. To the extent that the flames of familism have seared the American political landscape, public argument suffers a devastating loss of a language for public engagement and collective struggle for justice and equality rather than atonement, therapeutic consolation, and self-blame.

<h2>▨ Notes</h2>

1. © 1996 New York Times. Reprinted with permission.
2. de Goede (1996) describes strategies of misuse of statistics and argument from anecdote characterizing this conservative strategy.
3. © 1994 The Nation. Reprinted with permission.
4. © 1996 New York Times. Reprinted with permission.
5. © 1992 St. Louis Post-Dispatch. Reprinted with permission.
6. © 1992 St. Louis Post-Dispatch. Reprinted with permission.
7. © 1992 Washington Post. Reprinted with permission.
8. © 1991 HarperCollins. Reprinted with permission.
9. Naomi Warren (personal communication, October 1996) comments, "It is my observation that these films have traditionally been announced by media as 'anticipating violence.' "

10. © 1992 Los Angeles Times Syndicate. Reprinted with permission.

11. See Upton (1985); this essay, written before the L.A. uprising of 1992, provides a very cogent critique of the ways in which the Watts riot in 1965 was explained in the mainstream media. He condemns "pseudotheories" that are widely accepted but do not account for material causes or political motivations for urban violence. He states that "most are 'scapegoat' hypotheses often blaming the victim. Most fall in the category of 'pop' social science, often politically motivated" (243).

12. The rap music soundtracks to these films provide an important contextual element, but one that is beyond the scope of this analysis. I suggest, however, that the political economy of rap music allows for oppositional artists such as Public Enemy and the late Tupac Shakur to produce popular but extremely critical views about the roots of city violence in racism, poverty, lack of opportunity, and police violence. One does not have to embrace gang violence itself (as Shakur did, to his demise) to embrace the scenic critique offered by hip-hop music. Thus, the soundtracks of the films under consideration here might help frame the messages of the films in terms of social critique. For commentary on the economic interrelationship of rap and film, see Jeffrey (1993, 47; see also Dyson, 1993).

13. Copyright © 1993 K-III Magazine Corporation. All rights reserved. Reprinted with permission of *New York* magazine.

14. See St. Pierre (1991); this article argues that Reagan's supply side economics (revisited by Dole and Kemp) disproportionately and negatively affected the poor and blacks. Reagan's cuts in federal expenditures on family support (Aid to Families with Dependent Children) and food, housing, education, and employment programs, while increasing defense funding, hurt the poor. During Reagan's terms, black one-parent families increased from 51.9% to 59.4%, whereas one-parent white families increased from 17.1% to 21.7%. Between 1980 and 1988, the poverty level of black families with related children increased from 35.5% to 37.3%, whereas the poverty level for whites increased from 11.2% to 12.4% (338, census statistics; *Journal of Black Studies*, 213, 338.

15. Interestingly, new evidence revealed by the San Jose *Mercury-News* does indict the Central Intelligence Agency for importing drugs into urban areas to make money for the right-wing Nicaraguan Contras.

16. For an analysis of Garvey's United Negro Improvement Association, see Shawki (1990).

17. © 1993 Cineaste. Reprinted with permission.

18. *Boyz N the Hood* advocates a political perspective similar to that of the march. Furious is clearly intended to represent a member of the Nation of Islam because he engages in Muslim practices and espouses black nationalist self-help. Like the march, the film takes legitimate black anger and turns it in a therapeutic direction.

19. © 1996 New York Times. Reprinted with permission.

20. © 1996 New York Times. Reprinted with permission.

21. © 1996 New York Times. Reprinted with permission.

22. © 1996 New York Times. Reprinted with permission.

4 The Support Group Nation

We're a support group nation. We don't talk about whether something is right or wrong, we just talk about making it through it.

—Kathleen Farrell (as quoted in May 1991, 3A)[1]

Since World War II, psychotherapeutic techniques have been an explicit tool of governments at war. On the premise that individual psychology held the key to wartime morale, the United States Committee for National Morale was formed in 1940, with prominent psychologists and sociologists among its members (Herman 1995, 49). Emergency committees and pollsters combined forces during World War II to manage public opinion and bolster support for the war effort on the home front. The Persian Gulf War (1990-1991) was no different on this score because psychotherapeutic motives dominated public discussion of support for troops and for the war.

During the Persian Gulf War, U.S. television news played a key role in domesticating dissent by rearticulating political outrage as personal anxiety and reconfiguring the will to resist as the need to support our troops. The mobilization of the themes and language of psychological crisis and emotional support domesticated the home front because images of military families quietly coping with the threat of war served as the key icon for the manufacturers of appropriate public response.

This case study reveals the power of the therapeutic to guide responses to political crisis into the grooves of personal and emotional ministration. During the war, the American nation was itself figured as a unitary body—the body antipolitic—in need of comfort and reassurance. News stories from national magazines to CNN defined questioning or protest or both of the war as harmful to the U.S. social body. Protest was labeled a social disease, a resurgent epidemic of the "Vietnam syndrome."

Over and over again, news stories in print and on television suggested the mystical argument that troops were killed in the Vietnam War because of a lack of unified support on the home front. Any voice of protest—and any news story covering that protest—was accused of being somehow complicit in the possible death of the troops in Desert Storm. The therapeutic texts offered silent coping and emotional unity, along with support for not only the troops but also the war effort itself, as cures for the Vietnam syndrome. The framing of responses to the war in terms of emotional support represented a therapeutic displacement of political energy, effectively cordoning off and muting the voices of opposition to the war, thereby protecting the fragile social space from the anger of protesters.

This strategy depended on a particularly gendered mapping of the home front. During this and other U.S. wars, the discourse of family support for the troops feminized and personalized the "home" front. Gender divisions in society and their reinforcements in ideological texts are deployed during wartime to mobilize uncritical support for the war effort. The maintenance of prowar interests thus depends on a particular definition of feminine support and domestic space. As women and families were constructed within support roles, a potentially divided and conflicted country was also "domesticated." This chapter will show how a pattern of initial anxiety and critique of the war in news texts was answered by themes of comfort and consolation. Most widely watched news texts moved from reporting moments of incipient political critique to encouraging personal and emotional avenues for the expression of anxiety. This rhetorical move constituted the nation as a unified family supportive of the war. During the war, "coping," "waiting," and "healing" were the watchwords of families with members stationed in the Persian Gulf. Stories depicting families—especially military wives and children—were ubiquitous before and during the war, occurring for the most part at the end of television news broadcasts. These stories seemingly appeared in direct response to anxiety-producing coverage of war technologies, tactics, casualties, and protests. Almost without exception, coverage of troops' families began with statements of ambivalence, anger, and opposition to the war on the part of the interviewed family members. By the end of each segment, however, the interviewees had resigned themselves to coping with their fears and helping others to do the same.

More than consoling the interviewees, support group news during the Persian Gulf War consoled the nation as a whole. These stories, I argue, effectively personalized the political in a therapeutic discourse that contained widespread unrest and resentment toward the deployment of U.S. troops. The themes of therapy—consolation, coping, support, and adaptation—translate political problems into personal and emotional terms. During the war, this discourse moderated the antiwar edge of "harder" coverage (of casualties, danger, prisoners, and protests). "Support group" stories contained and recuperated news about antiwar protest through their placement in the broadcasts and their invocation and reinflection of the history of the U.S. "defeat" in the Vietnam War. Because therapeutic themes and motifs acknowledge unhappiness and anger while encouraging personal solutions to social problems, they are ideal for the expression and containment of "dis-ease" in popular culture. Theories of hegemony are thus a natural way of framing and talking about the therapeutic discourses of the Persian Gulf War.

Hegemony and the News: Domesticating Dissent

Hegemony theory enables critics to explain how popular and political texts can give voice to opposition yet simultaneously mute critical voices.[2] In elaborating a theory of how culture, broadly conceived, works to ensure consent to the social order, Antonio Gramsci argued that cultural texts play an integral role in defusing resistance to the established social system by manufacturing the consent of its subjects through persuasion rather than coercion.

This is not to say, however, that criticism and resistance to hegemonic ideas are impossible or that any compromise with the terms of the prevailing ideological system is suspect. My goal, however, is to call attention to the extent to which such rhetorics as the therapeutic can successfully contain and reframe oppositional movements and discourses. During the Persian Gulf War, the therapeutic discourse of coping, unity, and healing took what might have been resistance to the familial (and broader social) disintegration caused by the war and reflected it as unconditional support for the war.

The news participates in maintaining the hegemony of established economic and political interests. Herbert Gans's landmark study of newsmaking routines and texts argues that journalistic habits and the ideological commitment to liberalism have made television news a short-sighted undemocratic enterprise that depoliticizes the public realm (Gans 1979). By *liberalism,* I do not mean the commonsense "opposite of conservative" but rather the political philosophy and set of core ideological assumptions of Western, capitalist nations. Liberalism's core values include individual autonomy and responsibility over and above collective identification and action (Hall 1986, Hartz 1955). Thus, liberal discourses typically frame social movements and other forms of collective protest as aberrations from an individualist norm. Gans (1979, 190-91) notes that newsmakers working within the assumptions of liberalism thereby promote an ideology, although that reality is obscured by journalistic constructs of "objectivity" and the liberal assumption that liberalism itself is not an ideology; journalists portray anyone with a distinct ideological position as a special interest with an ax to grind. Furthermore, the structuring of news stories (especially on commercial television) follows a narrative format of introduction, rising action, crisis, falling action, and conclusion (Collins and Clark 1992, Gitlin 1979a, 1979b). This structure, like narratives in general, poses news events in terms of authority, social cohesion, and order. News narratives often frame oppositional viewpoints as disruptive challenges to that order, then undermine or discredit the oppositional perspective in a narrative restoration of order and unity.

Most studies of news content and form suggest that mainstream news preserves the social order, reinforcing the everyday liberal common sense of its viewers and defining any event or statement that challenges that common sense as a disruptive force.[3] Especially during a social crisis (such as a war), news reinforces the values of national unity, individualist solutions to problems, consumerism, and a sense of self that is fundamentally isolated and passive. Because journalists operate within the "routine structures of everyday thought" (Gitlin 1979a) and perceive perspectives outside of those structures as belonging to "biased special interests," news narratives tend to frame social conflict in terms of the dominant value system. Gans (1979, 295) writes, "To the extent that journalists help maintain order, warn against disorder, and act as moral guardians, they function as agents of social control." From this perspective, the most important question relates to how news deals with political opposition to established ideological common sense during times of political crisis, such as the Persian Gulf War (Gitlin 1979a, 1980; Hallin 1991, Kellner 1992).[4] The news works rhetorically to neutralize events categorized as social disorder news. As a result, each broadcast, or even segment, ends with the restoration of order. During the Vietnam War (and the ongoing civil rights struggle), marches, protests, sit-ins, and other political challenges were covered as "social disorder news." Gitlin's (1980) study of media coverage of the New Left during the Vietnam conflict provides additional evidence for the claim that media frames[5] incorporated New Left events and arguments but undercut them with implicit assumptions reinforcing the liberal ideology. The result for the New Left was marginalization, distortion of central contentions, and, most important, the false opposition between activism on the one hand and rational, moderate debate on the other hand (as if activists never made rational sense). This process of marginalization produced "discrepant statements of reality [that] are acknowledged—but muffled, softened, blurred, fragmented, *domesticated* at the same time" (Gitlin 1980, 271). Thus, the news frames demonstrations and conflict not as legitimate alternative suggestions but rather as disruptions of an order presumed to be the only legitimate option. Reporters attend to radical activists not to give their views supportive airplay but to call attention to the threat activists pose to the security of the social system. One key way in which the news attempts to undermine the persuasiveness of activists is through personalized news that reduces viewers' involvement in the world to the affairs of their personal lives.

Personalized News

Personalized news refers to the attempts of news producers and writers to link national and international events to the "real" lives of individuals in their home towns. Normally, this kind of news serves to "wrap up" the day's events in cheerful stories at the end of the broadcast to leave the listener or viewer with a pleasant sense of security.[6] Through personalized news, producers can structure information about opposing interests and events in narrative forms that make illegitimate any opposition to the basic assumptions of liberal capitalism. Since its emergence in the middle of the nineteenth century, this form of news has been symbolic rather than informational, designed to achieve audience identification with certain national values in dramatic form (Hughes 1940). The human interest story is a key component of "wrapping up" a news segment or broadcast featuring social discord. It can serve to restore a sense of unity and coherence, providing a "solution" to the problems posed in the text's earlier moments. The problem with this kind of news is that it tends to suggest that the resolution of social problems lies in individuals rather than on the structural or political causes of problems. This individualistic and personal focus can persuade people that they do not need to work politically for social change as the solution to social problems (Rucinski 1992, 92). Personalized news was a pervasive component of Persian Gulf War coverage, portraying ordinary families coping with the stress of war and taking personal responsibility for getting through the crisis. Family support stories at the end of national news broadcasts served to wrap up earlier news about the war (and opposition to it) in a neat, clean package with a yellow ribbon, putting a tidy end to dissent and disunity.

Yellow (Ribbon) Journalism

Reassuring family support stories seemed like a direct response to war-induced anxiety. "24-Hour War Coverage Makes Viewers Anxious," proclaimed one headline (Selby 1991). The news described how military families sometimes avoided footage of combat and favored the suggestion that the news be totally blacked out due to fear of trauma (Scott 1991).[7] The day after the war began, the *New York Times* interviewed marine wives. One said, "I try not to watch the news. It disturbs me too much." Another agreed: "I don't watch the news . . . I do not pretend to understand what makes the world tick. I know only how it affects me" (Reinhold 1991).[8]Around the country, support groups (numbering in the dozens in each major metropolitan or military community) sprang up to help people deal with the emotional stresses of war. Although the groups themselves consoled the individuals and the families wracked with worry, news coverage of support groups and family crisis—or yellow ribbon journalism—served to console the nation as a whole. Two important patterns emerge in this coverage. First, although some men were left at home to care for children and wait for the return of the troops, the stories (except a few investigating single fatherhood as an anomaly) focused on stressed-out women (military wives) and children. Second, in the accounts of these families, a dialectic of anxiety about the war and therapeutic solutions to that anxiety plays itself out. Operation Desert Storm is answered on the home front by "Operation Desert Comfort" (a phrase coined by Noam Neusner, 1991).[9] Many military families were critical of the war.[10] A national organization called the Military Family Support Network (MFSN; an antiwar group of military families) had 136 chapters and 6,500 supporters at the height of the war (Creighton 1991).[11] Although many military support networks refused disturbing political debate in favor of comfort strategies, the MFSN located blame for stress with public political factors rather than interpersonal ones.

The MFSN and the coverage of its particular version of "support the troops" rhetoric, however, were not featured in the popular media. Some articles from the war pointed out that if the war were to become drawn out and bloody, support for Operation Desert Storm would wane. Most stories, however, were structured around the principle of ameliorating anxiety and finding ways to cope. Personal conflict over the war was the dramatic crux of military family news coverage; personal solutions made for a comforting (and rhetorically effective) denouement to the drama. For example, an account in the *Baltimore Sun* of a military support group reported initial anger toward the war but went on to say that the group was composed of both war supporters and war opponents (Neusner 1991). The article stated, "But whatever their differences, these groups share a common goal: helping people cope with the loneliness, fear, and frustration that comes from separation from loved ones" (1G).[12] This passage marked the transition to suggested strategies for coping with the stress of war: swapping information, "getting things done for others," avoiding television, and talking about their fears. The article concluded with a list of support groups in the Baltimore area. A list of antiwar organizations was, predictably, absent.

This article was typical of most coverage of support groups in its movement from anger to coping, its emphasis on women, its plea for therapeutic unity between anti- and prowar citizens, and its assumption that women work through anxiety by helping other people rather than acting on their own behalf. In many of these articles, protesting the war is upheld but trivialized, on the one hand, as just another coping strategy (a way to "pretend" that one has some control over events). On the other hand, protest is articulated within the context of family support news as just another source of stress.

The inclusion of war supporters and protesters under the umbrella of "support" was a common framing device during the war. Support for the troops is an ambiguous construction, often becoming equated with support for the war. The rhetorical upshot of the imperative to community support is that we must be so careful of each other's feelings that politics is out of bounds at such a meeting. In other words, when political issues are framed in emotional terms, outright criticism and dissent are excluded in favor of nurturing and protecting others from potential critique. Support—translated to mean uncritical acceptance of existing conditions and one's ultimate powerlessness to do anything to change them—is the order of the day. The therapeutic functioned to nullify anger and to silence debate in the context of an emotional mutuality that precludes political discussion.

The focus on women and especially children played a large part in this work. Articles on how to talk to children about war and death, respond to their questions, and deal with the absence of one or more parents proliferated in the press. In response to what was called a "national collective anxiety attack" (Kobren 1991), the press advised adults and children alike to do two things: unite and adapt to the situation. One psychiatrist (as cited in Moore 1991) advocated yellow-ribbon wearing as a signifier of group identity.[13] The psychiatric discourse invoked in the popular news deployed therapeutic motifs of consolation and identification to encourage adaptation to the crisis rather than protest against it.[14] In addition, readers were encouraged to find comfort in the private sphere rather than take public action. The obsession with children's needs during the war thus might be regarded as an attempt to render the entire home front docile and childlike, seeking comfort and refuge from the war. Like the press, television overall took the therapeutic advice of one reporter to "temper reality with reassurance" (Sataline 1991).[15]

Television's Cure for the Vietnam Syndrome

The therapeutic went national as television news and national news magazines picked up and ran with coverage of families coping with war stress. *Newsweek* divided its war news into "Desert Storm" and "The Home Front," the latter devoted to news about protests, media coverage analysis, opinion polls, and—last but not least—coverage of military families coping with the war. *Time* employed a similar format, as in a story about a peace activist who had changed her mind and joined in the community "support the troops" campaign (Gibbs 1991a, 34).[16] Photographs or televised images of tearful good-byes and anxious families huddled around the television further personalized the experience of war. Coverage of families supporting the war followed and reframed coverage of protests, emphasizing the need for emotional unity so as to avoid another Vietnam War. Steven Roberts (1991, 11) stated in *U.S. News & World Report* that "Vietnam etched an indelible pattern on our identity, fragmenting our families and poisoning our patriotism."[17] His article featured young prowar activists who have ostensibly gotten over the cynicism and shame of the Vietnam War era and can rally around the flag in good conscience. National pride and emotional support for the troops function in this kind of coverage as therapy against the Vietnam syndrome.

In February 1991, *Time* covered the construction of an enormous human flag in San Diego, under the headline "Land That They Love: Patriotism and Its Symbols Dominate the Debate Over the Gulf War as Both Sides Emphasize Concern for the Soldiers and for the Fate of the Nation" (Gibbs 1991b, 52). The reporter wrote, "There is a measure of atonement in this by a country that treated Vietnam veterans with unjustified contempt" (52). This passage identifies what was so compelling about "support the troops" rhetoric: It served the therapeutic function of assuaging national guilt in the wake of the Vietnam War.[18] News writers, conservative pundits, and politicians blamed television newscasts for reinvoking Vietnam War-related anxiety. Headlines read "Just Watching the War Is Stressful"[19] and "War Takes Toll on TV Viewers"[20] (Calhoun and O'Hanlon 1991, O'Connor 1991). Meanwhile, President George Bush and Vice President Dan Quayle kept insisting that Desert Storm would not become another Vietnam War (Bush 1991, Quayle 1991).[21] Persian Gulf War presidential and news versions of that conflict continually suggested that lack of support was a major cause of the "failure" of the U.S. troops in the Vietnam War. In this revised historical account, the media were partly to blame for bringing vivid scenes of the horror of war before the U.S. public. If reporters of the Persian Gulf War were to escape blame this time around, they needed to "temper reality with reassurance."

During the first week of the war, one *Newsweek* article noted the eruption of a dedicated antiwar groundswell once fighting began (Adler, 1991). The article stated,

> The gulf-war protests start off with a legitimacy that it took years for other movements to win. Protest as such is no longer regarded as unpatriotic by most Americans and the rhetoric this time around is not as offensive. . . . But some protesters are conspicuously more radical than others. (37)[22]

The article went on to describe a split between mainstream patriotic protesters and the more radical wing of the movement. This strategy attempted to define the outer margins of acceptable dissent and, as in other similar stories, warmly accepted antiwar activists who still waved the American flag and paid emotional lip service to the support the troops mantra.

The article reported that 57% of Americans wished that all protests would stop. To drive that suggestion home, an additional short article within a box inside of the protest coverage carried the headline, " 'One Big Family' in Crystal Springs" (Smith and Miller 1991). It featured a city with 160 of its residents stationed in the Persian Gulf. Acknowledging that the residents were experiencing some anxiety over the fates of their loved ones, the article emphasized the community's support of the troops, the administration, and the war:

> Now the people of Crystal Springs continue to pray for a speedy end to the conflict, banding together for strength and solace. In the morning, many congregate at Hamilton's bakery to exchange news and lend support; in the afternoon and evening they drop by Trinity Cafe, where words of consolation come free with the hamburger steak and fried chicken. (40)[23]

Newsweek upholds Crystal Springs as a kind of public lesson in proper community response to the war, suggesting that despite anxiety and fear, the proper response is consolation, solace, and support—in other words, therapy. The juxtaposition of a unified community or "family" alongside the condemnation of protesters made an implicit argument. In contrast to the community of Crystal Springs, antiwar demonstrators, by implication, lacked strength and solace. They were constructed as outsiders to the national community enacted in the media and were rhetorically scapegoated for the anxieties and risks attendant to the war. Such stories constituted ritual expulsion of dissent and difference. The war and discussion about its merits was a subject reserved for the domestic space of the community family, a space in which consolation is more appropriate than dissent as a response to the crisis.

According to one study, the television networks (including CNN) spent more time (measured in minutes) on "yellow-ribbon" stories (focusing on domestic support for the troops) than any other war-related news stories by a ratio of almost two to one (Media Studies Center 1991, 48-9). The Media Studies Center explains this as a consequence of a similar rhetorical ploy in presidential discourse: "The President united the country under the umbrella of support for the troops [in his State of the Union speech] rather than seeking to win over skeptics to his approach" (48).[24] Todd Gitlin and Daniel Hallin (1992, 15-21) have argued that local nightly news emphasized support groups and rallying around the flag in an effort to build community morale and support for the war. Between November 1, 1990, and March 17, 1991, the three primary networks (CBS, ABC, and NBC) ran a total of 115 stories about the families of troops and domestic support for the war during the evening news (ABC, 36; CBS, 34; and NBC, 45) (Vanderbilt Television News Archive Index and Abstracts 1990/1991).[25] These stories always ran after "harder" news about troop deployments, battle developments, casualties and prisoners, and—most important—after news about anti-war demonstrations or criticisms of the war. For example, an NBC reporter interviewed a black soldier eating his Thanksgiving rations. The soldier criticized the racism of the military, noting that the nation's wealthy would not be fighting this war and that military service is often the only option for blacks seeking their way out of impoverished ghettos. This critical story (occurring 20 minutes into the newscast) was followed immediately by a family support story, in which a (white) military wife expressed her support for her husband via satellite video (Vanderbilt Television News Archive Index and Abstracts 1990/1991, 1976-77).[26] Similarly, stories about support groups, good-bye parties, and family reunions also framed stories about medical readiness for war, American hostages—and Vietnam War flashbacks. Like the other networks, CNN juxtaposed yellow-ribbon therapeutic news with hard news—only they did it around the clock in continuous newscasts that recycled story after story about support for the troops on the home front.[27] The sheer number of such CNN stories is impossible to know. According to CNN archivist John Robinson (personal communication, July 21, 1992), stories with themes of family support groups and the psychological effects of the war were so numerous as to render a thorough database search unwieldy.[28]

▓▓▓▓   In Every Hamlet, It's a War of Emotions

A close examination of two representative CNN clips from January 26 and 28, 1991, reveals that the pattern of critique and consolation occurred within news segments as well as across them. On January 26, 1991, CNN *Headline News* introduced into its rotation a segment about a black family in Houston with 30 of its members stationed in the Persian Gulf. Pearlie Cooper, the mother of several of these soldiers, was first shown in a close up, saying, "I really feel sad. It's just too high a price to pay." Throughout the story, family members expressed critical attitudes toward the war. Bettie Cooper, a young woman (presumably a sister or cousin) made the following case against the war from a black perspective:

> **Bettie:**   Now they're over there in a bad fix. They're scared, wondering whether or not they might not be coming back home.
>
> **Andrea** (brief close-up):   I wish they hadn't joined the army.
>
> **Bettie:**   And they say they don't want to go over there and die over nothing they don't have anything to do with or know anything about. . . . We're over there fighting a war and when we come back here we're fighting civil rights! It's like we're on the front lines out there, and that's not fair.

Bettie's opposition was reinforced by the CNN correspondent who provides background in a voice-over, "Like the rest of his enlisted relatives, Ronnie Johnson and his brother Russell joined the army. They wanted a job, the money, and a free education. Their sisters . . . now regret it." During this summary, the camera panned a photograph of all the members of the Johnson clan currently serving Uncle Sam. The image of rows and rows of solemn black faces strengthened the emerging critique.

Three elements of the text, however, resisted the critical edge. First, a reference to the Vietnam War occurred right after Bettie's quotation. Pearlie said, "I had several family members in the Vietnam War, and when they came back they got no recognition whatsoever." The correspondent said, "This war could wipe out an entire generation of men in this family. It's one more reason the Johnsons are ready for the fighting to end." Next, the text appealed to unity and to religion. Sherry Hawkins (another relative) said, "We're such a close-knit, tight family. All we can do now is pray and put it in God's hands, 'cause he can take care of, he will take care of us." This verbal expression of the theme of family unity was echoed here in the visuals of the segment. There were four long shots of the entire family clustered unnaturally close together, watching CNN on television. As Sherry concluded her remarks, the camera pulled out into an extreme long shot, foregrounding a dome clock, possibly symbolizing the need to wait patiently—or to suggest that for the Johnsons, time was running out.

The brief attempts at the end of the story to contain Bettie's clearly stated critique seemed desperate. The black, working-class women refused, for the most part, to take up the faithful supportive roles required of white middle-class women during the war. The critique of racism offered by Bettie politicized the personal in this story in a way that significantly injured the fragile rhetoric of support for the troops. In this way, the segment offered viewers a critical stance toward the war.

"Doing Something for the Emotional End of It"

More often than not, family support news on television resembled a segment aired by CNN on January 28, 1990. Anchor Lynn Russell introduced a story about a support group in Concord, New Hampshire. Over her left shoulder (our right), a map of New Hampshire was framed in a box. Below it, in blocked capitals, appeared the word "SUPPORT," itself both a label and an implicit command. The segment cut to a scene of the town, where, as Russell said, people were "coping with the war." The story moved from street scenes to interviews with women in a mall, to houses bedecked with yellow ribbons and American flags against a background of sparkling snow and crystal-blue sky, to more interviews at the mall followed by a cutaway to a rural woman alone at home and then with a group of supporters, then finally to Norma Quarrels, the correspondent, who wrapped the whole thing up: "On the home front, the Persian Gulf conflict is a war of emotions—as evidenced in small towns like Concord, New Hampshire."

Unlike the January 26 segment, however, the war of emotions here was one-sided. Concord, as the town's name suggests, was a place of unity and mutual support, not division, critique, or conflict. All the people in the story were white and clearly middle or upper class, dressed in furs or fashionable sweaters, their hair carefully coifed. They inhabited malls and shining white suburban homes. Dissent spoke here in a lonely voice. Coral Nieder, a rural woman with two sons in the Persian Gulf, described her initial reaction to news of their deployment: "Oh God, I wish we weren't there. I wish my sons weren't there." Earlier in the story, a token protester (a well-dressed, young white woman) walking alone in a shopping mall provided the illusion of journalistic balance: "I think we should get the hell out of there," she told the reporter. These statements were subject to several strategies of recuperation, however. Foremost among these was the appeal in both language and imagery to rural, traditional family and community values.

Introducing the story, correspondent Norma Quarrels stated, "The war in the Persian Gulf is reaching into towns, villages, and hamlets across the United States, touching many lives." The choice of nouns, "towns, villages, and hamlets," evoked a rural, small-town image of people who pull together for the common good and whose sense of community has not become a casualty of modern urban life. The text constructed such a space in its choices of images of Concord and Bow, both towns in New Hampshire. Nostalgia for community saturated the text, rhetorically exhorting viewers to emulate the supportive solidarity exemplified by these small-town residents.

In one passage, the reporter made the following statement in voice-over:

> People in Concord, New Hampshire are doing whatever they can to show their support for the troops serving in the Gulf. In addition to the flags and the yellow ribbons, there are letter writing campaigns, and this month, pictures are being taken and sent to the Gulf in time for Valentine's Day.

The visuals accompanying these words were a white, spacious two-story house, crusty with glistening snow. A man shoveled the sidewalk, but the camera focused on the yellow ribbons adorning the house and on the flag waving in the breeze. The segment cut to a closer view of the ribbons, yellow on white, then to a bumper sticker on a pickup truck: "I Support Our Troops in Operation Desert Shield." The segment concluded with an aestheticized low-angle shot of the flag with yellow ribbons in the foreground. The camera, using a starburst filter, zoomed in on the flag and captured the sun glistening on the waving fabric. Later in the story, similar shots constructed a pastoral, patriotic vision of the rural community of Bow, New Hampshire.

When the segment moved from the quiet outdoor scene to the bustling shopping mall, where families gather for a photo session and letter-writing stint, viewers were asked to connect the positive images of patriotic domesticity with the support group effort. The woman quoted previously who spoke out against the war is shown alone, in contrast to framing scenes that showed large numbers of community members engaged in a letter-writing campaign to the troops for Valentine's Day. The lone woman was young and angry, whereas the support group members were more mature, community identified, family oriented, and respectful. The report did not tell us her name or provide any information about her identity in or attachments to this community. In this mythic opposition of characters, protest was defined as the willful abnegation of community spirit and belongingness.

The iconography of the photograph contributed to this process. A common emotional ploy of support group segments was to zoom in on or to pan across photographs (usually adorned with yellow ribbons) of relatives stationed in the Persian Gulf, evoking a kind of emotional connection with the soldiers and an anxiety over their absence. In this story, one woman at the mall wore a photograph of her son pinned to her chest; later in the segment, the camera panned across the images of Coral Nieder's four sons on a wall. Images of those whose lives are at stake could be read oppositionally (as I think the Johnson photograph discussed previously encourages us to do). The fetishization of the absent soldier indicated a measure of anxiety over the lives of the troops and a desperate desire to have some control over the fate of those lives.

One way in which the anxiety evoked by the photographs was channeled into support for the war was through Vietnam War references. The woman who wore the lapel photo in this segment said, "They really do need our support. I don't want them to be unsupported like the men in Vietnam felt that they were unsupported." This statement preceded the brief cutaway to the unidentified woman who speaks out against the war, as if to chastise her for potentially creating another Vietnam War with her words.

Despite her initial anger at her son's fate, Coral Nieder was lauded for channeling her energy into community support work, collecting more than 400 names of New Hampshire families with members in the Persian Gulf and organizing letter-writing campaigns. She recalled her initial reactions: "It hit me . . . during the church service that they could die. My sons could die over there. But they chose to be there and I'll back them one hundred percent." The reference to the church service reinforced the theme of small-town values. The emphasis on the voluntary nature of military service can be read as an implicit response to the critique illustrated by Bettie Johnson—that African Americans joined the army out of economic necessity, not out of choice. Like the Johnsons, however, Coral Nieder resolved simply "to do something for the emotional end of it," as she says toward the segment's end.

The Support Group Nation

Support group news during the Persian Gulf War constituted a hegemonic dislocation of social anger and anxiety. The Operation Desert Comfort theme reinforced traditional and oppressive constructions of womanhood and family to enforce a sense of national emotional unity as a diversion from political fragmentation, conflict, and criticism of a brutal war that decimated a country and slaughtered 200,000 people, all essentially over the control of oil.[29] Emotional unity, however, created in the language of therapy, precluded the possibility of critical awareness and political action.

This study of therapeutic discourse during the Persian Gulf conflict reveals that the popular news media actively constructed a dysfunctional democracy based on the metaphor of family support. They persuaded audiences to find comfort in the flight from independent thought and action. They told us it was all right to be clients instead of citizens.

The imagined interpersonal harmony and emotional unity of the family are a metaphor for an ideal national consensus. When private sphere virtues and spaces are constructed as models for public discussion, however, therapy also forecloses on the perceived desirability of public debate, conflict, and change. In the private sphere, the scope of one's power as a social agent is limited to interpersonal negotiation and, ultimately, passivity in the face of structured events in the public sphere that affect our lives. Thus, the rhetoric of therapy strips us of public agency when acting and speaking out in protest are most vital.

Notes

1. Reprinted with permission of The Daily Iowan © 1995. Farrell's comments inspired this work.

2. This chapter develops a broad critical sketch of the family support coverage in network news, the popular press, and CNN Persian Gulf War coverage. My method has been to engage in wide critical reading of primary news sources (including the *New York Times,* the *Los Angeles Times,* various other city daily newspapers, popular national news magazines, and alternative news periodicals such as the *Nation*), in addition to nearly constant viewing of mainstream news coverage (particularly CNN's Headline News) of the war. I also consulted with CNN archivists and scanned the Vanderbilt Archives television index and abstracts to the network nightly news over the course of the war, counting the numbers of stories related to family support groups.

3. There is some debate over whether journalism routines (Eliasoph 1988; Herman and Chomsky 1988; Tuchman 1978); structures of ownership (Kellner 1990); advertising and control (Bagdikian 1990); narrative generic constraints [Epstein (1973, 164-65) describes the limited repertoire of news "plots"]; conscious "bias"; internalized liberal and anti-Communist ideologies (Herman and Chomsky 1988); or a combination of these elements produces the uniformity that characterizes commercial broadcast news in the United States.

4. I am particularly indebted to Kellner's (1992) comprehensive analysis.

5. Gitlin (1980, 6-7) stated, "Frames are principles of selection, emphasis, and presentation composed of little tacit theories about what exists, what happens, and what matters. . . . We frame reality in order to negotiate it, manage it, comprehend it, and choose appropriate repertories of cognition and action. *Media frames,* largely unspoken and unacknowledged, organize the world both for journalists who report it and . . . for us who rely on their reports. *Media frames are persistent patterns of cognition, interpretation, and presentation, of selection, emphasis, and exclusion, by which symbol-handlers routinely organize discourse."*

6. For a review of this issue and bibliography, see Dianne Rucinski (1992).

7. © 1991 Dallas Morning News.

8. © 1991 New York Times. Reprinted with permission.

9. © 1991 Baltimore Sun. Reprinted with permission.

10. For example, see Alex Molnar (1991). Molnar first published this piece, which is critical of the war, in newspapers across the country.

11. © 1991 Mother Jones. Reprinted with permission.

12. © 1991 Baltimore Sun. Reprinted with permission.

13. In the *New York Times,* Russell Banks (1991) reads the yellow ribbon phenomenon differently. He suggests that the ribbons signify "our desire to bring home Americans who were being held against their wills in foreign lands (which, since Vietnam, is how I have regarded enlisted men and women anyhow)." Other commentators have noted that the yellow ribbon phenomenon has roots in ancient folkloric rituals of communicating with spirits or date the practice to the civil war ("Collective Conversations" 1991, 138). Banks argues that it is only when the yellow ribbon gets inextricably linked to the American flag and patriotism (which he argues contradicts the motive of getting the troops home) that it becomes an unequivocal nationalist symbol (© 1991 New York Times. Reprinted with permission).

14. © 1991 Berkshire Eagle. Reprinted with permission.
15. © 1991 Hartford Courant. Reprinted with permission.
16. © 1991 Time Inc. Magazines. Reprinted with permission.
17. © 1991 U.S. News & World Report. Reprinted with permission.
18. © 1991 Time Inc. Magazines. Reprinted with permission.
19. © 1991 Cincinnati Enquirer. Reprinted with permission.
20. © San Francisco Examiner. Reprinted with permission.
21. © 1991 New York Times. Reprinted with permission.
22. From *Newsweek,* January 28, 1991; © 1991, Newsweek, Inc. All rights reserved. Reprinted by permission.
23. From *Newsweek,* January 28, 1991; © 1991, Newsweek, Inc. All rights reserved. Reprinted by permission.
24. © 1991 Media Studies Center. Reprinted with permission.
25. The ratio is approximately five stories every 6 days for all networks in 137 days of coverage. This count includes only those stories containing the words "family" and "support" in the same context. The occurrence of support group stories peaked at times of crisis and stress—Thanksgiving and Christmas 1990, as the troops celebrated holidays away from home; news of American hostages in Iraq; news about the failure of diplomacy; the beginning of the air war; the beginning of the ground war; and, most notably, immediately framing news about antiwar demonstrations.
26. © 1991 Vanderbilt Television News Archive Index and Abstracts. Reprinted with permission.
27. At the war's beginning, a record 10.7 million people tuned in to CNN, whereas other stations tallied losses. Nielsen ratings showed CNN with a 19.1, ABC with a 14.4, NBC with a 13.8, and CBS with a 10.9 rating the day after the war (see *Broadcasting* 1991, 23). A *Times-Mirror* poll late in the war found that 61% of those questioned thought CNN had the best war coverage compared to 12%, 7%, and 7%, for ABC, NBC, and CBS, respectively (Thomas 1991; © 1991 Los Angeles Times Syndicate. Reprinted with permission).
28. Because CNN does not index its programs (and thus information is available only by commissioning a search by the professional archivists there), numerical data on CNN family support coverage are inaccessible.
29. See Kellner (1992) for detailed accounts of economic and political motives for the war.

5 The Therapeutics of Feminism

From Self-Esteem to Suicide

> In helping us to make the transition from a modern to a postmodern world, with the help of feminist ideas, the recovery movement also does a dangerous and depressing thing. By using spiritual and disease words, instead of political ones, it encourages us to disregard the economic and political roots and benefits of the system in which we live and distracts us from the possibility that the system itself is flawed.
>
> —*Elayne Rapping (1996, 123)*

"The personal is political." This tenet, established early in feminism's second wave (Hanisch 1971),[1] generated a new definition of politics, one in which traditional public-sphere activities—speechmaking, strikes, demonstrations, and electoral campaigning—are not centrally valorized. Thus, feminism, whose practices (especially consciousness-raising) focus on understanding personal issues of power in sexual and familial relationships, is potentially a therapeutic politics, or a political therapy. As the authors (Mander and Rush 1974) of a book called *Feminism as Therapy* suggest, "It is precisely because feminism

103

includes the political that it is therapeutic. It is therapeutic to integrate the personal and the political" (49).

Recently, feminist political theorist Jane Flax (1990) has attempted to explore the connections between feminisms, postmodernism, and psychoanalysis, suggesting that feminism is a cluster of discourses united in their concern with questions of consciousness and subjectivity. Feminism locates power and resistance in the realms of identity, discourse, and personal life, in contradistinction to materialist and liberal approaches to politics. Historian Ellen Herman (1995, 303) has noted that feminism and therapy underwent a "curious courtship" in the 1960s: Feminists rightly challenged many of the sexist assumptions of psychological experts who blamed mothers for every social ill and mandated female domesticity. They also incorporated many of therapy's assumptions into the practice of consciousness-raising (CR).

In this chapter, I interrogate the feminist conflation of public and private and the commonplace claim made by some radical and cultural feminists that personal work is in and of itself constitutive of political change on behalf of women. So far, I have argued that therapeutic discourse dislocates political energy, anger, and activity into the realm of personal life, where opposition to systems of oppression and exploitation can do little damage and exert minimal long-term influence on relations of power as they exist. I have suggested that the therapeutic is a containment strategy that insinuates itself into and transforms radical political rhetoric.

My privileging of public, agonistic, and collective political work is subject to the feminist critique that notions of the public have historically excluded the domains of women's oppression: the body, sexuality, and the family as sites of male power. On feminism's own terms, however, what are the ends of politics? If they are the achievement of women's liberation in economic, cultural, and political realms and the winning of reforms such as abortion rights and equal pay, and if the goal of feminist struggle extends beyond the liberation of consciousness to include also the achievement of emancipation from the material and physical effects of oppression, then my definition of politics must have a place within feminism. After all, only when people take to the streets in demonstration for change are reforms won. The rollback of reforms such as abortion rights since 1976 corresponds with a period of minimal public women's movement activity.

Even so, we must seriously consider feminism's challenge to any easy opposition of therapy and politics. Feminism, a multifaceted liberation struggle taking as its starting point that the personal is political, poses the greatest challenge to the presumption that a liberatory politics must be public and collective. Is feminism therapeutic, political, or both? Is the therapeutic always contradictory to political action? If so, what are the implications of feminism's personal politics for a theory of the public sphere and social change?

Since the beginning of feminism's second wave (starting between 1963 and 1967), personalized politics have come up against both liberal-capitalist and Marxist political visions, resulting in both polarized antiliberal and anti-Marxist feminisms, as well as various ambivalent amalgams of liberal-feminism and Marxist or socialist feminism. I argue that although feminists offer a great deal of insight in the critique of liberalism's division between public and private and the way in which that binary structure positions women as subordinate to men, radical feminists' rejection of the Marxist analysis of gender relations in capitalism constituted a partial retreat from politics. A personal politics is politics insofar as understanding of self and the social analysis generated in CR activity lead to the generation of public political activity and discourse aimed at transforming public structures of power. In other words, feminism is necessary as a critique of woman's place in sexist society. Critique and self-awareness, however, are in a sense prepolitical events. When personal work and intellectual understanding become ends in themselves for feminist theory, the therapeutic motive cannot be far away.

To the extent that feminist theory rejects public collective action and focuses exclusively on the personal as the site of analysis and change, it collaborates with the liberal ideology's attempts to contain issues of power and struggle in the private sphere. As Alice Echols (1989) argues, radical feminism developed out of the collective projects of the student antiwar movement and the civil rights movement so that originally feminists argued for public militancy in the face of public structures of exploitation and oppression. Extreme sexism in Students for a Democratic Society and other groups motivated feminists to distance themselves from their predecessors and insist on the significance of women's personal experience as a political question. In vilifying the New Left, feminists put themselves in the position of having to defend a politics that became increasingly focused on the personal. This polarization in combination with the emerging backlash against feminism and the general decline of radicalism shaped the evolution of feminism from a radical collective project to an introspective, "cultural feminism" concerned with issues of sexual identity, self-esteem, and lifestyle change (Echols 1989). Ellen Willis (1984) stated,

> Cultural feminism is essentially a moral, countercultural movement aimed at *redeeming* its participants, while radical feminism began as a political movement to end male supremacy in all areas of social and economic life, and rejected the whole idea of opposing male and female natures and values as a sexist idea. (91)

If this description is accurate, cultural feminism represents the complete reconciliation of feminist politics with the therapeutic.

It is misleading, however, to see the convergence of feminism and the therapeutic as a simple decline from an original political ideal. From the outset, feminist activity and theorizing have encouraged privatized, idealistic responses to the political problem of women's oppression. I do not mean to suggest, however, that feminism is itself entirely responsible for these constructions. The availability of the therapeutic as a frame for "dis-ease," compounded by feminism's legitimate critique of liberalism's public-private bifurcation, overdetermined the emergence of a therapeutic politics. As I have argued, privatization and idealism are hallmarks of the therapeutic recuperation of political energy. The expression of women's anger and resistance in sole terms of private life participates—if unwittingly—in this hegemonic process.

This chapter takes two contemporary popular feminist texts, Gloria Steinem's 1992 best-seller *Revolution From Within* and the controversial 1991 film *Thelma & Louise* as instances, respectively, of persuasive liberal and radical feminist rhetorics. With these texts as the center of my investigation, I join a long-standing debate among feminist activists and theorists over the proper balance of the personal and political, the individual and the collective, the family and the workplace or the state, and the discursive and the material.[2] *Thelma & Louise* and *Revolution From Within,* although not representative of the full range of feminist rhetorics, are key indicators of how mainstream (liberal-capitalist) culture interprets and reframes political opposition and offers it in persuasive form to audiences.

Feminisms: Difference in Unity

Of course, feminism is not monovocal; it generates several competing theories, both practical and academic, of the subordination and liberation of women (Jaggar 1983, Snitow 1989). It is important to distinguish among liberal feminism, which seeks simply to apply liberal individualist standards of citizenship and opportunity to women; radical feminist theories of patriarchal domination; socialist feminist definitions of the gender-class system that stress women's role and exploitation as laborers both inside and outside the home; antiracist feminist theories that insist on interrogating both race- and gender-based oppression; and, finally, recent poststructuralist feminisms that attempt to deconstruct the category "woman" itself. More specific theoretical variations exist within and across the basic liberal-radical-Marxist triad, including psychoanalytic feminism and what is known as "identity politics" (see Joeres and Laslett 1992, Mitchell 1974; on identity politics, see Phelan 1994).

Despite the various inflections of feminist political theory, Catharine MacKinnon, among others, has suggested that there is a core feminist philosophy recognizing women's oppression and male power and committed to the epistemological assumptions of CR, or the idea that political practice and theory must be generated out of an understanding of the personal life experiences of women. Feminists of whatever stripe, however, generally share certain other theoretical presumptions. First, women are oppressed, and male power over women is the most significant axis of power in all cultures. Second, women's oppression is primarily rooted in private-sphere relations of family, sexuality, and sexual violence (rape). Third, oppression is a significantly psychological issue because men have a psychosexual interest in dominating women. Fourth, women will be liberated if they can come to a sense of their internal worth that has been denied by the patriarchal culture. Finally, feminism assumes that political change will happen through gradual shifts in consciousness and alterations in personal lifestyles and social norms.

Furthermore, feminists in general are committed to the epistemological assumptions of CR, or the idea that political practice and theory must be generated out of an understanding—achieved through women-only encounter groups and through analysis of private-sphere activities—of the personal life experiences of women. Consciousness-raising is the centerpiece of feminist politics. This foundation is expressed in its most "pure" form in radical feminism but is central in shaping the political agendas of other feminisms, even in the amalgamated forms of liberal- and Marxist-feminism. Whichever expression feminism has taken, the politicization of the family and sexuality has profoundly troubled the class liberal division between the public and private. Any argument on behalf of a revitalized public politics must take this critique into account.

▓▓▓ The Public, the Private, and Politics

Feminism and Marxism share a critique of the division in liberal society between public and private. Both Marxists and feminists argue that the ideal of public citizenship legitimating state power in the public sphere obscures the material conditions of unequal power relations in what liberalism designates as private and thus outside the boundaries of political activity: the economy and the family. Feminist political philosopher Carole Pateman (1989) writes, "The dichotomy between the private and the public obscures the subjection of women to men within an apparently universal, egalitarian and individualist order" (120). Pateman argues that liberalism is highly contradictory in its commitment to political democracy alongside its subordination of women in the private sphere.

Marx, too, of course, criticized the illusion afforded by individualist democracies that their citizens were actually free. He distinguished between the "political state," or the abstract formal constitution of modern governments, and the "material state," or the sphere of actual social relations of power that, by virtue of ideological obfuscation, appears to be separate and distinct from the political state (Marx 1843/1978b; Schwartz 1979). In liberalism from Locke forward, the ideal government is a representative democracy in which political decision making is abstracted from the material conditions of life so that competing economic interests are set aside as a precondition for political activity. This ideal presumes the general economic and social equality of individual citizens (or assumes that only property holders are citizens). In this model, the state's central function is the protection of individual privacy—including private property. As Pateman and many others have pointed out, however, the liberal state contradicts its ideal because it depends on the formation of a private sphere in which people toil on behalf of the property owners. The exploited labor of women and workers is obscured in the liberal rhetoric of public citizenship.

Liberalism, however, does not present the only model of public politics available. Although some theorists have taken Marx's critique of the liberal public-private split to indicate that in communist society, there would be no distinction and thus no realm of freedom from the state, Nancy Schwartz (1979) argues differently. Schwartz explicates the *Grundrisse* to show that Marx, although condemning the ideological uses of the public-private division in liberal capitalist society, held as an ideal the notion of people as political animals engaged in *praxis* (transformative social activity that includes labor, creative work, and political decision making) for the common good. Such activity is more than the totalized administration of the necessities of life; it is the collective public striving to enact a good life in the *polis*. This chapter argues that feminism does itself a disservice when it abandons any goal of public instrumentality. Feminisms have provided a critique of women's places in an oppressive gender system and have offered many women a powerful political identity, but often feminist political work stops short at the point of CR.

Consciousness-Raising

Consciousness-raising, or the development of insight into the experience of oppression and the discovery of social experiences shared by a group through the analysis of personal life, represents ostensibly the central political practice of feminist organizations and feminist criticism and theory. Originally popular within radical feminist circles, CR began as a method of small group exploration of the problems of femininity. Any social critique or group exploration process that generates an understanding of structures of power, the subordination of groups within those structures, the role of ideologies in winning those groups' adherence to their own subordination, and the need for collective action to overcome oppression and dismantle the system can in some sense be said to raise the consciousness of those it addresses. In this way, most attempts on the part of film, television, criticism, and theoretical texts to constitute and win identification from a politically embattled audience meet my definition of CR.

Consciousness-raising can be inflected variously depending on whether it is employed in radical or liberal feminist contexts. In either context, CR represents at least a partially therapeutic moment. Feminists in general define CR as the epistemological method invented by and in radical feminism and the enactment of the principle, "the personal is political." The following early Redstockings (a radical feminist collective) manifesto (as quoted in Shreve 1989) illustrates that CR primarily attempts to generalize outward from individual experience and to mobilize collective action:

> Our chief task is to develop female class consciousness through sharing experience and publicly exposing the sexist foundation of all our institutions. Consciousness-raising is not "therapy," which implies the existence of individual solutions and falsely assumes that the male-female relationship is purely personal. (11)

Inevitably, however, one must decide to what degree CR itself as the guiding metaphor for most feminist practice is inherently an internalization of the therapeutic imperative within the feminist movements. In her ethnographic study of contemporary 12-step recovery groups and talks shows, Elayne Rapping (1996) concludes that those groups have been inspired by feminist CR. Although the progressive edge of recovery culture gets its capacity to acknowledge collective problems and identify with sufferers from its similarities to feminism, it also shares the privatizing aspects of CR. Rapping's (7, 61) critique demonstrates the ways in which therapeutic or "recovery"-oriented texts and programs tap into real anger and disability, but work to affirm traditionally ideological solutions to suffering. She writes, "Addiction is no more than a metaphor itself for a much larger human and social problem" (65).

Although Rapping (1996) argues that feminist CR is better politically than the recovery movement, I fear that an epistemological and political reliance on CR might promote an implicit acceptance of the conceptualization of "woman" as belonging to the private sphere of healing and consolation. One additional problem with CR as a political method even within feminism was that it attracted middle- and upper-class women who had little interest in the fundamental social change envisioned by radical feminists. Even among radical feminists, CR was and is a limited political option. Often, feminists could see no avenues for action beyond CR. One feminist (Payne 1973) asked whether CR might be a dead end, criticizing the practice as stagnation:

> It is pointless to develop the self-confidence to challenge assumptions about women's roles and an understanding of the way society channels women without then collectively doing something about these problems . . . I am not sure where to go from here. (284)

When the raising of consciousness is seen as an end in itself, feminist practice runs up against the wall of the therapeutic, as the working over of identity replaces politics.

Within the boundaries of a discourse designed not to develop a systematic analysis or to plan strategies for action, enormous pressure exists for participants to focus on themselves, their feelings, and their pain. Most CR groups prohibited explicit political analysis, synthesis, abstraction, or commentary on another person's contribution, thereby ensuring that no coherent political agenda would emerge from discussion.

When the sharing of feelings and the generation of incipient political analysis becomes an end in itself, however, the project of liberatory change is thwarted and contained. In other words, CR is necessary as a tool for understanding the gender system but is inadequate as a *telos*. Consciousness-raising is the swinging gate between isolation and identification, feeling and analysis, self-consciousness and collective consciousness, the simply personal and the political analysis of personal life, and the private and the public. Pamela Allen (1973), a radical feminist who conceptualized CR as "free space" for women, explained,

> It is clear to us that the small group is neither an action-oriented political group in and of itself nor is it an alternative family unit. Rather, *this is where ideology can develop* [italics added]. . . . The total group process is not therapy because we try to find the social causes for our experiences and the possible programs for changing these. But the therapeutic experience of momentarily relieving the individual of all responsibility for her situation does occur and is necessary if women are to be free to act. (278)

Again in this passage we hear the (defensive?) insistence that CR does not constitute therapy, although it contains a therapeutic moment en route to other goals. The gate between ideology and action, however, either opens up onto a broad critique of socioeconomic power (in conjunction with Marxist analysis, I argue) or it closes shut, containing feminist political energy within the prison house of therapy. Radical feminism stalled out as enthusiasm for CR hit its zenith in the early 1970s and began to dissipate, merging in the popular culture with liberal humanistic self-help psychology. Despite its revolutionary intent and the possibility of creating a mass movement, CR "moved into the orbit of the group therapy movement" (Rosenthal 1984, 309).

From the outset, radical feminism offered a model of social life in which power is predominantly a psychological and ideological (rather than economic or political) phenomenon. Rather than seeing masculine aggression and feminine subordination, the objectification of women, and the isolation of the nuclear family as expressions or functions of material interests, feminists (apart from socialist feminists) have attacked the ideological and the psychological almost exclusively.

Radical feminism offers a constitutive rhetoric—one aimed at identifying a group with a common interest and consolidating it as a group in opposition to others. This kind of rhetoric is one step closer to a public politics than is a simply expressive discourse that does not transform audience into an agent of change. Political change, however, requires an instrumental rhetoric—one geared toward mobilizing a newly constituted and self-conscious class toward public action.

Perhaps because of CR's radical, collectivist origins, liberal feminists did not embrace CR immediately; nevertheless, one finds liberal interpretations of CR goals. (Both the New York Radical Feminists and the liberal National Organization for Women circulated CR guidelines in the early 1970s.) Instead of a political epistemology of the personal, CR offered liberal feminists a therapeutic space in which to discover and enact their individuality and to enable career shifts and changes in personal life (Sorensen and Cudlipp 1973): "CR is the exploration of individual oppression through examining personal, cultural, social, sexual, and religious roles with the options of keeping some roles, dropping others, and modifying still other roles in an effort to increase personal functioning and potential" (5). The language of personal potential and liberation as a matter of individually decided role shifts reflects liberal feminist emphases on the individual as agent and on irrational social roles as the cause of women's oppression. Liberal feminist CR embodies liberal feminist ideas about individual agency, rationality, and citizenship in the public sphere.

Indeed, *Revolution From Within* (Steinem 1992) works as liberal feminist CR; *Thelma & Louise* persuasively constructs a radical feminist theory of oppression out of its protagonists' lives. Readings of these texts reveal that when the raising of consciousness is seen as an end in itself, feminist practice runs up against the wall of the therapeutic.

Liberal Feminism's "Revolution From Within"

Liberal feminists are put into a curious bind—that of founding a politics on the individualistic principles of liberalism, while at the same time recognizing women's collective oppression and acknowledging the difficulties faced by women, oppressed in the private sphere, in the task of entering public life as equals to men. The liberal ideal depends on a meritocracy that presumes individual agency, consciousness, and rationality. Feminism, however, recognizes the irrational and unjust systems of power that the ideology of individual achievement masks. For this reason, liberal feminism is a contradictory discourse.

Gloria Steinem's *Revolution From Within* (1992) exhibits these contradictions. On the one hand, it is clearly an unmitigated resort to the therapeutic to attempt the construction of a liberal feminine subject who possesses self-esteem as an individual and who as such is enabled to participate within the system. On the other hand, it pushes against its own assumptions in some interesting ways, exposing the limits of liberalism for feminism. In this light, it can be read as much as a critique of therapeutic discourse as an exemplar of it.

Hailed by *Ms.* magazine (Morgan 1991) as the feminist manifesto for the 1990s, Steinem's *Revolution From Within* (1992) articulates the liberal feminist project in the language of the self-help psychology movement.[3] In her advance introduction to the book in *Ms.*, Steinem (1991) announced that "In the '70s and '80s, we learned that the personal is political. In the '90s, the world must learn: *the political is personal*" (224).[4] The book hit the *New York Times* best-seller list as women crowded into bookstores to meet Steinem and have her autograph their copies.

Throughout most of the text, Steinem (1992) offers a liberal feminist therapeutic vision (as opposed to a radical feminist vision) of a "universal I" and "core self" esteem, exhorting individuals to participate in public life. Steinem locates the blame for low self-esteem in childhood experiences; her solutions are therefore therapeutic outlets such as meditation, looking for and rehabilitating the inner child, refusal of feminine ideals of physical beauty, shunning traditional romance, body image work, respect for old age, and so on.

The book's topics range from problems of the white U.S. middle class to urban ghettos and developing nations, recommending self-esteem as the solution to problems of poverty, hunger, and despair. For example, Steinem (1992) celebrates California Assemblyman John Vasconcelos's social therapy campaign (a program that offers self-esteem workshops to ghetto residents), and holds up Gandhi as a self-actualized role model who had to overcome his own sense of inferiority relative to British colonials to organize others. She wrote, "Self-esteem is a 'social vaccine' against an epidemic of school dropouts, teenage pregnancy, domestic violence, drug and alcohol addiction, child abuse, and other destructions of the self and others" (27). Steinem's choice of the words *epidemic* and *social vaccine* to describe the politics of self-esteem signals a therapeutic thematic at work. Steinem's endorsement of the therapeutic interpretation of social problems appears to be a collaboration with the liberal hegemony.

Reviewers expressed surprise and even rage at the book's self-help focus and apparent retreat from politics. In the *Washington Post,* Beryl Benderly (1992) wrote,

> All I could think of was that 20 years ago, the movement Steinem spear-headed gave women a liberating insight: The personal is political. . . . That knowledge helped shape two decades of social change. So what are we to make of a Steinem who now tells us that the personal is . . . well, personal, and even the political is personal? That the key to social change . . . is not economics or power relationships but, of all things, self-esteem? That competition arises not from scarcity but from low self-esteem? That wars and oppression happen not because nation-states have always battled over limited resources like tillable land, warm-water ports and oil fields but because leaders lack self-esteem? (3)[5]

Socialist-feminist Dierdre English (1992) similarly bemoans Steinem's emphasis on self-nurturing: "To improve the lot of America's women, the pressing need is not an ever greater focus on the self" (13).[6]

In its reversal of the personal and the political as cause and effect—for example, in the claim that low self-esteem causes oppression and not vice versa—the book clearly exhibits all the hallmarks of therapeutic discourse: idealism, privatism, and individualism. It offers consolation instead of compensation for social ills. It locates responsibility for change and fulfillment with the individual woman seeking a sense of self.

Revolution From Within (Steinem 1992), however, might be read against its grain as a muted critique of its own limits. Such a critique strains the text along two seams: where Steinem describes self-esteem as a prepolitical rather than political process, and where her examples suggest that self-esteem is a liberal code word for class consciousness. It becomes clear early on in the book that Steinem employs the language of the therapeutic to talk about other forms of confidence and action that characterize collective liberation struggles (for civil and women's rights, for autonomy and dignity in the developing world, and for workers' rights and gay rights)—all of which might more accurately be called collective or class consciousness rather than self-esteem:

> When India and England continued their Commonwealth and other relationships after India's independence, one might say that, as George Sand once suggested men and women do, they had broken the marriage bond and reformed it as an equal partnership. When "Negroes" became "blacks" and then "African Americans" in the United States, it was part of a long journey from the humiliation of slavery to a pride of heritage. When I myself started to say "we" instead of "they" when speaking of women, it was a step toward self-esteem that was *at least as important as* identifying with one's true ethnic heritage. (44)

To compare on equal terms political and economic struggles of national liberation with the linguistic effort of a bourgeois woman to name herself independent of her husband is potentially to trivialize and demean collective struggles against capitalism, imperialism, and racism.

Steinem (1992), however, could be more favorably read as stretching an individualist category such as self-esteem in a more collective and engaged direction. At other points in the text, Steinem celebrates the formation of SEWA, a women's trade union in India that gave women power in economic terms, and applauds Wilma Mankiller and the growing collective consciousness of the Cherokee Nation as lessons in self-esteem building (Steinem 1992, 42, 96). Carol Sternhell (1992) stated in the *Women's Review of Books* that "What Steinem calls self-esteem I would often call activism" (5).

In the shift from self- to collective orientation as a necessary political moment, Steinem (1992) redefines self-esteem. In her analogies between self-liberation and collective struggle, Steinem transgresses the ideological boundaries of liberal individualism, offering a new definition of selfhood and agency that can be inflected as either individual or collective. She expands the language of the therapeutic to evoke the power inherent in numbers of people, not just individuals. Her occasional breaches of her contract with liberal individualism align her with the project of CR—the expansion of one's perspective on the world that generates collective identification.

Even as the discourse of self-esteem enables Steinem (1992) to make the notion of political struggle accessible to many people, however, the process renders politics in terms of self-help, prescribing laughing, singing, drawing, writing, and other forms of middle-class self-expression as cures. Such a limited personal politics is not confined to Steinem's book but is characteristic of the decline of feminism and of social movements generally.

Can feminism go beyond CR? Its theory and its tasks center on reproduction, analysis of sexuality, and identity issues. Its method is symbolic, educational, and theoretical because its central assumption is that oppression is a psychological, culturally produced, identity-forming phenomenon. What is the motive for the production of certain gender identities and certain cultural arrangements? Who benefits and in what way do they benefit? Against whom should feminists struggle?

Thelma and Louise: Radical Feminism's Dead End

Radical feminism answers the previous questions by saying that women constantly struggle for power against men, that the oppression of women is primary and fundamental, and that men's motives for oppressing women are primarily sexual and psychological (New York Radical Feminists, 1973). The centrality of the psychological motive for male power in the feminist analysis limits the possibilities for feminist politics. In addition to CR in small groups, these possibilities include symbolic protests against cultural practices or censorship of some cultural practices or both (e.g., protests against beauty pageants and the antipornography movement); withdrawal from heterosexual relationships; feminist counseling and psychotherapy; and the establishment of a separate, marginal women's culture in business, literature, theology, and the arts.

Short of an all-out war against men, radical feminist politics do not directly confront systems of power. Instead, the basic assumptions of feminism lead to a withdrawal from political activity and a process of self-marginalization in an attempt to escape from power's effects. *Thelma & Louise,* like *Revolution From Within* (Steinem, 1992), is double-edged in this regard. Although the film dramatically displays the central features of a therapeutic radical feminism, it also deploys a critique of the radical feminist vision and can be used as a resource for understanding the political limitations of feminism.

Thelma & Louise (1991) is a film about two women who confront sexism, take a journey together across the desert Southwest, and transform themselves from waitress and housewife into women who refuse to settle for powerlessness in the gender system. This film's narrative, in addition to reviews both outraged and supportive, defines the movie as a feminist text.

Although a few reviewers (and screenwriter Callie Khouri) attempted to deny the film's feminist politics (Carlson 1991, Rohter 1991, Shapiro 1991), most critics either heralded or lambasted the film for portraying what happens when women realize they have nothing to lose. The *Village Voice* insisted that "*Thelma & Louise* strikes a nerve . . . because it's about power, *female power*" (Dargis 1991, 22). *Ms.,* of course, argued that "It is their rejection of patriarchy that make Thelma and Louise controversial" (Maio 1991).[7] Even the fashion magazine *Glamour* discussed the film, not once but twice, in the context of women's fight against social inequality and the misogyny of the Hollywood establishment (Krupp 1991, Tevlin 1992). Tevlin credits the film for launching "a pop-culture expedition into sexual politics" (265), noting that women in the audience cheered as the film's protagonists exacted revenge against their male oppressors. These authors acknowledged—and celebrated—the film's feminist agenda.

Reviewers on the other end of the political spectrum found the film's feminism "unsettling" (Simon 1991),[8] "guerrilla" (Baber 1991, 45), and, in *U.S. News & World Report,* "toxic" and "fascist" (Leo 1991b, 20). John Leo wrote, "The scene is set in the Southwest, but the real landscape is that of writer Andrea Dworkin and the most alienated radical feminists" (20).[9] Despite the political polarities of the debate over *Thelma & Louise,* the film was defined and framed in the literature of its reception as a paradigmatic feminist text. The questions remain, however: What is the film's construction of feminism, and how does it attempt to reach audiences with its vision?

Combining elements of the woman's film, the buddy film, and the road movie, *Thelma & Louise* uses the metaphor of the journey to chronicle the transformation of its protagonists' consciousness. As Thelma and Louise get their consciousness raised about the realities of being a woman in a male-dominated culture, the film itself attempts to raise the consciousness of its audiences by encouraging identification between women in the audience and the film's protagonists. Ultimately, this strategy builds a radical feminist analysis of social power and of women's place in U.S. culture. I suggest that although the text constitutes a radical feminist audience in an act of CR, the narrative's final solution to the problem of women's oppression calls the political choices of the protagonists into question. By implication, the film is ambivalent about its own therapeutic feminist vision.

At the film's outset, Thelma (Geena Davis) and Louise (Susan Sarandon) set off on a weekend fling, Thelma momentarily escaping her domineering but fundamentally insecure husband Darryl (Christopher MacDonald), and Louise looking forward to a weekend off from her job as a diner waitress. At a roadside honky-tonk, the women stop for a drink, and Thelma dances with a man named Harlan (Timothy Carhart). Harlan attempts to rape Thelma in the parking lot (hoisting her body onto a car, which is a symbol of male terrain and power). Louise witnesses the attempted rape and shoots and kills Harlan after he has let Louise go. The women's joyride turns into a flight from justice.

The rest of the film depicts the women's journey to the realization that to be a woman is to be either a victim or a fugitive. This journey constructs a radical feminist political critique through five semiotic clusters, which are developed with examples in the following pages: (a) the rape as motivation for critique and as a symbol of a patriarchal social order; (b) the use of editing to make analogies among all the men in the film and their positions of power over the women (the visual evocation of a patriarchy); (c) the narrative of female bonding, the flight into utopia, and deliberate self-marginalization as solutions to the problem of women's oppression; (d) the transgression of the traditional feminine role and the position of Thelma and Louise as outside the laws of the masculinist state and culture; and (e) the critique of adaptation or "settling" for life in feminine abjection and the refusal of therapeutic adaptation by Thelma and Louise.

Late in the women's journey, Thelma rejects the idea of going back to life with a sexist husband and a job waiting tables: "Something's, like, crossed over in me and I can't go back. I mean, I just couldn't live." Riding in the car at dawn across the desert, Thelma says, "I feel awake. Wide awake. I don't ever remember feeling this awake. Everything looks different." By the end of the film, Thelma's newly awakened feminist consciousness has led her to a new analysis of society in which relationships she had taken for granted look completely different to her. The viewer is positioned as envisioning a radical shift in perspective along with Thelma. What has led to this transformation in consciousness?

First, of course, is the attempted rape itself, which *Thelma & Louise,* like other radical feminist texts, places at the center of its analysis of male dominance. Harlan, the rapist, comes to represent synechdocally other male power figures in the film. In addition, the film puts forward the feminist analysis of the rape to the audience through Thelma and Louise's gradual reinterpretation and discussion of it.

At first, Louise blames Thelma for their predicament as they fight in the car after Harlan's murder. Indeed, Louise's predictions that no one would believe Thelma's account of the rape bear out in the "reality" of the film's reception, as *Playboy* proves the film correct by openly blaming Thelma (and all women who "ask for it"): "You might ask what signals Thelma is sending Harlan with her behavior, since she has been dancing and drinking and flirting openly with him for some time" (Baber 1991, 45).[10]

If indeed we do not live in the kind of world that accepts a woman's word about rape, the film must convince the real-world audiences of the validity of the feminist analysis. Gradually, viewers who identify with Louise must also identify with Thelma because Louise and Thelma change places and merge into almost one character in appearance (tan, tough, and windblown) and action over the course of the film. Viewers caught up in identifying with the protagonists before they come to feminist consciousness are gradually introduced to a more critical view of gender relations as the narrative progresses.

Later in the film, as the women drive through a catacomb of eerie desert monuments, Thelma asks Louise, "It happened to you, didn't it. In Texas. You was raped." Defensive, Louise asks Thelma to drop the subject and Thelma reassures her, "It's okay." Here, Thelma frees herself and Louise from culpability for the rape(s). Later, Louise also admits to mistakenly blaming Thelma. Louise asks, "We could both get killed. Why didn't we go to the police?" Thelma says,

> Nobody'd believe us. That guy was hurtin' me. He woulda hurt me worse and nothin' would have happened to him. My luck would have been a whole lot worse than it is now. At least now I'm having some fun. I'm not sorry that son of a bitch is dead. I'm just sorry it was you who did it and not me.

This exchange replies directly to Louise's original anger at Thelma. Now, the fact that no one would believe them about the rape and murder is not an indictment of Thelma but of a culture that lets rapists go free. Now, a righteous anger and the knowledge that the rapist deserved to die empower Thelma. The film's audience, who might have been reluctant to admit such a claim at first, is encouraged to undergo a similar transformation in point of view along with Thelma.

As Thelma and Louise are visually merged together in their common cause, the men in the film are also constructed as interchangeable by the editing techniques of director Ridley Scott. For example, after Louise kills Harlan, Thelma stops to call Darryl. The phone rings in an empty house, as a shot of Thelma's note on the microwave stands in for the absent (presumably philandering) Darryl. Immediately, the scene cuts to a shot of Harlan, dead on the ground, surrounded by the flashing lights of police cars. Detective Hal (Harvey Keitel; a benevolent if paternalistic force in the film) interrogates a waitress. The image of Hal gives way to Louise calling her on-again, off-again boyfriend Jimmy. No one answers.

Sequences such as these throughout the film build a visual equation among all men, even when absent or dead, united in their tyranny over the women. In addition, when men in the film are represented collectively, they are revealed as uniformly sexist. For example, when three detectives and Darryl watch a video of Thelma robbing a store, they echo each other in the invocation of a male deity: "Jesus Christ," "Good God," and "My Lord." For Thelma and Louise, the act of robbery generated a sense of liberating transgression; for the men, in contrast, the act (like Harlan's murder) is beyond their understanding. In another collective indictment against men, the camera shows the men watching sports and reading pornography in shots that frame Thelma and Louise's discussions of rape and rape culture. Male reviewers of the film comment that there are no likable male characters in the film, and, indeed, most of the male characters—an authoritarian police officer, a tyrannical beer-guzzling angry husband, and a lecherous truck driver—are caricatures in the film's attempt to establish itself as an allegory of patriarchal power and feminine flight.

During the flight of Thelma and Louise across the Southwest United States, the film's cinematography emphasizes the wide open spaces of the desert, evoking comparisons with the photography of Ansel Adams in scenes of breathtaking awe. The sweeping vistas, other-wordly passages through mesas under a wide-open sky, and seemingly endless horizons constitute a utopian vision for women seeking solace from the perils of civilization. The remotivation of Western conventions to feminist ends results in an alternative genderscape. Although the feeling of openness and transport into another world can be read as a metaphor for women's liberation into unlimited space and corresponding roles as outlaws and adventurers, the masculine is always figured symbolically as a looming presence in the film.

While Thelma and Louise drive along deserted roads singing happily, a shadow of a crop-dusting plane crosses their path. Oil rigs form a morass of mightily pumping black towers, in an obviously symbolic gesture. Day and night, huge trucks bear down on the women in their convertible, honking and hissing as they pass through the landscape. Therefore, even when men are absent, symbols of an omnipresent male power dominate the scene.[11] In its clearly emerging analysis of male power as patriarchal, the film partially excludes men as its audience, or perhaps invites male viewers to identify with the transgressive feminine subject positions of the protagonists. It remains to be explored what political avenues the film as a rhetorical text exhorts the women in its audience to follow.

The film poses one solution to the problem of patriarchal persecution: the construction of a "no-man's-land" or free space for women to explore their identities and problems. Thus, the women's journey through the desert is the construction of the free space characteristic of CR groups. The film's omnipresent symbols of male power might serve as a warning to the viewer that marginalizing oneself is a naive and risky response to domination. The film, however, does not offer an alternative to self-marginalization and flight from power enacted by its protagonists.

As with radical feminism generally, part of this flight from male power in the film involves increasingly intimate woman identification or female bonding. John Simon (1991), writing in *National Review,* manages to ask a question that is to him almost unthinkable: "Are these women, consciously or unconsciously, in love with each other? Is this perhaps not just a feminist but also a lesbian feminist movie?" (49).[12] In the framework of the film's critique of the various forms of masculine domination (especially the police state and the family, which are metaphorically linked in the interactions between Darryl and the Federal Bureau of Investigation), further intercourse (social or sexual) with men becomes unthinkable as Thelma and Louise grow closer in the knowledge of their common oppression. Because lesbian identity becomes a logical outgrowth of radical feminism's critique of compulsory heterosexuality (Rich 1980), *Thelma & Louise*'s lesbian subtext lies only barely beneath the narrative's surface. For example, before the women are scheduled to leave on their trip, Louise calls Thelma from the busy kitchen of the diner. Louise's manager, overhearing the conversation, calls out "When are you going to run away with me, Thelma?" Louise retorts, "Not this weekend, sweetie, she's running away with me." At the film's end, after Thelma nods toward the cliff over the Grand Canyon and the women's final destiny, the women kiss. Holding hands, they drive into oblivion.

These interactions walk the fine line between female friendship and lesbian identity. As Rich (1980) argues, woman identification is somewhat natural for most women, who, Rich claims, exist on a "lesbian continuum." The pun made by Louise between "running away" from oppressive lives (although she does not know at this point that they will become literal fugitives) and "running away together," with all its sexual implications, elides the positions of friendship and erotic love on that continuum.

The hint of lesbian identity is not the only transgressive position that Thelma and Louise take up in the course of the film. Other volatile enactments of women's power and gender role transgressions have generated explosive anger in the mainstream press and appreciation among feminists for the portrayal of a long-overdue cinematic revenge in retribution for violence against women. Louise's shooting of Harlan and Thelma's knack for convenience-store holdups are but two of these instances; the women also lock a policeman in the trunk of his patrol car (warning him that he should be sweet to his wife or perhaps she would turn out like Thelma) and blow up the oil tank truck of a trucker who had harassed them on the road when he refused to apologize to them for his disgusting behavior.

Thelma in particular makes the most dramatic shift from timid housewife to feminist outlaw, eventually trading places with Louise as leader of the duo. "I've had it up to here with sedate," she says at one point, and, in a sense, the film is about her transformation as she realizes how oppressive her existence in Darryl's household had been. After a taste of freedom, she crosses over into a new persona: one who can rob stores, command a cop, ignite a truck, and make hard decisions about her own fate. The outlaw and road movie genres (along the lines of *Butch Cassidy*) are typically narratives about male rites of passage and heroic individualism. In *Thelma & Louise,* women fill the male roles in a rhetorical statement about women, power, and representation.

In all the ways I have outlined, the film apparently argues for a radical feminist analysis and course of action for women. Its journey exemplifies a rhetoric geared to reconstitute women as feminists in their identification with Thelma. In addition, it warns men (if men serve as a rhetorical audience for the film at all) not to push women over the edge. In these ways, the film itself works as CR; it offers critique and analysis but also reveals the feminist strategies of flight from patriarchy and unprogrammatic resistance tactics as tragically unsuccessful. In the context of a critique of therapy, this reading of *Thelma & Louise* as feminist CR reveals the film as a therapeutic text, constituting a feminist subject with nowhere to go and nothing to do but express herself. The *New York Times* (Maslin 1991) defended the film as follows:

> Its heroines, during the course of a few brief but wildly eventful days, crystallize their thoughts and arrive at a philosophical clarity that would have been unavailable to them in their prior lives. . . . *Thelma & Louise* is transcendent in every way. (Section 2, 11)[13]

This review provides a textbook definition of CR and of therapy: transcendent clarity achieved through interpersonal discussion.

The double-suicide ending of the film, however, poses a challenge to the film's own vision. Schickel (1991) writes,

> It is toward self-destruction that Thelma and Louise's road inevitably winds. For all the time they have been out there expressing themselves, a posse has been relentlessly closing in on them. . . . [T]he message here is that "self assertion and awakening lead to death." (56)

Greenberg (1991/1992) worries about the hegemonic implications of a film that celebrates suicide as feminist victory, whereas other reviewers insist that the film is actually antifeminist (Doody-Vermilya 1991).

By the criteria established previously, the film is a feminist text. The film's ending, however, serves as a warning to the politicized women it addresses—a warning that the practices of self-marginalization and retreat from power are ultimately a dead end. Like the heroine of Kate Chopin's Victorian novel *The Awakening* (1851/1904), Thelma and Louise refuse to "settle" for the system as it exists. Given a radical feminist agenda of individual acts of transgression, female bonding, and deliberate flight into a false utopia, however, their options are slim. The film poses those options very starkly: settle for patriarchy or kill yourself. In my view, feminism also gets what it settles for, and the antipolitics of CR have spelled near-suicide for militant approaches to women's liberation. In this sense, the film itself critiques its own version of feminism for posing apolitical solutions to women's oppression.

Thelma & Louise lays this conclusion on the line as the two women drive off of the edge of the Grand Canyon. The film's final image is a still of their convertible suspended in midair. Although this final shot and the celebratory music that accompanies it might be read as a gesture toward transcendence of the women's double bind, it falls terribly short of being a happy ending.

Thelma and Louise pay for their freedom with their lives. I believe that feminism, in its investment in therapeutic rhetorics, has paid a similarly dear price for its personal politics: the figurative death of woman as political agent. The film *Thelma & Louise* is disturbing because although it levels such an incisive critique of the gender system, it also starkly reveals the shortcomings of the feminist response. It leaves the question open: Is CR a dead end? Like radical feminism, *Thelma & Louise* offers a rich and persuasive critique of sexist culture and the woman's place within it as ultimate victims—but it, like radical feminism in general, cannot see a future after the critique. Because radical feminism upholds the definition of the feminine as marginal, its vision remains fundamentally apolitical.

Here, my argument may seem to echo the indictments of antifeminists such as Camille Paglia (1992) and Katie Roiphe (1993), who argue that feminists construct a privileged but puritanical and powerless "victim" persona for women. Their positions, it seems to me, ignore the reality of women's oppression: Feminism does not "construct" victims out of thin air but rather aims to mobilize women whose bodies are routinely violated and whose opportunities at work, at school, at home, and in politics do not measure up to those afforded men. In light of this reality, my critique stems from fundamental sympathy with feminist goals.

Still, feminists who employ the language of self-esteem, consciousness, and the valorization of private life would do well to interrogate these metaphors as ways of understanding how to overcome women's oppression. Are these metaphors still operating in feminist talk? Much recent critical and theoretical work, influenced by poststructuralist discourse theories and the work of Michel Foucault, rejects the gender essentialism and lack of complexity in the radical feminist analysis. Do these theories attenuate or extend the therapeutic politics of radical feminism?

Postfeminist Therapies

Chris Weedon's (1987) book, *Feminist Practice and Poststructuralist Theory*, sets out the guiding principles of a poststructuralist feminism (see also Alcoff 1988, Butler 1990, Nicholson 1990). Central to this project is the insight that subjectivity, or one's individual sense of self (in addition to one's desires, agency, and sense of embodiment) in relation to the social world, is socially constructed in language and culture in a matrix of competing discourses in which one is always multiply and contradictorily located.

The project of debunking the illusion of individual subjecthood can lead to a critique of the structures of power that have a stake in perpetuating certain forms of the subject (e.g., as Marxism attempts to understand how racist and sexist ideologies undergird capitalism). Poststructuralism's rejection of notions of material reality and interests and stable structures of power, however, in addition to its suspicion of collective organization, work against the possibility of political work as an outgrowth of a critique of subjectivity.

For this reason, although poststructuralism resists the gender essentialism (the assumption of and reliance on a definition of a core, essential femininity as the basis for liberation) of radical feminism, it mimics radical feminist politics in its focus on the critique of culture and the "subversion of identity" (Butler 1990) as the only possible acts of women's liberation. In fact, Weedon (1987) even insists that CR is the political form of poststructuralist feminism:

> The collective discussion of personal problems and conflicts, often previously understood as the result of personal inadequacies and neuroses, leads to a recognition that what have been experienced as personal failings are socially produced conflicts and contradictions shared by many women in similar social positions. This process of discovery can lead to a rewriting of personal experience in terms which give it social, changeable causes. (33)

Poststructuralism might help feminists challenge the assumption of a unified, essential, and universal womanhood, but it perpetuates and reinforces the therapeutic dimensions of feminism.

Judith Butler's (1990) book, *Gender Trouble*, sets out a critique of "the compulsory order of sex/gender/desire" (6), with the goal of understanding "how the category of 'women,' the subject of feminism, is produced and restrained by the very structures of power through which emancipation is sought" (2). Influenced strongly by the theories of Michel Foucault, Butler focuses on the production of feminine subjects and the tendency of feminism to reproduce hegemonic articulations of "woman" as a stable, unified category. Indeed, as Marxists have pointed out in dialogue with feminism, women as a group possess no unifying identity that is not fractured along axes of race and class.

The poststructuralist approach, however, is obsessed with the constitutive to such a degree that it becomes impossible to envision instrumental collective political activity. Thus, poststructuralist feminist Barbara Biesecker (1992) advocates, as an alternative to instrumental politics, "a kind of 'getting through' or ad hoc 'making do'" on the part of "an agent that does not necessarily take herself to be anything like a subject of historical or cultural change" (155-56). Although Biesecker rejects liberal individualism as a basis for understanding historical agency of women, she resorts to a model in which the only available strategy for change comes from localized strategic raids on meaning systems.

The poststructuralist analysis of discourses producing subjects located in networks of power generates a politics of "subversive bodily acts" (Butler 1990, 79), or the parodic performance of gender-ambiguous identities (transsexualism and transvestism) that deconstruct the illusion of ontologically given gender or sexual identity. Still, Butler argues that "the deconstruction of identity is not the deconstruction of politics; rather, it establishes as political the very terms through which identity is articulated" (148).

Ironically, despite the poststructuralist critique of radical feminism's universalizing category labeled "woman," Butler (1990) offers a personal politics very much like radical feminist CR. In this vision, "the personal [the terms through which identity is established] is political." If, as I have argued, radical feminism tends toward the therapeutic in its lingering in the realm of consciousness and culture, poststructuralist feminism is also suspect. In other words, both feminisms are idealist in their formulations of power as matters of language, discourse, culture, and psychology— and never as matters of material benefits for real people who deploy discourses in the maintenance of an oppressive social system. Thus, it makes sense for poststructuralists to discuss the "economy" of the sign and the "regime" of discourse. For poststructuralists such as Foucault and Butler, power exists without agent or motive, resulting in a focus on agency, or the discursive means by which power constitutes its subjects.

Furthermore, in condemning the collective project of radical feminism in favor of subversive acts of individual parody and critique, poststructuralism replicates the individualism of the liberal ideology in addition to the privatism of feminism generally. It is the total deconstruction of social categories and the total rejection of any understanding of power as stable, structured, and dominating that has led some feminists to label poststructuralist feminism "postfeminism." In her book, *Feminism Without Women,* Tania Modleski (1991) argues forcefully against post-feminism's abandonment of the category woman as well as notions of patriarchal or capitalist structures of power. Noting that the works of Lacan, Althusser, Foucault, and others mark the shift in critical emphasis from material conditions of oppression to the positioning of subjects in language and discourse, she writes,

> [T]hinkers like Lacan and Foucault have provided the analytical tools by which we may begin the arduous task of unbecoming women. . . . It is not altogether clear to me why women, much more so than any other oppressed groups of people, have been so willing to yield the ground on which to make a stand against their oppression. (15)

Along with Linda Alcoff (1988), Susan Bordo (1990), Teresa Ebert (1992/1993), and bell hooks (1990), Modleski contends that the postmodern turn in feminist theorizing has partially undermined the project of feminist politics, giving up the possibility of collective identification and action among women (or anyone else). Interestingly, Modleski (1991, 14) notes that a liberal reviewer of a postmodernist feminist book actually approved of its content, which the reviewer read as symptomatic of a breakdown of the women's movement in the deconstruction of common identity and cause. Poststructuralist nihilism at times runs in the same riverbed as atomistic liberal individualism. Also, the playful strategies of subversion advocated by poststructuralists—gender-bending explorations of subjectivity—sound remotely akin to Steinem's (1992) play therapies.

Clearly, neither radical feminism nor poststructuralist feminism provides a way out of therapeutic individualism, privatism, and idealism. Although radical feminism offers a vision of a collective project against a structured power, its emphasis on consciousness and on changes in personal life works against political action. Poststructuralism, although it challenges gender essentialism, maintains the emphasis on the private, the ideological, the sexual, and the cultural, and it exhibits the further problem of lapsing into therapeutic individualism, actually encouraging the refusal of political collective identifications in favor of quasi-subversive self-expression. Where at least feminism's second wave attempted to raise consciousness of women who shared their oppression in common as a first step toward political change, postfeminism theoretically undermines even this achievement.

A public, collective politics of women's liberation needs an analysis of women's oppression that can account not only for the ways in which women's identity and consciousness are constructed in language and culture but also for the material motives for those constructions. In whose interests is women's oppression maintained, and to what end? What form does that oppression most often and most effectively take? How can it be overcome? In my view, some feminists have come closest to answering these questions in a political (rather than therapeutic) way in the sometimes acrimonious dialogue between feminism and Marxism.

Feminists and Marxists have been embroiled in a long-standing debate over whose politics best represent the project of women's liberation (Hartmann 1981). Feminists tend to argue a series of claims against Marxism, including the charges that Marxism's categories are sex-blind; that Marxists fail to recognize the relative ideological autonomy from the mode of production of the gender system (or patriarchy), which is based on relations of reproduction in the private sphere; that Leninism (democratic centralist organization) is unsuitable for organizing women, who prefer comforting consensus-based groups; that women's oppression is universal, predating capitalism and therefore distinct (as a power relation) from capitalism; that all men have an interest in controlling all women's bodies and labor; and that women are a sex class in a patriarchy. Catherine MacKinnon (1989) states in an often repeated formulation that "Sexuality is to feminism what work is to Marxism: that which is most one's own, yet most taken away" (3).

Marxists, however, argue that women's oppression has a material basis in class society's need to control the inheritance of wealth and, later, for the services performed by the nuclear family. On this analysis, the bourgeois nuclear family developed with capitalism as the mechanism of inheritance and the reproduction and nurturance of labor for capitalism. Far from being autonomous from capitalist relations of production, the sphere of reproduction is, using the Marxist argument, determined by the mode of production. For this reason, it is important to understand how gender ideologies, contradictory and complex as they are, attempt to secure women's place in the household and their status as second-class (and therefore lower-paid) workers (Engels 1843/1978b, Zaretsky 1976).

Marxist politics take the goals of the women's liberation project to be the achievement of economic equality with men (in the context of generalized economic justice), the end of ideologies that reinforce the capitalist family and discriminatory wage system, and the socialization of the labor and responsibility now performed by women (mostly) in the private sphere of the family (Harman 1984). Challenging prevailing construction of gender identities is surely part of this project.

These goals, however, cannot be achieved—indeed, have not been achieved—by the inward-looking therapeutic politics that have characterized feminism's second wave. Feminists have overlooked Marxism and its important warnings about the consequences of a politics of personal life. These consequences are starkly revealed in both liberal and radical contemporary feminist texts, as this chapter's readings of *Thelma & Louise* and *Revolution From Within* illustrate.

Indeed, too great an emphasis on personal life—on consciousness, identity, and lifestyle—has hindered progress toward women's liberation. Furthermore, it is important to keep in mind that the translation of politics into the discourse of the private, emotional, cultural, sexual, and psychological is not unique to feminism but is rather the hallmark of liberal-capitalist hegemony, corresponding to the steady erosion of political gains made by women, workers, and minorities earlier in this century. In this light, "the personal is political" may not be a revolutionary challenge to the status quo but rather an unwitting collaboration with the forces of stability in contemporary capitalist culture.

Chapter 6 makes a similar argument regarding post-Marxist politics, which seem to me to offer therapeutic consolations akin to those provided by "New Age" philosophies. The final chapter of this book turns to a discussion of what might constitute a revitalized, but inclusive, public life, an antidote to the therapeutic created in and by struggles for social change.

Notes

1. This piece, originally published informally in the context of feminist consciousness-raising groups, is credited as the first use of the phrase.

2. Despite the recent poststructuralist conflation of material and discursive levels of reality, I maintain the dualism because of the political consequences of arguing that discourse is material, as argued in Chapter 6. Some feminisms (as I will elaborate) assume that oppression is primarily a discursive, ideological phenomenon. This assumption entails therapeutic consequences.

3. © 1991 Ms. Magazine. Reprinted with permission.

4. © 1991 Ms. Magazine. Reprinted with permission.

5. © 1992 Washington Post Book World Service/Washington Post Writers Group. Reprinted with permission.

6. © 1992 New York Times. Reprinted with permission.

7. © 1991 Ms. Magazine. Reprinted with permission.

8. © 1991 National Review. Reprinted with permission.

9. © 1991 U.S. News & World Report. Reprinted with permission.

10. © 1991 Playboy Magazine. Reprinted with permission.

11. Shapiro (1991) noted that in the film, "the landscape is alive with symbols of male power" (63; from Newsweek, June 17, 1978, © 1978, Newsweek, Inc. All rights reserved. Reprinted by permission).

12. © National Review. Reprinted with permission.

13. © 1991 New York Times. Reprinted with permission.

6 The New Age of Post-Marxism

A good many movement veterans gravitated toward the milieu
which in the late sixties had begun to call itself "the human potential
movement." This melange of encounter groups, therapies, and
mystical disciplines promised to uncover authentic selves. . . . However you defined the problem, your task was to "work on yourself."
If there was going to be a New Age at all, it was going to come—
going to have to come—from the purification of the self.

—*Todd Gitlin (1987, 424-25)*

The New Age movement is perhaps the definitive instance of
the therapeutic. A cluster of discourses and practices—ranging from
Erhardt seminars training, meditation, and Eastern mysticism to vege-
tarian evangelism and New Age entrepreneurship and from antinukes to
environmentalism and crystal worship—New Age philosophy centers on
the care of the self in an oppressive society. The aim of this chapter is to
posit and elaborate an analogy between a New Age politics and the
post-Marxism represented by Ernesto Laclau and Chantal Mouffe
(1985). Through this analogy, I hope to reveal the shared, therapeutic
political and social contexts of otherwise seemingly diverse ideologies.
Most New Age texts argue for personal responses to social, economic,
and political practices.[1] At first glance, the rhetoric of the New Age would

seem to have little to do with post-Marxist social theory. Nevertheless, this chapter will detail what New Age and post-Marxist politics have in common and will critique both theoretical systems for participating in the idealism, individualism, and relativism of the therapeutic. Idealist (spiritual or text-centered) explanations for material (economic or physical) problems generate from therapeutic rhetorical strategy, which is often couched in the language of sickness and healing to code social "ills." The therapeutic approach, which demands not activism but self-transformation and not collective work but individual consumerism, appeals to upper-middle-class intellectual elites. On the whole, New Agers fit this demographic category (Wilson 1988).[2] An illustrative case of the New Age approach to struggle can be found in the resistance of New Agers to a 1992 labor protest against Berkeley's Whole Foods Market, a "politically correct" grocery store that offered its (mostly black and Latino) workers lower wages and fewer health benefits than other stores in the Berkeley area. When the workers attempted to unionize and went on strike, both management and shoppers (ostensibly members of the Left counterculture) criticized them for interfering in the process of transformative consumption. *Nation* reporter L. A. Kauffman (1992, 74) described the event as "a parable of the fate of countercultural politics: a tale of *what happens when the personal overwhelms the political* [italics added]." Kauffman argues that the shift in the Left reflects

> a larger shift in advanced capitalist countries from a politics centered on the point of production (the workplace) or the point of distribution (the state) to a politics oriented toward the decentered sites of consumption and daily life. (75)

Kauffman describes the Whole Foods store's politics as a hybrid of the New Left and the New Age. The personalization of the political is a therapeutic move insofar as most formulations of "personal politics" (including feminism, gay rights struggles, consumerist environmentalism, the impulse to "unlearn" racism through encounter groups, etc.) formulate a project of emancipation that depends on transformations of identity and consciousness. Therapy, likewise, works with a person's identity and consciousness as the solution to life problems.

The description of the antilabor aspects of the New Age bears directly on the analogy I hope to establish in this chapter between the New Age movement and the politics of post-Marxism. Like the New Age, post-

Marxism represents a shift to a politics of consumption, identity, and everyday life. Both the New Age movement and the New (post-Marxist) Left have refused participation in the struggles of the working class (defined simply as those people who must work for a wage to survive, without whose labor the capitalist system of production could not move forward) in favor of "a politics oriented toward the decentered sites of consumption and daily life" (Kauffman 1992, 75). Far from being grounded in the struggle of the exploited and oppressed for liberation, the New Age movement encourages upper-middle-class professionals to consume politically and environmentally correct products as the panacea for social change.

Mark Satin's (1978) movement-encompassing treatise, *New Age Politics,* calls for a new "revolutionary" strategy appropriate to our time and focuses its efforts on the discursive plane, at the level of consciousness. The book outlines a plan to build a radical pluralist democracy, although it lacks specific criteria for the ideal world or ideal political work. Moreover, it explicitly rejects the working class as the primary agent of change, endorsing instead a range of local activities involving the transformation of one's consciousness.

This chapter argues that the New Age does not represent an adequate political response to the conditions of late capitalism. Rather, it is a hegemonic therapeutic discourse that dislocates political movements of the late 1960s into a track of personal lifestyle work and conspicuous consumption. Alex Callinicos (1990) has argued that postmodernist, post-Marxist political theories (which I will define in detail later in the chapter) constitute an ideological justification for the post-1968 withdrawal of many intellectuals from politics altogether. My purpose here is to construct an analogy between the discourses of New Age and of post-Marxism to show that both are therapeutic rhetorics generated to console activists after the failure of post-1968 revolutionary movements and to legitimate participation in liberal politics (or the adoption of an explicit antipolitical stance).[3] Although the New Age movement and post-Marxist social theory may seem at first glance to be completely incongruous, it is possible to reveal quite extensive similarities in commitment between them. This comparison, however, does not completely dismiss the complex contributions that post-Marxist and poststructuralist theory offer political activists today.[4] Philosophically, the therapeutic impulse in political rhetoric is linked with tendencies toward idealism, or the assumption that the revolution will happen at the level of discourse and consciousness rather than at the level of economics (Callinicos 1990, 63, 70, 73-80); humanism (the belief, emergent with liberal capitalism, in the sovereignty and boundedness of the individual as agent)[5] and ethical and political relativism. The therapeutic relationship is founded on the ethical and ontological neutrality of the therapist; similarly, post-Marxism rejects any attempts to ground a political project in claims of truth or reality. These tendencies, in part, also characterize the New Age movement.

More important, however, this chapter attempts to reveal that—despite claims to radical, oppositional, antihumanist, and revolutionary import—poststructuralism's contributions to political theory and practice are undergirded by the same idealist and textualist, liberal humanist, and relativist assumptions—with significant debilitating consequences for Left politics. These assumptions represent a "retreat from class" as the foundation of oppositional politics (Wood 1986).

Post-Marxist Theories of Discourse and Politics

The work of Gramsci (1936/1971) and Althusser (1984) marked a turn in Marxist theory toward the ideological or discursive levels of society. Their work initiated a still-evolving theoretical discussion in Left circles as to the relationship between base and superstructure and between the material relations of production and the cultural or ideological expressions that win social consent to those relations.[6] As Wood (1986, 18-9) explains, Althusser inaugurated an academicist obsession with the structures of language and consciousness within Marxist theory and rejected any notion of the subject as political agent within a class. The postmodernists have taken this turn to its logical conclusion by interjecting arguments that discard the economic and political realms as primary sites of struggle.[7] Now, the theoretical focus shifts to discourse (the symbolic articulation of social relationships) as both the source and the site of contradictions and political struggle.[8] Baudrillard (1975) takes this position to its extreme, arguing that people can be "oppressed by the code" that establishes relations of consumption, which he views as more foundational to late capitalism than the relations of production. Since 1929, Baudrillard argues, capitalism has exerted its control on the level of consumption, on which subjects are positioned in ways that subordinate them to the code, whether or not they happen to be workers. Thus, social control happens through discourse and ideology: "prolonged education . . . endless personal development. . . . All the institutions of 'advanced democracy' " (132). Likewise, Mouffe (1988a) argues for recognition of social antagonisms that are the product not centrally of class relations but rather of relations of subordination at the level of consumption, resistance to bureaucracy, mass culture, sexism, racism, homophobia, and so on (see Laclau and Mouffe 1987, Mouffe 1988b, 1990). Mouffe argues that the Left should accommodate the proliferation of new antagonisms or, in other words, accept as legitimate struggles not involving class conflict. Mouffe, however, does not consider that the dissolution of class politics into myriad fragmented movements (in "postmodern" social space) opposed in vague ways to "the system" may actually collude with the system in some ways. As with the New Age phenomenon, other new social movements may represent capitalism's recuperation of radical political challenges.

For Laclau and Mouffe, as for Baudrillard, revolutionary agency is located not in the working class as a discrete entity but rather in other groups subordinated within the complex and shifting discursive formation. In *Hegemony and Socialist Strategy* (Laclau and Mouffe 1985) and "Post-Marxism Without Apologies" (Laclau and Mouffe 1987), Laclau and Mouffe offer a definition of political struggle with five basic components: the discursive nature of the state and its autonomy from the economic base; the subject as site of overdetermined contradictions, out of which agency arises; the rejection of the working class as agent of change in late capitalism; the concept of resistance defined as discursively articulated antagonism to the system; and a definition of revolution as the establishment of a new hegemony within the democratic imaginary.

Overall, Laclau and Mouffe view the social as the site of struggle because social relations, including those of class, are discursively constituted in a system of differences and equivalencies. Regularities in this system make the concept of opposition and struggle meaningful in that social space is more or less seamlessly structured, and clear positions of subordination and oppression exist. Struggle emerges out of contradictions in social space, but struggle does not produce antagonism (the systematic expression and coordination of collective opposition) until some identity among struggling forces is rhetorically established, dividing social space into two camps.

I argue that the post-Marxist collapsing of the discursive and the real results in an idealist and relativist political model analogous to the therapeutic consolations of the New Age movement. In the second half of their book, however, Laclau and Mouffe (1985) do posit a political program based on the rhetorical articulation of the interests of the subordinated. The call to participate in on-the-ground, emancipatory social movements is not an instance of therapeutic dislocation. As Terry Eagleton (1991) suggests, implicit here is a theory of oppression of certain categorically defined groups—workers, women, racial minorities, and so on—even if the categories involved are discursively constituted. It is at this point that Laclau and Mouffe's two projects—one deconstructive of the Marxist political tradition and one reconstructive of a political program—become unhinged, suggesting that the authors actually do acknowledge the relative stability of a social formation whose discourses, although not entirely sutured, are still constitutive of dominated and dominating groups. Like Laclau and Mouffe, I acknowledge the importance of the rhetorical constitution of oppositional consciousness, and I recognize that Laclau and Mouffe themselves do not promote self-absorption and lifestyle politics as emancipatory.

Unfortunately, however, their emphasis on discourse as the only site of struggle (indeed, as all there is) leads to an abandonment of the working class as the agent of historical change and prevents them from linking their rhetorical perspective to the project of formulating collective consciousness among the working class. According to Laclau and Mouffe (1985), society does not consist of material and discursive levels but is rather purely discursive (although *discourse* here is defined broadly to include any symbolic utterance, action, or relation). In this work, culture becomes theoretically detached from material reality.[9] Therefore, political struggle is now something that takes place not at the site of production but rather through the unevenly progressive expressions of oppositional cultural identity. In discourse, ideological elements are discursively linked to other elements and to subject positions, forming a complex, dispersed, but relatively stable totality (Laclau and Mouffe 1985, 105). Laclau and Mouffe (1985) state that it is in the provisional order of this totality that relationships of domination and subordination are constituted:

> The practice of articulation, therefore, consists in the construction of nodal points which partially fix meaning; and the partial character of this fixation proceeds from the openness of the social, a result, in its turn, of the

constant overflowing of every discourse by the infinitude of the field of discursivity. (113)

Thus, the state is a constellation of discursive nodal points, around which subjects are positioned in the process of articulating and rearticulating social identities and relations. For example, "woman" and "nature" are by themselves floating elements of discursive space until they are articulated together so that historically womanhood has been identified as close to nature. Such moments are relatively permanent but open to challenge when contradictions arise that point out the constructedness of this articulation (e.g., when women's association with beauty, achieved through artifice, runs up against the definition of woman as "natural"). More to the point, Laclau and Mouffe's (1985, 115-17) example of the nodal point "human being," defined as having inalienable rights, contradicts the fact that certain people are deprived of those rights. According to this analysis, the state is discursive; because contradictions can occur around nodal points (such as race, gender, environment, etc.) independent of class conflict, the state is completely autonomous from the economic base. For this reason, the working class is no longer the privileged site of disruption and conflict. Laclau and Mouffe (1985) write, "Hence, there are a variety of possible antagonisms in the social, many of them in opposition to each other" (131). Later, they state,

> Today it is not only as a seller of labour-power that the individual is subordinated to capital, but also through his or her incorporation into a multitude of other social relations: culture, free time, illness, education, sex, and even death. There is practically no domain of individual or collective life which escapes capitalist relations. (161)

Struggle is displaced from class relations onto other social relations—namely, those involving people as consumers of culture, leisure activity, medical care, and so on. It is important to note, however, that although the working class is no longer the sole agent of change, the enemy to be fought is still capitalism for Laclau and Mouffe (1985). Because of the autonomy of the state from the relations of production, however, any struggle against any subordination, whether or not it is perceived to be subordination to capitalism, is a legitimate struggle. This openness about what constitutes a legitimate political practice has its pitfalls, as I will explain.

Struggles against subordination become antagonisms when they are articulated together to present a unified front and when these articulations divide social space into a clear "us" and "them." According to Laclau and Mouffe (1985), relations of economic domination and exploitation do not make these divisions a priori; rather, antagonisms appear in discourse, involving alliances that go beyond boundaries of economic classes. Laclau and Mouffe write that antagonisms emerge from "equivalential displacement between distinct subject positions" (159). I take this statement to mean that when unequal relations of power exist between subject positions constructed in a relationship of difference to each other (e.g., woman-man), there is potential for antagonism. Furthermore, in a discourse that unifies various subordinate positions (i.e., expresses commonality in the suffering of various oppressed groups), there is hegemonic power.

Hegemony, for Laclau and Mouffe (1985), involves more than the engineering of consent of the dominated by the dominators. It consists of the establishment of a social order based on the ability to articulate together a variety of subject positions, unified in their antagonism to a discursively identified enemy or evil (189). In their phraseology, "A situation of hegemony would be one in which the management of the positivity of the social and the articulation of the diverse democratic demands had achieved a maximum of integration" (189). It does not suffice to be simply antisystem; one must take the pieces of the social order and put them together in a new vision. This process can take place on the Left, as the "attempt to establish different nodal points from which a process of . . . reconstruction of the social fabric could be instituted" (189), or on the Right in the maintenance of the nodal points that are already fixed in place. Because hegemony is a process of positivity, of not only antagonism and deconstruction but also social reconstruction, the Left must work within the "democratic imaginary" (the dominant liberal ideology, with its core values of individual liberty, equality, and responsibility) of the liberal state to achieve its goals. Laclau and Mouffe (1985) suggest using the primary nodal points of this imaginary—the rights of liberty, equality, and the human being itself—as elements that can be rearticulated in the interests of those struggling against the current limiting and oppressive understandings of those terms:

> In the face of the project for the reconstruction of a hierarchic society, the alternative of the Left should consist of locating itself fully in the field of

the democratic revolution and expanding the chainings of equivalents between the different struggles against oppression. *The task of the Left therefore cannot be to renounce liberal-democratic ideology, but on the contrary, to deepen and expand it in the direction of a radical and plural democracy.* . . . The *meaning* of liberal discourse on individual rights is not definitively fixed; and, just as this unfixity permits their articulation with elements of conservative discourse, it also permits different forms of articulation and redefinition which accentuate the democratic moment. (176)

This new formulation of the Left's task is not unique to Laclau and Mouffe but rather is characteristic of all Western Marxisms after 1968, including poststructuralist discourse theory and especially the Eurocommunism of the British journals *Marxism Today, Rethinking Marxism,* and *Strategies.*[10] The debate between Marxists and post-Marxists rearticulates the perennial question of the role of culture in perpetuating capitalism. Although Gramsci and Lukács inaugurated a turn toward discourse in understanding how cultural hegemony is the product of struggle (Eagleton 1991, 93-123), Althusser and Baudrillard complete the rotation. Althusser (1984) argued for the relative autonomy of the ideological realm from the economic base, opening the door for the postmodernists and the post-Marxists to posit the absolute autonomy of, and indeed a lack of distinction between, cultural expression and class relations. The argument follows that because domination is stabilized through construction of cultural hegemony, resistance to that domination should take place on a cultural level as well. What this argument forgets is that the cultural hegemony of the Right is geared toward, rooted in, and dependent on the cooperation of laborers in the system of production. No social movement devoted to the articulation of oppositional identity will effectively challenge that system unless the workers also stop cooperating. The post-Marxist argument suggests not only that consciousness not only participates in relations of production (an argument I can accept) but also, and more problematically, that consciousness (ideas in culture) determines or constitutes those relations. Thus, shifts in cultural representation and in the consciousness of certain antagonistic groups become the end goal of politics.

Clearly, poststructuralism and Eurocommunism constitute explicit reactions against a Marxist practice based on class politics. This tendency includes the post-Fordism/"New Times" hypothesis, which argues that postmodernity represents a break with organized capitalism and mandates new forms of dispersed, local, and nonworking-class organizing (Rustin 1989; see also Clarke, 1991). Stuart Hall (1988, 58-60) provides a definition and summary of this theoretical development, endorsing a view of our times as representing a "postindustrial," post-Fordist epoch in capitalism. This epoch is ostensibly characterized by flexible, decentralized forms of labor; the preponderance of "soft," "information age" technologies; the dispersal of industries into hives of segmented work activity; the rise of multinational corporations and a new corresponding division of labor; an elaboration of a consumer culture targeted toward groups according to lifestyle and taste rather than class; and multiple subject forms inhabiting a complex social world. Paramount in the shift to New Times, argues Hall (1988), is the return of the subjective in Left political theory—in other words, a focus on the elaboration of the self through consumption and discursive expression rather than on transformative politics. Interestingly, that shift to and exclusive focus on the subjective also marks New Age thinking as well as therapeutic discourse in general.

New Age Politics?

Mark Satin's (1978) *New Age Politics* is, like *Hegemony and Socialist Strategy* (Laclau and Mouffe 1985), a concentrated version of a dispersed set of ideas. This 1970s polemical vision of and strategy for New Age society resonates strongly with Laclau and Mouffe on several points, including the acknowledgment of a need for a new political model appropriate to the current conjuncture, the idea of politics as articulation of many interests together across classes, the focus on the discursive sphere and consciousness as sites of struggle, and the ultimate goal of a radical plural democracy, achieved through working with already-established democratic ideals. Particularly, both political visions are characterized by therapeutic idealism, individualist humanism, and relativism. After treating each of these tendencies in both discourses, I turn to the ways in which a critique of New Age as represented by Satin—specifically regarding the problems of idealism and textualism, individualist humanism, and political relativism—reflects back onto post-Marxist prescriptions for revolutionary strategy.

Like Laclau and Mouffe, Satin labels himself a post-Marxist. Having abandoned socialism after becoming a draft resister during the Vietnam conflict, he sought a new approach to politics. He argues, like Laclau and Mouffe, that the situation in the United States since the 1970s is so different from the context of much Marxist theorizing that "a whole new way of looking at the world" becomes necessary—"one that comes out of our own experience" (Satin 1978, 7).[11] Like Laclau and Mouffe, he finds this new perspective in the diverse "fringe movements" of his time:

> It dawned on me that the ideas and energies from the various "fringe" movements—feminist, ecological, spiritual, human potential, and the rest— were beginning to come together in a new way . . . in a way that was beginning to generate a coherent new politics. (1)[12]

Insofar as Satin's expressed project in this book is to bring together all the "bits and pieces" of the new politics and to articulate them together in a new way, he is attempting to establish a hegemonic antagonism that represents a dissatisfied people.

The Idealism of the New Age

This attempt to establish a hegemonic antagonism that represents a dissatisfied people takes place in discourse, against an allegedly purely discursive social system. Like Laclau and Mouffe, Satin (1978) wants to get beyond a Marxism that sees the problems of the world in simple economic terms: "Our problems are only superficially economic, and . . . they have much more to do with culture: with who we are and what we want from life" (17).[13] Although Laclau and Mouffe would disagree with Satin's point that economic struggle is superficial (as if there were levels of reality, which Laclau and Mouffe refute), Satin's concern with subjectivity and culture resonates with their idea that subjects are struggling against subordination at the level of the code, identity, and consumption. The goal of analyzing and reconfiguring identities ("who we are") is a therapeutic one—a practice that offers psychological insight as a consolation for the impossibility of structural transformation. Throughout his book, Satin argues that because our problems inhere not in our institutions but in our consciousness and belief systems, we must struggle to rework our beliefs before meaningful change can happen.

According to Satin (1978), our current belief system poses the biggest obstacle to founding a new society. Satin calls this belief system the

Prison. The Prison has six components or walls: patriarchal attitudes, egocentricity, scientific single vision, the bureaucratic mentality, nationalism, and the big city outlook (23). For Satin, none of these is the product of capitalism, which is not in itself an obstacle to freedom. Similarly, racism is not a product of modern capitalist imperatives but rather is a symptom of a mental prison. According to Satin, the Prison leads to what he calls "monolithic institutions," or institutions with totalizing, controlling power: transportation, medicine, schooling, religion, the nuclear family, nuclear power, the defense system, the monolithic state, the governing elite, and so on. Again, these institutions are enabled not by the capitalist mode of production but by our negative belief systems. Satin writes,

> Basically the Prison is a way of *seeing* the world, a *mental construct, or an illusion* . . . that we create every day anew. And because we create it in our minds, we can undo it in our minds. We *can change our consciousness* individually and collectively so that we're not prison bound.
>
> And if enough of us do this . . . then *and only then* would the institutions, goods, and services that are set up to meet the needs of Prison-bound people lose the Prison-bound aspects of their appeal [italics added]. (24)[14]

Clearly, Satin is calling for therapeutic, self-oriented work within the democratic imaginary—a reworking of individual consciousness in place of public struggle. Notice how similar his definition of the Prison-bound mentality ("a way of seeing the world, a construct, or an illusion") is to an Althusserian definition of ideology and to Laclau and Mouffe's (1985) "discourse," although they would reject the idea of calling discourse an illusion. As with discourse for Laclau and Mouffe, altering the Prison is, for Satin, a matter of altering one's consciousness and envisioning a new symbolic universe.

In *Hegemony and Socialist Strategy* (Laclau and Mouffe 1985), this new social order (or hegemony) takes the form of a radical, plural democracy based on the ideals of liberty (autonomy or difference) and equality (sameness and collectivity). In this regard, Satin (1978) offers his readers a satisfying utopian vision of a New Age world—a globally connected but locally focused set of communities of androgynous, peaceful, spiritual people who depend on "biolithic" [sic] ("grounded in life?") or life-centered institutions for their well-being. All these institutions would encourage diversity and autonomy in balance with community needs. This notion again resonates with Laclau and Mouffe's vision of a radical democracy—radical in its lack of a hierarchy of meaning and rules for conformity, but democratic in that each element or member of this plural democracy is valued equally (167). Laclau and Mouffe might well agree with Satin's statement, "Autonomy and community: Marxism stresses community at the expense of autonomy, and liberalism does just the reverse" (106).[15] Both Satin and Laclau and Mouffe are concerned with "deepening the democratic imaginary" to include both terms.

The Relativism of the New Age

In such an open plurality, however, there can be no criteria for a "correct" strategy or society, and the result is political relativism. Satin (1978) writes, "New Age people aren't interested in creating a 'perfect' or 'utopian' America run according to the 'correct' political principles. Instead, *diversity* would be treasured" (106).[16] Similarly, Laclau and Mouffe (1985) argue that one cannot tell a person where and how to struggle because such discourse would be totalizing and suturing—that is, inherently undemocratic (179). They write, "The first condition of a radically democratic society is to accept the contingent and radically open character of all its values—and in that sense, to abandon the aspiration to a single foundation" (101). To me, it seems that generating a true antagonism out of such open plurality would be difficult. How does one create an "us" and a "them" (a directed antagonism based on the ability to locate blame for the problem, an enemy) if there is no basis on which to evaluate a political practice? In this view, any collective expression of dissatisfaction from the Ku Klux Klan to Earth First! would represent an appropriate antagonism. To enact a transformative politics, one must identify correctly the source of the problem. From a relativist perspective, however, there can be no such thing as a correct analysis.

Satin (1978) does not provide a much-needed set of guidelines in his discussion of political strategy. Action loosely involves cultural change, "group work," and political and institutional change, but Satin holds these impulses in check, citing the "emerging consensus among many New Age people that would avoid all talk of stages and . . . all advice to others about what they 'should' do next" (211). Therefore, instead of a program, he advances the concept of "critical mass":

If enough of us, a "critical mass," share the New Age ethics and political values and are active in the areas that are most accessible to us or that "feel right" to us when we've begun to meet our needs of love and esteem and self-actualization and self-transcendence—then society will begin to move in a New Age direction. (211)[17]

In the language of humanist psychology, this passage equates the therapeutic goals of love, esteem, self-actualization, and "feeling" right with a political program. Although Laclau and Mouffe (1985) do not describe the process of hegemony-building in terms of feeling and self-actualization, they put forward a conception of hegemony in which subjects struggle locally and in discourse until the democratic imaginary takes on new shape. In its idealism, this vision resembles Satin's assurance that given enough work on consciousness, the real structures of power will transform themselves.[18] Michael Rossman (1979) explains the process in New Age terms as follows:

Our social reality is a construct also, a coherent but arbitrary web of relations which could well be other than it is. . . . We can imagine yet other arrangements. At certain transcendent moments of history, political or spiritual, we become aware of the power we have to change the rules we play by—not piecemeal but throughout all the dimensions of life, creating a changed and integral conspiracy of social reality. (67)

Is a "conspiracy of social reality" a synonym for cultural hegemony? Like Rossman, Laclau and Mouffe express faith in the power of human beings to transform society through shifts in consciousness and cultural expression.

So far, we have seen that with regard to the goals and strategies of politics, the New Age movement as represented by Mark Satin fits a post-Marxist model. New Age falls short of radical antagonism in many ways, however, all of which hinge on the problem of individualist, voluntaryist humanism.

The Therapeutic Individualism of the New Age

Like Laclau and Mouffe (1985), Satin (1978) explicitly rejects the working class as the privileged agent of social change. Satin devotes an entire chapter to this question, in which he divides the world into life-seekers and death-seekers instead of into capitalists and workers. He writes,

According to Marx, socialism would be fought for by the proletariat, by the working class, by all those whose basic needs were frustrated by predatory capitalism. In the United States, most members of the working class weren't willing to fight for socialism. But they did change capitalism enough so that they could meet their material needs, their physiological and security needs.

The working class finds it incredibly hard to meet its nonmaterial needs, but so do the rest of us. We're all in the same boat when it comes to these needs, when it comes to the Prison and its institutions.

But we can't expect all the classes to join together and work for New Age society. In fact, we can be almost certain that none of them will. For every social and economic class, *as a class* . . . has a substantial stake in monolithic society.

No, New Age society won't be brought about by any particular class acting in its interests as a class. But it may be brought about by all those *individuals* who are able to see that Prison society is making it impossible for them to meet their needs as individual human beings. (82)[19]

Satin's concept of nonmaterial needs is reminiscent of Baudrillard, who argues that needs are a construct of a society that worships labor and consumption. In other words, to posit a set of noneconomic needs is to posit a set of noneconomic relations of subordination and thus to allow for agents of change other than those who are victims of economic subordination. This position does not differ greatly from Laclau and Mouffe's (1985) idea that no one has an "objective" or material stake in change, but rather that we all have constructed interests on many levels of society.

For Laclau and Mouffe (1985), contradictions in social space locate people in overdetermined subject positions, enabling them to act strategically as agents despite the provisional and discursive nature of the positions they take up. Laclau and Mouffe renounce the liberal "category of subject as unitary, transparent and sutured entity," but they argue for a kind of strategic humanism to resolve the paralysis that results when conceiving of a completely dispersed and fragmented social subject (117, 166). Although recognizing that subjects are not the origin of social relations, Laclau and Mouffe (1985) argue that when people located in overdetermined subject positions engage in antagonistic relations in the democratic imaginary (their Left-lingo phrase for the liberal ideology), those relationships are necessarily embodied in humanist subjects. For the Left, they advise taking advantage of the rhetoric of rights and freedoms associated with the humanist subject, working to articulate those rights with the needs and interests of subordinated groups. They write,

Insofar as of the two great themes of the democratic imaginary—equality and liberty—it was that of equality which was traditionally predominant, the demands for autonomy bestow an increasingly central role upon liberty. For this reason many of these forms of resistance are made manifest not in the form of collective struggles, but through an increasingly affirmed individualism. (The Left, of course, is ill prepared to take into account these struggles, which even today it tends to dismiss as "liberal." Hence the danger that they may be articulated by a discourse of the Right, of the defence of privileges.) (164-65)

This passage critiques the Left's unwillingness to use the rhetorical tools or elements provided by the democratic imaginary for assuming antagonistic positions (although, in fact, Marxist organizations have, at certain historical junctures, joined with reform struggles in a united front). This critique has its merits. The affirmation of individualism, however, is a risky undertaking for any movement seeking economic justice in terms of collective interests. Any Left struggle that attempts to articulate its demands in the terms of individual rights risks cooptation.[20] It is the translation of socioeconomic problems and responses to them into an individualist framework that most centrally characterizes therapeutic discourse. Indeed, I suggest that post-Marxism's rhetoric of the individual resembles Marxism less than it resembles liberalism; it is a dressed-up concession to the stability of liberal capitalism. In the New Age movement, the consequences of articulating an almost-oppositional vision in the terms of liberal individualism become quite clear. According to this analysis, individuals choose workaholism or leisure and success or poverty in much the same way as one chooses between organic and nonorganic produce. Liberation is equated with the transformation of selves presumed to possess the economic and cultural means of self-articulation and enlightened consumption. Collective struggle or public work is ruled out in the refusal to develop a coherent program for suprapersonal change. The values of liberal individualism embed the movement in the upwardly mobile middle class, whose interests do not lie with fundamental economic transformation of society.

Although Laclau and Mouffe (1985) are aware of the dangers of strategic individualism, their analysis of non-working-class agency gives us no grounds on which to critique the New Age's conception of agency. Likewise, for Satin (1978), agency resides within the individual. He believes that social change inevitably follows self-change, as reflected in the critical mass hypothesis. Also, self-change is possible because of what

Satin calls the "trans-material world view" (91-101).[21] We escape the Prison through encounters with our spiritual or religious selves, through meditation, religious ritual, or (more to the point here) therapy. Through such practices we find (or, as I see it, are hailed by the illusion of) power in ourselves and transcend the material level of reality and the Prison. Here, the agent is the individual, isolated humanist subject—imagining a new world in isolation and substituting the project of self-transformation and imagination of new worlds for actual political struggle.

There are two problems with Satin's (1978) conception of the human agent. First, its spiritual idealism leads to a definition of action as withdrawal and isolation. Instead of taking the power discovered through consciousness-raising practice (whether it be individual or group) and organizing a confrontation with the state or corporate interests, on this argument one simply waits for everyone to come to the same realization and automatically the world will be a better place. In this way, the possibility of a real collective, public struggle is subverted.

The second problem is that the notion of isolated, individual human agent is inextricably linked with liberal capitalism. As Wood (1986, 150) explains, capitalist hegemony rests on the separation of the political and economic, and in the political sphere, people are defined as individual sovereigns without reference to their economic position or interests.[22] The consequences of this separation are the preclusion of radical change occurring on the plane of the political and the mystification of the collective and structural foundations for power. Both the New Agers and the post-Marxists accept this separation between political activity and economic interests. To translate the radical project of structural economic and political transformation into the language of individual agency and individual freedom is to self-destruct. The ideology of liberal individualism subverts the analysis of economic exploitation and oppression that characterizes a radical, as opposed to a simply liberal, political program. Satin's (1978) discourse exemplifies this problem. In fact, Satin cites the historically embedded connection between capitalism and individual freedom as a significant reason behind his choice to defend capitalism in his book. This defense is based on the following assumptions: First, capitalism supposedly disperses power away from the center of the state.[23] Second, capitalism is not the problem in modern society: Once we are free of the Prison mind-set, capitalists will not exploit people any more (166). Finally, economic oppression is not serious. Satin fallaciously argues (in a major therapeutic move) that United States society has overcome the problem of material deprivation and that what we are really hungering for is "strokes," or affirmations of our self-esteem. For these reasons, Satin celebrates entrepreneurship and worker-managed (but, of course, not worker-owned) enterprises. At one point, he celebrates a General Foods plant for its work team approach that gave workers control over their production. The result was a marked increase in efficiency and cost-effectiveness. Of course, the workers did not receive a corresponding control over the profits of their supposedly self-actualized labor.

Critiques of the New Age

Predictably, the New Age movement has been soundly taken to task by Left critics in the popular press for its celebration of capitalism, its elitism, its retreat into individualism, and its lack of real political action. Richard Blow (1988) writes,

> The New Age way is not to deny differences between people, but to deny that they matter. It's an attempt to create an egalitarian society based not on equal distribution of wealth or property, but on spiritual equality—a sort of *socialism of the mind*. It's an illusion. But for New Agers, even an illusion can become real if you believe in it long enough [italics added]. (27)[24]

Blow notes that New Age denies the importance of material differences among people. Other authors might level the same critique against Laclau and Mouffe (1985) because they argue that all interests are discursively constructed and that no one has more of a stake in social change—or more of a say in the form that change should take—than anyone else. Both New Age and post-Marxism represent a "socialism of the mind"— an idealist project without grounding in material interests or working-class political strategy.

Blow (1988) accurately and succinctly expresses a second flaw in New Age thinking: the merging of "liberal political views with the ability to earn a profit":

> New Age language sounds suspiciously like Republican social policy. Economic growth leads to personal growth, and that is always worthwhile. Even better, the pursuit of profit will also take care of social concerns, like poverty, hunger, and war. In the New Age lexicon, there is no mention of

sacrifice, duty, or responsibility. Those concepts are regressive, unprofitable in any sense. (26)[25]

Although the New Age has a politics that is generally left of center—"anti-war, pro-environment, anti-nuke, pro-feminist" (26)—its therapeutic individualism keeps it from articulating a truly radical agenda that addresses the need for the redistribution of wealth as a necessary precondition for true democracy. The *New Age Journal* 15th anniversary retrospective ("Where We've Been," 1990) stated that the Left counterculture went from "Abbie and Jerry to Ben and Jerry's"—from political activism to profit-making ice cream chains. Blow (1988) criticizes New Agers for their therapeutic responses to political problems, including their unwillingness to confront problems in a way that would involve challenging another person or group ("They never tackle issues; they hug them") and the inefficacy of the critical mass strategy ("No one really seems to know what happens when an idea becomes unstoppable") (27).[26] The therapeutic discourse of the New Age provides an idealist, individualist frame for some people's dissatisfaction with their material lives—discontent that, given access to alternative and truly political social analyses, might fuel public political activity.

If the New Age movement (along with its more mainstream therapeutic variations) now constitutes a familiar and widely accepted worldview, what does that say about the state of Left politics? To me, the New Age, as represented by Satin (1978), reveals the risks of therapeutic hegemonic politics in late capitalism. It is clearly not antagonistic to the capitalist system. It demonstrates the ease with which a radical pluralism can be recuperated by the dominant ideology when one preaches inclusiveness where judgments are necessary. The New Age's therapeutic notion of the subject, one firmly embedded in the democratic imaginary, leads to withdrawal from political life and an endorsement of capitalism. Finally, New Age, by focusing so intently on consciousness, turns what should be a political struggle into a moral one involving a battle between "the forces of life and the forces of death."

The "New Age" of Post-Marxism

Like New Ageism, post-Marxism has been subjected to extended critique in Left publications.[27] Norman Geras (1987) argues that Laclau and

Mouffe (1985) set up and dismiss a straw version of Marxist arguments about class, discourse, and the state. One does not, as Geras points out, have to hold untenable views of economic determination to embrace notions of relatively stable cultural formations in which some groups are systematically subordinated to others. Geras's strongest point, I believe, is that Laclau and Mouffe themselves are forced to adopt some version of a theory of fixed, stable class relations that require subverting (77). Terry Eagleton (1991) has added his voice to the fray, critiquing the "inflation of discourse" represented by Laclau and Mouffe (1985) and other post-Marxist theorists. He, along with Alex Callinicos (1990), argues convincingly that the theoretical conflation of discourse and material conditions undercuts the critique of ideology (Eagleton, 219). In addition, he notices that the anticapitalist political vision of Laclau and Mouffe is at odds with their relativist and idealist philosophical commitments because a politics of liberation must assume the real existence of exploitation and oppression (216-17).When one leaves behind class interests and agency, one makes it easy to imagine that the problems of society, all the relations of subordination that the discursive formation of the state produces, are not inherent in any real structure of power. Without a notion of class interest, moreover, it is not necessary to struggle for socialism because it is possible to envision a political democracy that does not meet the needs of the economically exploited. Finally, a radical pluralism does not provide adequate criteria by which to judge political strategies and goals.

It is a hallmark of therapeutic discourse to redirect attacks on capitalist society toward a reformist strategy that does not challenge liberal individualism, idealism, or relativism—much less world capitalism. Unless joined with a working-class struggle based on fundamental material class interests, articulation of the elements of the democratic imaginary will necessarily be recuperated in favor of the dominant order. Furthermore, the centerpiece of the democratic imaginary—the idea of the self-contained, responsible, and autonomous individual—is incompatible with the Marxist goal of collective working-class emancipation.

If political organizing and rhetoric on the Left is to surpass the celebration of self-expression and co-opted social movements, it must retain a notion of collective "interests." Laclau and Mouffe (1985) reject the idea of a priori class interests as an outmoded, totalizing realist formulation. It is absurd, however, to argue for an emancipatory politics without presuming that some real group or groups of people need emancipating and thus have a material stake in the project of change. Laclau and Mouffe affirm that the discursive totality of the state is relatively fixed around certain nodal points (i.e., that domination of certain social groups is systematic and real). They reject, however, any essentialism or reductionism (or any privileging of any social category as unit of analysis or as historical agent). Mouffe (1988b) writes,

> A person's subjectivity is not constructed only on the basis of his or her position in the relations of production. . . . There is no reason to privilege, a priori, a "class" position as the origin of the articulation of subjectivity. Consequently, a critique of the notion of "fundamental interests" is required. . . . Interests never exist prior to the discourses in which they are articulated. (90)

The notion that there are no extradiscursive (material) interests directly contradicts a classical Marxist perspective, which argues that although a person's subjectivity is not a simple matter of class determination, his or her oppression and exploitation are directly connected to his or her economic status and position in the relations of production. Marxists believe there is more to liberation than the articulation of alternative subjectivities; an end to poverty, hunger, exploitation, and abuse are more central to a politics of liberation and require a notion of class position, agency, and interests.

To a certain extent, Laclau and Mouffe (1985) would agree with this critique of the New Age project, but their politics of discursive antagonism bears some resemblance to the New Age in its idealist, individualist, and relativist foundations.

Post-Marxism as Therapeutic Consolation

A successful socialist strategy must acknowledge the interests of the working class as the central organizing principle of a radical democratic struggle. Laclau and Mouffe (1985) do have in mind such a confrontation when they argue for the articulation of a new hegemonic bloc based on a coalition of a collection of radical social movements. Perhaps the post-Marxist embrace of the student, gay rights, and environmental movements—all cross-class struggles of consciousness and identity rather than projects of revolutionary transformation—offers a palatable radicalism that might move some readers to the Left.

I believe, however, that it is more likely that the availability and hegemony of the postmodern, post-Marxist view in the academy is attractive to intellectuals as a way to justify continued lack of engagement in nonacademic radical politics. Post-Marxism tells academics that they do not have to struggle with issues of class. When post-Marxism (and postfeminism and poststructuralism generally) becomes the dominant critical theory in the academy and the Marxist insistence on class politics is derided as passé, these new theories might not move people to the Left but rather offer readers a cloak with which to dress up their ossified liberalism.

As my analysis of the New Age movement demonstrates, the articulation of progressive antagonisms at the level of discourse or consumption will not likely result in a society free from exploitation and oppression. At best, such a coalition can build support for legislative reforms such as those won by the civil rights and women's movements. At worst, the messages of individual freedom in the context of radical democracy may be appropriated by the New Right and reframed in terms of consumer choices within capitalism, self-fulfillment, property ownership, and right-wing libertarianism.

As Alex Callinicos (1990) argues, post-Marxist, poststructuralist, post-Fordist, and postindustrial theories are (like the New Age movement) ideological buttresses of an upwardly mobile intellectual elite, disillusioned over the failure of revolutionary politics since 1968 and distant from the revolutionary project.[28] The late capitalist epoch is characterized by a "process of personalization" that is not liberating for the individual but rather complicit with the ideology of liberal individualism that obscures structural oppression and the need for collective struggle against it. Callinicos writes,

> "Personalization" involves an intense investment of private life and the reduction of the public sphere to the merest shell. And the limits to the participation on offer are plain enough. The classical democratic tradition from Machiavelli to Rousseau and Marx had something more extensive in mind when they spoke of freedom rather than the ability . . . to choose between various items of consumption offered by competing multinational corporations. (153)

Callinicos goes on to say that alienation "seems as good a term as any to sum up this society of privatized activity and public apathy" (153).

Callinicos's critique could apply equally well to the New Age movement as it does to his immediate object, the endorsement of personalized politics by post-Marxist theorists.

Since the Vietnam War era, Americans have lived in a society who's ruling class and media gatekeepers encourage "privatized activity and public apathy." Therapeutic discourses such as the New Age movement contribute to the demise of the public political realm by dislocating political oppositional energy and tracking it into individualistic, idealistic, and relativistic pursuits. Therapy offers consolation instead of compensation in the face of war, starvation, poverty, overwork, alienation, oppression, and abuse. The New Age movement obviously exemplifies this rhetorical strategy; post-Marxism, perhaps simply an idealist theoretical rejection of historical materialism, is nevertheless partially complicit with the forces of stability in late capitalist society.

Furthermore, the motives behind post-Marxist theories include the therapeutic solace offered in the retreat from class after 1968. Perry Anderson (1976, 1991) has argued that the story of Western Marxism in general has been a tale of decline and betrayal of revolutionary political principles in the context of material abundance, upward mobility for intellectuals, and the entrenchment of academic Marxism. Callinicos (1990) notes the therapeutic dimension of this decline when, after summarizing the political upheavals of 1968, he suggests that the narcissistic individualism identified by Lasch, Sennett, and others grew out of disillusionment with and betrayal of a Left politics rooted in the working class (166). He states,

> What could be more reassuring for a generation, drawn first towards and then away from marxism by the political ups and downs of the past two decades than to be told . . . that there is nothing that they can do to change the world? "Resistance" is reduced to the knowing consumption of cultural products. (170)

Like post-Marxism, the New Age movement offers a definition of resistance as consumption and self-therapy. The New Age clearly fits the model of struggle within the democratic imaginary posited by Laclau and Mouffe (1985) and other post-Marxists. I have attempted to set the New Age movement, as represented by Mark Satin (1978), and the radical democratic politics espoused by Laclau and Mouffe against each other to support the idea that there is a fundamental incompatibility between certain aspects of the democratic imaginary and radical political and critical goals. To embrace poststructuralism's or post-Marxism's vision of a fluid and unsutured democratic social space is, in my view, both inaccurate and disabling to the Left.

Capitalism may be global and flexible but it is still founded on the expropriation of the labor of workers for the profit of capitalists (Harvey, 1989). In the face of such a system, a project such as the New Age movement is revealed to be a pacifier—a discourse of therapeutic consolation over deeply felt effects of the system. The goal of radical democracy is something to be achieved through real-world struggle against capitalist relations of power and not "articulated" into being out of a collection of social movements without structural power to overthrow the system. Without a foundation in the working class, radical democracy will be, like the New Age, a "socialism of the mind."

Notes

1. I refer the reader to a 1990 retrospective of *New Age Journal* (Jan./Feb. 1990) as a representative example that includes excerpts and letters from the past 15 years of the New Age movement. Several readers (including Abbie Hoffman) in the selection criticize the journal and the movement for encouraging self-centered responses to political problems.

2. Wilson (1988) notes that "Affluent baby boomers are the group most likely to embrace the so-called New Age movement. . . . New Agers tend to be educated, affluent, and successful people. They are hungry for something that mainstream society hasn't given them. And they are willing to pay for it" (34). Ninety-one percent of New Agers are college educated. Most make more than $40,000 a year and are in their thirties. They are three times as likely to travel internationally for business or pleasure than are working-class people. They are concerned with "ethical investing, organic food, holistic health, and mind/body awareness" (36; © 1988 American Demographics. Reprinted with permission). *New Age* summarized, "Where We've Been: From Abbie and Jerry to Ben and Jerry's" (Jan./Feb. 1990, 39).

3. The wholesale collapse of Stalinist so-called communist states since 1989 has reinforced the disillusionment of the Left and added fuel to the argument that the current historical period calls for a politics not of working-class revolution but of reforms within liberal market capitalism. If one views bureaucratic state "socialism" as the betrayal rather than the consequence of socialist revolution, however, it is not necessary to interpret its demise as a vindication of liberal capitalism.

4. In particular, post-Marxist political theory is attractive to scholars of discourse and power because it focuses so extensively on how the hegemony of

any power bloc is rhetorically constituted and maintained. M. Rustin (1985, 55) stated that post-Fordist Marxism is concerned more with "the reproduction of the social relations of capitalism" than with the system of production itself. Insofar as the social relations of race and gender are discursively constructed and maintained in late capitalism, it is important to have a rhetorical understanding of how discourse functions in the service of power. If the social relations of capitalism are generated in the interest of capitalists, however, revolutionary workers' struggle is necessary to end those relations—they cannot be eliminated through the production of alternative rhetorical constructions. The New Age movement, in comparison, has little theoretical or political subtlety, constituting a consumer haven for upwardly mobile seekers of comfort and mystical redemption.

5. By humanism, I mean the illusion of agency as inhering in the individual alone, the dominant ideological individualism that serves to obscure our position in structures of class, race, and gender in capitalism. By critiquing the humanism of post-Marxist politics, I do not mean to endorse the radical antihumanism of Foucault or Althusser, whose theoretical erasure of the agent has been so complete as to render political activity for change theoretically impossible. Sue Clegg (1991) states that any political theory should accept that to some degree "human beings engage in conscious political activity and can transform social relations" (71).

6. For a critique of the discursive turn in social history, see Brian Palmer (1990).

7. I have in mind Jean Baudrillard (1975) and Michel Foucault (1980). For other contributors to this shift, see "Beyond the Modern" (1988) and "Marxism Now" (1990).

8. Laclau and Mouffe are at the center of my analysis because their text, *Hegemony and Socialist Strategy* (1985), is the most-cited and most "beautifully paradigmatic" (Wood 1986, 47).

9. As I have argued elsewhere, the materiality of discourse hypothesis (the argument that there is no distinction to be made between linguistic or cultural phenomena and economic relations) is a theoretical hedge around this problem, with two variations. Either one argues that discourse has real effects in the social world (an argument I accept), or one argues that material reality (including economic social relations) is purely a discursive phenomenon. I reject the latter position because of its political relativism (see Cloud 1994).

10. See the Introduction to the first issue of *Rethinking Marxism* (1988, 5-13) and Hall (1988), and Lazarus (1991) provides a particularly useful critical survey of this tendency.

11. © 1978 Bantam, Doubleday, Dell. Reprinted with permission.

12. © 1978 Bantam, Doubleday, Dell. Reprinted with permission.

13. © 1978 Bantam, Doubleday, Dell. Reprinted with permission.

14. © 1978 Bantam, Doubleday, Dell. Reprinted with permission.

15. © 1978 Bantam, Doubleday, Dell. Reprinted with permission.

16. © 1978 Bantam, Doubleday, Dell. Reprinted with permission.

17. © 1978 Bantam, Doubleday, Dell. Reprinted with permission.

18. Post-Marxism is linked theoretically with the (unsubstantiated) hypothesis that capitalism itself has become disorganized in the transformation from national

to international capital. Therefore, political responses to the oppressions generated in capitalism must remain disorganized, plural, and local to be effective. Implicit in much of this argument is the idea that capitalism will eventually undo itself without the organized self-activity of the working class, an idea that has much resonance with the New Age "critical mass" formulation. For a summary and critique of this position, see Callinicos (1990, 121-171).

19. © 1978 Bantam, Doubleday, Dell. Reprinted with permission.

20. To her credit, Mouffe (1988b) argues that the post-Marxist project of a radical democracy differs in principle from the assumptions of liberal democracy, rejecting separation of power and politics, the presumption of individual responsibility and agency, and so on. Mouffe states, "To value the institutions which embody political liberalism's principles does not require us to endorse either economic liberalism or individualism" (58). The problem with this statement is that economic liberalism (the free market and the separation of the market from the sphere designated as politics) and individualism are foundational to political liberalism, which cannot be willy-nilly disconnected from its economic and ideological counterparts.

21. © 1978 Bantam, Doubleday, Dell. Reprinted with permission.

22. This is not, of course, to reject entirely the humanist discourse of rights, liberty, equality, justice, and so on that emerged with liberal capitalism. Marxism itself begins with the assumption of human rights but argues that real human liberty, equality, and justice cannot be achieved so long as rights are conceived in political but not in economic terms.

23. This is also a central argument of post-Marxism (see Callinicos 1990, 132-144).

24. © 1988 New Republic. Reprinted with permission.

25. © 1988 New Republic. Reprinted with permission.

26. © 1988 New Republic. Reprinted with permission.

27. In particular, see the *New Left Review* exchange: Geras (1987, 1988), Laclau and Mouffe (1987), and Mouzelis (1988). Recently, a collective based in Syracuse has begun a new journal to respond to post-Marxism. Teresa Ebert, Donald Morton, and Mas'ud Zavarzadeh are coeditors of *Transformation*, a journal devoted to a rehabilitation of classical historical materialist critique of capitalist society. See "On Transformation Now" (1995). Also see Morton and Zavarzadeh (1994) and Ebert (1996).

28. For another Marxist perspective on post-Marxism, see Smith (1994).

Conclusion

Antidotes to Therapeutic Hegemony

A catalogue of some of the essentially most important or interesting problems, even if at first sight they do not appear to be in the forefront, [includes] psychoanalysis and its enormous diffusion since the war, as the expression of the increased moral coercion exercised by the apparatus of the State and society on single individuals, and of the pathological crisis determined by this action.

—*Antonio Gramsci (1936/1971, 279-80)*

This is not about women being stupid or crazy or masochistic or co-dependent. It's about women not having options.

—*University of Texas Law Professor Sarah Buel*
(as quoted in Brice, 1996, A1)

In her comments about how best to teach law students about domestic violence, Professor Buel (as quoted above) self-consciously resists common therapeutic framings of domestic abuse and insists that abused women are not crazy, masochistic, or codependent—the latest therapeutic explanation for oppression. In addition, her remarks suggest public, material solutions—giving women options regarding jobs, housing, and child care, presumably—to aid women's escape from batterers. Professor Buel's comments struck me as an important and hopeful reminder: Despite the hegemonic force of the rhetoric of therapy in

157

contemporary American political life, every day one can find scholars and activists pushing against the personalistic and privatizing explanations of social reality offered in therapeutic discourse.

Antonio Gramsci (1936/1971) noticed in his prison writings the increasingly persuasive and pervasive power of psychotherapy. He also encouraged intellectuals to attend to the necessity of and potential for creating a counterdominant hegemony, the point at which workers and other activists articulate a common counterhegemonic perspective in revolutionary struggle.[1] In this chapter, I argue for the continuing relevance of these two sides of the hegemony coin. On the one hand, contrary to liberal and postmodern redefinitions of cultural hegemony as either happy compromise or a discursive process by which a historic bloc takes symbolic but not material power,[2] I suggest that a notion of hegemony as the persuasive means by which a ruling class maintains its power is still necessary to explain discursive phenomena such as the rhetoric of therapy. On the other hand, this conclusion points to activism and critique as counterhegemonic correctives—or antidotes—to the rhetoric of therapy.

This book has argued that in U.S. political culture, the themes and strategies of a therapeutic rhetoric have framed in terms of personal life and individual responsibility issues and problems (such as war, women's oppression, racism, exploitation, and poverty) that might better be understood in terms of structured, systemic injustice. This therapeutic rhetoric is a hegemonic discourse that shapes and contains responses to structural injustice, encouraging even feminists and Left activists and scholars to reject structural critique and public struggle.

Therapeutic discourse works within the hegemonic framework of liberal individualism, idealism, and privatism to channel social unrest and discontent into individualistic, private-sphere accommodations and adaptations. Chapter 1 developed a theory of the therapeutic as an ideological mechanism and rhetorical strategy of liberal capitalism. I argued that we must tie a theory of the therapeutic to the material interests that it serves. In Chapter 2, I argued for locating a rhetoric of therapy in the context of the rise of modern, capitalist society and its need for subjects who conceive of themselves as individual, self-responsible human agents. Later, during the consolidation of industrial capitalism, psychotherapeutic rhetorics in the workplace and in the broader society enabled managers to orient workers to the terms of wage labor on the assembly line. With regard to inegalitarian relations of class, race, and gender, the therapeutic has served to acknowledge outrage and resistance while reframing discontent as "dis-ease" in terms of individual psychological distress. In this way, the therapeutic has served the hegemony of liberal capitalism.

The case studies featured in this book also support a Gramscian interpretation of how a ruling class maintains power during times of crisis or unrest by offering persuasive messages that acknowledge "dis-ease" and thereby provide sites for audience identification and resonance with those messages. At the same time, rhetorics of therapy encourage those audiences to see those problems as purely personal rather than political in scope. As a result, public political engagement and social movement struggle have had to compete with the consolations of therapy for people's time, energy, money, and overall commitment.

The implications of this rhetoric are perhaps most serious when it is deployed in times of a national crisis such as war. One might argue that during such a crisis, in which many lives are at stake, open democratic debate should flourish. Chapter 4, however, demonstrated that during the Persian Gulf War, the rhetoric of therapy was one strategy whereby that debate was silenced in a domesticating discourse of familial support and coping. Similarly, Chapter 3 argued that in the contemporary debate over welfare and other social programs, politicians and popular culture deploy a "rhetoric of family values" to privatize social responsibility and discourage protest against racial injustice and cuts in support for struggling families. In the contexts of nationalist war propaganda and federal welfare policy, the therapeutic is a conservative rhetorical strategy of a system attempting to inoculate itself against dissent.

This book has also been concerned with the extent to which even potentially counterhegemonic political theories and movements are undermined when articulated as therapeutic. Chapter 5 argued that the therapeutic hinders achievement of feminist political goals when feminisms are defined by their shared core tenet that the personal is political. Similarly, post-Marxism, in its idealism, implicit therapeutic individualism, and political relativism, resembles the hypertherapeutic and procapitalist rhetoric of the New Age movement.

When advocates of once-radical political programs jettison their commitment to revolutionary social transformation, their retreat is often couched in therapeutic terms. Thus, the therapeutic is a rhetoric that encourages a reformist rather than revolutionary political stance. For example, the emphasis on psychological ministration and moral uplift in

the Progressive Era corresponded with a series of moderate, but benefi-
cial reforms in industrial capitalism. Recently, feminism's emphasis on
the personal as site of transformation can lead to either a political strategy
of gradual reforms in culture and consciousness in sexist society or,
worse, to a strategy of political disengagement. Post-Marxist politics,
despite its claim to Left politics and vocabulary, closely resemble liberal
reformism, especially in the call to work within the bounds of the
prevailing "democratic imaginary." Without attention to structural relations of class exploitation or a public strategy building on collective class
agency, any political program will advocate settling for what the current
system will allow.

I do not mean to suggest, however, that reforms obtainable within
existing sociopolitical relations and rhetorical constraints are worthless.
Voting rights, immigrant rights, desegregation, improvements in work
conditions, higher wages, womens' rights to reproductive choice, and
progressive reforms in health care, child care, welfare, and other social
services are worth fighting for and defending. It is dangerous, however,
to allow the therapeutic to set the bounds of our political imagination to
the extent that it becomes difficult even to conceive of revolutionary
change. Furthermore, the therapeutic asks activists to retreat from the
public struggle for even modest reforms in favor of private wound-
licking.

Therefore, although the therapy-politics continuum is just that—a
range of possible responses to social crisis and dissatisfaction and not a
simple binary opposition—it is justifiable to emphasize the debilitating
consequences of the therapeutic for social change and to pose collective,
public challenges to the capitalist system starkly against the therapeutic
recuperation of political energy in contemporary culture. The therapeutic discourse of healing, emotional support, identity constitution and
maintenance, spiritual growth, and personal identification has been a
natural ally of liberalism and capitalism. The therapeutic is rooted in
liberalism's assumptions about how change happens and how problems
are solved. This book has argued that people must be and are convinced
by the liberal ideology not only to give up their social and political being
and to perceive themselves first and foremost as individuals but also to
think of crisis, resolution, change, and stability as personal issues rather
than as structural ones. Liberalism assumes that change happens at the
level of ideas and values (idealism)[3]; that individuals are agents of their
destiny and are responsible for their own failures and successes (individu-

alism); that matters of justice and morality are individual and private and that the collective cannot decide on them (relativism); and that conflicts and differences of interest are related to the private sphere for interpersonal negotiation, and the economy and the household are separated from the site of public decision making (privatism).

An emphasis on private consumption of remedies for late capitalist distress also characterizes the therapeutic. The therapeutic is part and parcel of the constitution of the individual as private consumer, generating a discourse in whose terms people are free insofar as they can make choices of lifestyle, consumption, and identity. The personalizing of the political or the dislocation of issues of power into terms of emotional well-being and individual responsibility in the private sphere are characteristic of the public's decline. The intensification of this process—the blurring of boundaries between public life and private (Hutcheon 1989, 161-68), the pervasiveness of a shallow consumer culture that substitutes for political engagement, the rejection of "totalizing" or explanatory theories of society, and the obsession with identity and consciousness as political projects—has led some theorists to argue that we have entered a new epoch: postmodernity. I suggest that far from being a break with modern capitalism and its constitution of the subject as a private, sovereign agent, contemporary culture and its therapeutic variants represent the logical progress of liberal capitalism.

According to some theorists of postmodernity, the increasing shallowness and breadth of global cultural forms is an emancipatory expression of a new phase of late capitalism. For example, psychologist Kenneth Gergen (1991) argues that an obsession with the self as a reflexive project—the creation of a "saturated self" out of shards of globally transmitted multivocal culture—is an emancipatory characteristic of postmodernity. The case studies in this dissertation reveal that the consequences of a politics of self-constitution are not so benign. Indeed, postmodernism's focus on the self or private family as the site of political understanding and agency represents a logical development of a therapeutic imperative to translate political liberation into personal work.

Furthermore, it is doubtful that the process of self-saturation and the concomitant decline in public identification and commitment noted by Habermas (1989) are products of postmodernity. Rather, as I argued in Chapter 2, modernity is the setting for the constitution of the therapeutic self of the bourgeois subject. As part of this process, the modern family consolidates the subject as private person in the liberal ideology. As challenges to the capitalist system developed, popular and political discourse (e.g., the modern novel) worked to reinforce the ideology of individual identity, agency, and responsibility. Therefore, the therapeutic is neither new to contemporary culture nor a function of postmodern culture in particular; rather, it is a product of the exigencies of modern capitalism over the long term. Richard Sennett (1978, 262) stated, "The end of a belief in public life is not a break with nineteenth century bourgeois culture, but rather an escalation of its terms." Similarly, what contemporary theorists are hailing as "postmodernity" can be regarded as nothing more than an "escalation of the terms" of modernity. With Anthony Giddens (1991), I suggest that the rhetoric of therapy is an important characteristic of postmodernism (the ideology of late capitalism), in which "real" communities and explanatory political narratives (such as Marxism and feminism) are called into question and obsessive rituals of self-constitution take their place. Like David Harvey (1989) and Fredric Jameson (1991), I see postmodern cultural forms as the discursive support for global capital rather than as subversive celebrations of multiplicity and difference. Postmodernism represents the intensification of the dispersal of community, collective power, and meaningful public life in the late twentieth century. Harvey's (1989) argument is that postmodernism and what he calls "flexible" post-Fordist capitalism exhibit more continuity than rupture with modernism and the Fordist regime of capital accumulation. Both periods are crisis prone and governed by the logic of capitalist accumulation, generating cultural forms that call attention to social fragmentation, alienation, and disorder.

Even so, Harvey (1989) counters the excessive postmodern emphasis on incoherence and ephemerality with a call to theorize the still-stable realities of global capitalism. Harvey's claim that postmodernism is the ideological justification and reinforcement for multinational capitalism is similar to Jameson's (1991) argument that postmodernism is the "cultural logic" of late capitalism. Jameson, like Harvey, argues that far from being a chaotic state of unsystematic, heterogeneous, fragmented cultural practices, postmodernism is actually the systematic and logical manifestation of multinational ("late") capitalism. Although late capitalism produces differences in groups and representations, disconnects the signifier from the signified, and decenters the subject as agent, the mode of production is not itself disordered or impossible to explain in terms of totality. In Jameson's words, a system that produces differences is still a system. Jameson's arguments remind us that far from being the end of ideology, postmodernism itself is ideological. The point for Jameson is to map the system—ultimately, to restore consciousness of class and exploitation to subjects caught up in the dizzying impulse to retreat into therapy or "commodified micropolitics."

By commodified micropolitics, Jameson (1991) means that in the absence of public, collective political goals, politics becomes a matter of lifestyle—of consumers choosing who to be for the day. This shallow form of politics is epitomized in the therapeutic: self-help psychology, the New Age movement, and, as I have argued, in postmodernist social theories and feminisms that celebrate social fragmentation and self-definition by difference rather than by commonality.

Together, Jameson (1991) and Harvey (1989) warn us not to celebrate postmodernism's separation of time and space, production of social amnesia, fascination with cultural surface rather than historical depth, and the obsessive quest for elusive identity. Giddens's (1991, 9) thesis is that the alienating conditions of late modernity render us obsessed with the "reflexive project of the self." On a materialist critique, this project is no substitute for the traditional, collective struggle for human emancipation. In addition to demonstrating the degree to which our political life has been saturated by therapeutic rhetoric, a purpose of this work has been to argue for an alternative to therapy: a Marxist politics of public, working-class struggle for the common good, or praxis. As Richard Bernstein (1971, 63) explains, *praxis* is a central concept in Marx's thought, denoting the "essential productive dimension of human life" and emphasizing the person as historical agent and not as passive victim of economic forces. For Marx, praxis meant human activity aimed toward the revolutionary transformation of an unjust world. This transformation cannot happen if its agents behave as private, isolated individuals; rather, they must enter into public struggle with others who share their interest in changing society.

In contrast to liberal definitions of the public, which pose an idealized public of disinterested policy debate against a private sphere in which conflict and power reside, I argue for a conception of the public sphere constituted in and by struggle. Such a praxis is collective, rooted in the fight for material equality, and instrumental in the struggle against the forces of stability. This struggle assumes that suffering, exploitation, and oppression are real and not merely discursive products (although consciousness of exploitation must be rhetorically constituted). As a model of public engagement, praxis differs significantly from Habermas's (1989; see also Calhoun 1992) utopian liberal ideal in *Structural Transformation of the Public Sphere*. Seen from a Marxist perspective, Habermas's (1988) project is liberal and utopian in orientation. I hope, however, for this book to extend his critique of the increasing interpenetration of personal and political life and the displacement of critical debate by consumerist spectacle. Habermas's argument is that after the bourgeois public sphere reached its peak of vitality in the 1800s, the pressures of special-interest politics and privatized consumer capitalism began to take their toll on public life. In a society in which engaged public dialogue has been exchanged for mass culture media hype and commodity marketing, the ability to frame social issues as problems of structure and collectivity is weakened. The result is the "refeudalization" of the public sphere, in which a participatory public is exchanged for the spectacular display of power. As the sphere of the social is ever expanded to survey the most private aspects of life (e.g., in drug testing, regulation of reproduction, family life, and lifestyle), the possibility of a democratic public becomes more remote.

In contrast to a privatized social realm, Habermas (1989) poses the ideal of the public good achieved through rational debate. Habermas narrates the fate of the public sphere in contemporary capitalist society as a story of degeneration from an ideal. As Michael Schudson (as cited in Calhoun 1992, 143-64) points out, capitalism has never engendered a truly democratic realm and to the contrary has required the increasing commodification and atomization of social experience. Furthermore, liberalism's exclusion of economic relations from politics proper is an ideological buttress of capitalism. Where people are most affected by power—in their relation to work, wages, and the material necessities of life—they are granted no decision-making faculty. We do not vote over our wages, work hours, employment status, benefits, or the accessibility of child care and health care—all in realms designated under capitalism as private.

In this light, the nostalgia for the liberal public sphere is explicitly idealist. Habermas (1989) calls for a utopian sphere of public argument and decision making modeled on the polis and on the bourgeois public sphere at its height. Ultimately, Habermas defends a utopian liberalism that presumes that one can (and capitalists will voluntarily) set aside economic interests during political deliberation. He laments the emergence during the 1800s of class struggle and the labor movement as symptoms of the public's decline in interest in politics rather than of its democratic expansion. By privileging dialogue—in some imagined space of harmony and common interest—over dialectics—the process of social transformation through class struggle—his argument begs the question of whether one can achieve a democratic public life in a capitalist society divided by class in which the interests of the few control the institutional spaces, media outlets, and terms of discussion. In other words, socialism is a prerequisite of a democratic political life that cannot be "talked" into being.

Habermas's (1989) attempt to uphold the public as a realm of freedom, in addition to his rehabilitation of the modernist project of human liberation, is admirable. This vision, however, presupposes a measure of economic equality and the diminishing of the power of the market—conditions that can only be met in the present by way of a politics of struggle, in which the political is not rendered ever more pure and separate from the social (or from market forces of manipulation and domination) but is rather geared toward transforming economic relations. Clearly, the rhetoric of therapy is a mass culture strategy that works against this project.

Today, the rhetoric of therapy, combined with the liberal values of self-reliance and private transformation, has pervaded much of social life and has replaced other modes of understanding self and society. The systems of oppression and exploitation under which we live thrive on our inability to come together in meaningful ways. They thrive on the ability to sell us identities like pairs of shoes. They thrive on our isolation and fragmentation. Identities, like everything else, are for sale, produced by a cultural industry that feeds us lifestyle choices to assuage our hunger for real community life. We are asked to shoulder the responsibility for change as individuals, no matter the extent of our suffering or the structural causes of our despair. We enact rituals of self-definition and -transformation to locate ourselves in an increasingly complex world.

Therapeutic rhetoric foregrounds the tasks of emotional support and unity in the private realm, relegating to the background the public, structural, and material forces influential in our lives. In this period, we should look to Marxist critical theory and socialist organization, as well as to other progressive social movements, for public antidotes to therapy.

Liberalism relies on the therapeutic, but increasingly so do feminism and other progressive movements and ideologies. Post-Marxism is inadequate to the task of formulating an antitherapeutic politics because it rejects normative materialist criteria for struggle and itself is a symptom of therapeutic retreat from politics. Rather, we must counter the rhetoric of therapy with a discourse that insists that the society—not the individuals suffering within it—needs adjusting. Both activism and critique are necessary to the revitalization of collective political activity, organized from below, demanding justice and freedom.

Although therapeutic discourses discourage both systematic understanding of capitalist society and collective struggle against it, we can find moments suggesting that the therapeutic hegemony faces continual challenge. Opportunities small and large exist for critique and activism and could be built on to make a real challenge not only to the therapeutic but also to the unjust society that the rhetoric of therapy supports. Examples include the recent protests in defense of affirmative action on the University of Texas campus, strikes for pay increases and benefits among graduate students and staff at the University of California and Yale, the emergence of progressive and militant movements within the broader labor movement and the beginnings of renewed labor protest challenging the declining American standard of living, the 1996 demonstration for immigrant rights in Washington, and earlier marches on Washington for gay and lesbian rights and for the rights of children in the face of federal cuts in social services.

As activists become more angered and more confident in the face of cuts in services, racist scapegoating, and so on, we can expect this kind of struggle to erupt more often and in a more sustained way. In the meantime, there are continual opportunities to build social movements and to offer publics critical perspectives on contemporary society. In particular, critical scholars have an obligation to find diverse audiences and fora for our work, articulated in accessible language and designed to encourage not only more talk but also collective public action for social change.[4] Organized meetings—of socialists and progressives, civil rights advocates, and labor unions—offer one such site of political-critical engagement. In teaching, as well, we might introduce students to critical perspectives on social reality and encourage their public political engagement.[5] The envisioning and constitution of a public in struggle is a project from which we, as teachers, scholars, and activists, cannot abstain. Although therapy has its place as an enabler of individual healing after personal trauma, and sometimes as a necessary precursor to public engagement, it is inadequate as a stand-in for political activity. In contemporary culture, therapeutic narratives attempt to neutralize anger and obscure the structures of power as contexts for our work. The task at hand is an emancipatory one. We need to be present where workers and other activists struggle for justice, where people seek political explanations for their personal suffering, and where we can meet to organize against exploitation, injustice, and oppression. Only in those places, engaged in social action, can we find the antidote to therapy.

Notes

1. Gramsci (1936/1971, 333) writes, "Critical understanding of self takes place therefore through a struggle of political 'hegemonies' and of opposing directions. . . . Consciousness of being part of a particular hegemonic force . . . is the first stage towards a further progressive self-consciousness in which theory and practice will finally be one."

2. For revisions of the concept of hegemony defining hegemony as compromise or concordance, see Celeste Condit (1994) and Ernesto Laclau and Chantal Mouffe (1985). For a critique of Condit's redefinition of hegemony, see Cloud (1996).

3. It is important to distinguish therapy, as a subset of idealist rhetorical strategies, from other idealisms, particularly religion. Spiritualist and moralizing rhetorics presume a suprapersonal set of ideals and guidelines by which the individual is exhorted to live. Therapy, in contrast, is a secular rhetoric particularly appropriate to liberalism's faith in the individual as agent. It places responsibility for change and adaptation to circumstance squarely in the realm of individual personal life, without positing any community standard or collective good to which that life might be dedicated. Furthermore, the therapeutic is marked by its tendency to translate social problems into organic terms of sickness and health, positing an individual, a social, or even a national body in need of nurturance, protection, and restoration. It could be argued that therapy is to the twentieth century what religion was to the nineteenth: the dominant expression of idealist worldviews, having taken on secular rather than supernatural implications.

4. This conception of the intellectual's role is based on Gramsci's (1936/1971) notion of the organic intellectual. Gramsci writes, "The task of the intellectuals is to determine and to organise the reform of moral and intellectual life, in other words to fit culture to the sphere of practice" (453). He notes that capitalism produces its own intellectuals to further the system's ideological agenda; intellectuals should be self-conscious about their tendency to conformity and should resist the isolation, elitism, and individualism encouraged in the universities.

5. In my experience, however, pedagogy is limited as a space of political transformation. First, one's audience is not entirely voluntary and consists only of people who have been admitted to and who can afford to attend college. Second, because student evaluations of teaching (rightly) factor into professors' performance and tenure evaluations, professors must be somewhat cautious—and respectful of diverse student views—in sharing critical perspectives with students. We can use the classroom to teach engagement skills but performing acts of specific political advocacy in the classroom can be problematic for teacher and students alike. For these reasons, the classroom does not fully constitute a public in practice but rather, as University of Texas professor of rhetoric and composition Rosa Eberly (1996) has noted, a "proto-public" in "practice" (or training) for practice.

References

Adler, Jerry. 1991. "Prayers and Protests." *Newsweek* 28 Jan.: 36-39.
Agel, Jerome. 1972. *The Radical Therapist*. New York: Ballantine.
Alcoff, Linda. 1988. "Cultural Feminism vs. Post-Structuralism: The Identity Crisis in Feminist Theory." *Signs: Journal of Women in Culture and Society* 12: 405-36.
Allen, Pamela. 1973. "Free Space." *Radical Feminism*. Eds. Anne Koedt et al. New York: Quadrangle.
Althusser, Louis. 1984. "Ideology and Ideological State Apparatuses." *Essays on Ideology*. London: Verso.
American Psychological Association. 1994. *Diagnostic and Statistical Manual of Mental Disorders*. 4th ed. Washington, DC: APA.
Anderson, Perry. 1976. *Considerations on Western Marxism*. London: Verso.
———. 1991. *In the Tracks of Historical Materialism*. London: Verso.
Ariès, Philippe. 1962. *Centuries of Childhood: A Social History of Family Life*. Trans. Robert Baldick. New York: Vintage.
Baber, A. 1991. "Guerrilla Feminism." *Playboy* Oct.: 45.
Back to the Future. 1985. Dir. Roger Zemekis. Hollywood, CA: Universal Studios.
Bagdikian, Ben. 1990. *The Media Monopoly*. Boston: Beacon.
Banks, Russell. 1991. "Red, White, Blue, Yellow." *New York Times* 26 Feb.: A15.
Barrett, Michele, and Mary McIntosh. 1982. *The Anti-Social Family*. London: Verso.
Baudrillard, Jean. 1975. *Mirror of Production*. Trans. Mark Poster. St. Louis: Telos.
Bellah, Robert, et al. 1985. *Habits of the Heart*. Berkeley: U of California P.
Benderly, Beryl. 1992. "Gloria in Excess." *Washington Post*, 23 Feb.: 3.
Berger, Warren. 1995. "Childhood Traumas Healed While-U-Wait." *New York Times* 8 Jan.: 33.

Bernstein, Richard. 1971. *Praxis and Action*. Philadelphia: U of Pennsylvania P.

"Beyond the Modern." 1988. *Strategies* 1 (Special issue).

Biesecker, Barbara. 1992. "Coming to Terms With Recent Attempts to Write Women Into the History of Rhetoric." *Philosophy and Rhetoric* 25: 155-56.

Blow, Richard. 1988. "Moronic Convergence." *New Republic* 138, 25 Jan.: 27.

Bordo, Susan. 1990. "Feminism, Postmodernism, and Gender-Skepticism." *Feminism/Postmodernism*. New York: Routledge.

Boyz N the Hood. 1991. Dir. John Singleton. Los Angeles: Columbia.

Bradsher, Keith. 1996. "Rich Control More of U.S. Wealth, Study Says." *New York Times* 22 June, sec. 1: 31.

Brandley, Bill. 1996. "In Person: Reasons to March: Bill Brandley on the Costs of Poverty and Racism." *New York Times* 29 Sept., New Jersey ed., sec. NJ13: 5.

Brecher, Jeremy. 1974. *Strike!* Greenwich, CT: Fawcett.

Brice, Alfred. 1996. "As a Former Victim of Domestic Abuse, a New UT Law Professor Hopes to Teach Others Their Rights." *Daily Texan* (Austin) 5 Nov.: A1.

Broadcasting. 1991. Jan.: 23.

Brodsky, Annette, and Rachel Hare-Mustin, eds. 1980. *Women and Psychotherapy*. New York: Guilford.

Brown, Laura. 1994. *Subversive Dialogues: Theory in Feminist Therapy*. New York: HarperCollins.

———. 1996. "Current Topics in Feminist Therapy: Theory and Practice." Seminar sponsored by the Austin Women's Psychotherapy Project, 13 April, U of Texas at Austin.

Brown, Laura, and Mary S. Ballou. 1992. *Personality and Psychopathology: Feminist Reppraisals*. New York: Guilford.

Burke, Kenneth. 1969a. *Grammar of Motives*. Berkeley: U of California P. (Original work published 1945)

———. 1969b. *Rhetoric of Motives*. Berkeley: U of California P. (Original work published 1950)

Bush, Barbara. 1992. Speech. Remarks to the Republican National Convention. Text obtained from Lexis/Nexis database, 19 Aug.

Bush, George. 1991. Transcript of the comments by Bush on the air strikes against the Iraqis. *New York Times* 17 Jan., sec. A.

Butler, Judith. 1990. *Gender Trouble*. New York: Routledge.

Calhoun, Craig. 1992. *Habermas and the Public Sphere*. Cambridge: MIT P.

Calhoun, Jim, and Kevin O'Hanlon. 1991. "Just Watching War Is Stressful." *Cincinnati Enquirer* 20 Jan.: B4.

Callinicos, Alex. 1990. *Against Postmodernism*. New York: St. Martin's.

Carlson, M. 1991. "Is This What Feminism Is all About?" *Time* June: 57.

Carnegie, Andrew. 1936. *How to Win Friends and Influence People*. New York: Pocket Books.

Chesler, Phyllis. 1972. *Women and Madness*. New York: Avon.

Chopin, Kate. 1904. *The Awakening*. Chicago: H. S. Stone. (Original work published 1851)

Clarke, John. 1991. *New Times and Old Enemies*. London: HarperCollins.

Clegg, Sue. 1991. "Remains of Louis Althusser." *International Socialism* Winter: 53.

Clinton, Bill. 1992. Speech. Remarks to the NAACP National Council Conference. Text obtained from Lexis/Nexis database, 11 July.

Clinton, Hillary. 1996. *It Takes a Village to Raise a Child.* New York: Simon.

Cloud, Dana, L. 1994. "The Materiality of Discourse as Oxymoron." *Western Journal of Communication* 58: 141-63.

———. 1995. "The Rhetoric of Family Values and the Public Sphere." Argumentation and Values: Proceedings of the Ninth SCA/AFA Conference on Argumentation. Annandale, VA, Aug. 3-6. 281-89.

———. 1996. "Hegemony or Concordance? The Rhetoric of Tokenism in 'Oprah' Winfrey's Rags-to-Riches Biography." *Critical Studies in Mass Communication* 13: 115-37.

"Collective Conversations." 1991. *Public Culture* 3.2: 138.

Collins, C. A., and J. E. Clark. 1992. "A Structural Narrative Analysis of Nightline's 'This Week in the Holy Land.'" *Critical Studies in Mass Communication* 9: 25-43.

Condit, Celeste. 1994. "Hegemony in a Mass-Mediated Society: Concordance About Reproductive Technologies." *Critical Studies in Mass Communication* 11: 205-30.

Coontz, Stephanie. 1988. *Social Origins of Private Life.* London: Verso.

———. 1992. *The Way We Never Were: American Families and the Nostalgia Trap.* New York: HarperCollins.

Cott, Nancy. 1977. *Bonds of Womanhood.* New Haven, CT: Yale UP.

Coyle, Kelly, and Debra Grodin. 1993. "Self-Help Books and the Construction of Reading." *Text and Performance Quarterly* 13: 61-78.

Creighton, Jane. 1991. "War at Home." *Mother Jones* May/June: 22-3.

Cushman, Philip. 1990. "Why the Self Is Empty: Toward a Historically Situated Psychology." *American Psychologist* 45.5: 599-611.

———. 1995. *Constructing the self, Constructing America.* Reading, MA: Addison-Wesley.

Daniels, Tom, et al. 1997. *Perspectives on Organizational Communication.* Madison, WI: Brown & Benchmark.

Dargis, M. 1991. "Female Trouble: Guns N' Poses." *Village Voice* 16 July: 22.

de Goede, Marieke. 1996. "Ideology in the U.S. Welfare Debate." *Discourse and Society* 7(3): 327.

Deleuze, Gilles, and Félix Guattari. 1983. *Anti-Oedipus: Capitalism and Schizophrenia.* Trans. Robert Hurley et al. Minneapolis: U of Minnesota P.

Denby, David. 1993. "Menace II Society." *New York* 31 May: 54-5.

Derber, Charles. 1995. *What's Left?* Amherst: U of Massachusetts P.

Dizard, James, and Howard Gadlin. 1990. *The Minimal Family.* Amherst: U of Massachusetts P.

Donzelot, Jacques. 1979. *The Policing of Families.* New York: Pantheon.

Doody-Vermilya. 1991. "The World Over, Women's Progress Is Uneven." *New York Times* 30 June, sec. 4: 14.

Dyson, Michael. 1992. "Between Apocalypse and Redemption: John Singleton's Boyz N the Hood." *Cultural Critique* Spring: 121-41.

———. 1993. *Reflecting Black.* Minneapolis: U of Minnesota P.

———. 1996. *Between God and Gangsta Rap.* New York: Oxford UP.

Eagleton, Terry. 1991. *Ideology: An Introduction.* London: Verso.

Eberly, Rosa. 1996. "Classrooms as Proto-Public Spheres." Paper presented at the annual meeting of the Modern Language Association, Washington, DC, Dec.

Ebert, Teresa. 1992/1993. "Ludic Feminism, the Body, Performance, and Labor: Bringing Materialism Back Into Feminist Cultural Studies." *Cultural Critique* 23: 5-48.

———. 1996. *Ludic Feminism and After.* Ann Arbor: U of Michigan P.

Echols, Alice. 1989. *Daring to be Bad: Radical Feminism in America.* Minneapolis: U of Minnesota P.

Ehrenreich, Barbara, and Deidre English. 1978. *For Her Own Good: 150 Years of the Experts' Advice to Women.* New York: Anchor.

Eliasoph, N. 1988. "Routines and the Making of Oppositional News." *Critical Studies in Mass Communication* 5: 313-34.

Engels, Friedrich. 1978a. "Socialism: Utopian and Scientific." *The Marx-Engels Reader.* Ed. R. Tucker. 2nd ed. New York: Doubleday.

———. 1978b. "The Origin of the Family, Private-Property, and the State." *The Marx-Engels Reader.* Ed. R. Tucker. 2nd ed. New York: Doubleday.

English, Dierdre. 1992. "She's Her Weakness Now." *New York Times* 2 Feb.: 13.

Epstein, E. J. 1973. *News From Nowhere.* New York: Random House.

Etzioni, Amitai. 1993. *Spirit of Community.* New York: Crown.

"Ex-Marxism Without Substance." 1988. *New Left Review* 169: 34-62.

Faludi, Susan. 1991. *Backlash: The Undeclared War on American Women.* New York: Crown.

Fenner, Elizabeth. 1994. "Generation X Strikes Back." *Money* June: 90ff.

Fiske, John. 1986. "Television: Polysemy and Popularity." *Critical Studies in Mass Communication* 3: 391-408.

Flacks, Richard. 1988. *Making History.* New York: Columbia UP.

Flax, Jane. 1990. *Thinking Fragments: Psychoanalysis, Feminism, Postmodernism.* Berkeley: U of California P.

Foner, Eric. 1990. *A Short History of Reconstruction.* New York: Harper.

Foucault, Michel. 1973. *Madness and Civilization.* Trans. Richard Howard. New York: Vintage.

———. 1980. *History of Sexuality.* Trans. Robert Hurley. Vol. 1. New York: Vintage.

———. 1987. *Mental Illness and Psychology.* Trans. Alan Sheridan. Berkeley: U of California P. (Original work published 1954)

Frank, Leroy. 1988. "Psychiatry as a Form of Oppression." *Issues in Radical Therapy* 13: 60-6.

Franks, Gary. 1992. Speech. Remarks to the Republican National Convention. Text obtained from Lexis/Nexis database, 18 Aug.

Frazier, E. Franklin. 1951. *The Negro Family in the United States.* New York: Dryden.

Friedan, Betty. 1963. *The Feminine Mystique.* New York: Dell.
Galbraith, Jane. 1992. "A: South Central (Q: What Movie Didn't Open in L.A.?)" *Los Angeles Times* 27 Sept., home edition: 25.
Gannett Foundation. 1991. *The Media at War.* New York: Media Studies Center.
Gans, Herbert. 1979. *Deciding What's News.* New York: Pantheon.
Garnham, Nicholas. 1995. "Political Economy and Cultural Studies: Reconciliation or Divorce?" *Critical Studies in Mass Communication* 12: 62-71.
"Generation X-Onomics." 1994. *Economist* 19 March: 27.
Geras, Norman. 1987. "Post-Marxism." *New Left Review* 163: 40-82.
Geras, Norman. 1988. "Ex-Marxism Without Substance." *New Left Review* 169: 34-62.
Gergen, Kenneth. 1991. *The Saturated Self: Dilemmas of Identity in Contemporary Life.* New York: HarperCollins.
Gibbs, Nancy. 1991a. "The Homefront: A First Thick Shock of War." *Time* 28 Jan.: 34.
Gibbs, Nancy. 1991b. "The Home Front: Land That They Love." *Time* 4 Feb.: 52.
Giddens, Anthony. 1991. *Modernity and Self-Identity.* Stanford, CA: Stanford UP.
Gilman, Charlotte Perkins. 1899. *The Yellow Wallpaper.* Boston: Small, Maynard.
Gilroy, Paul. 1992. "It's a Family Affair." *Black Popular Culture.* Ed. Gina Dent. Seattle: Bay Press.
Gitlin, Todd. 1979a. "News as Ideology and Contested Arena: Toward a Theory of Hegemony, Crisis, and Opposition." *Socialist Review* 9.6: 11-54.
———. 1979b. "Prime-Time Ideology: The Hegemonic Process in Television Entertainment." *Social Problems* 26.3: 251-66.
———. 1980. *The Whole World Is Watching: Mass Media in the Making and Unmaking of the New Left.* Berkeley: U of California P.
———. 1987. *The Sixties: Years of Hope, Days of Rage.* New York: Bantam.
———. 1995. *Twilight of Common Dreams.* Berkeley: U of California P.
Gitlin, Todd, and Daniel Hallin. 1992. "Prowess and Community: The Gulf War as Popular Culture and as Television Drama." Paper presented at the 42nd Annual Conference of the International Communication Association, Miami, FL, May.
The Godfather. 1972. Dir. Francis Ford Coppola. Hollywood, CA: Paramount Pictures.
Goffman, Erving. 1961. *Asylums.* Chicago: Aldine.
Gottlieb, Martin. 1995. "Not Guilty: The Racial Prism." *New York Times* 4 Oct.: A1.
Gramsci, Antonio. 1971. *Selections From the Prison Notebooks.* Trans. Quentin Hoare and G. N. Smith. New York: International. (Original work published 1936)
Gray, Herman. 1989. "Television, Black Americans, and the American Dream." *Critical Studies in Mass Communication* 6: 376-86.
Greenberg, H. R. 1991/1992. "Thelma and Louise's Exuberant Polysemy." *Film Quarterly* 45: 20-1.

Grob, Gerald. 1983. *Mental Illness and American Society, 1875-1940.* Princeton, NJ: Princeton UP.
————. 1985. *The Inner World of American Psychiatry, 1890-1940.* New Brunswick, NJ: Rutgers UP.
Grodin, Debra. 1991. "The Interpreting Audience: The Therapeutics of Self-Help Book Reading." *Critical Studies in Mass Communication* 8.4: 404-21.
Grossberg, Lawrence. 1995. "Cultural Studies vs. Political Economy: Is Anyone Else Bored?" *Critical Studies in Mass Communication* 12: 72-81.
Grove, L. 1992. "Women With a Ticket to Ride." *Washington Post* 16 July: C1.
Habermas, Jurgen. 1989. *Structural Transformation of the Public Sphere.* Trans. Thomas Burger. Cambridge: MIT P.
Hall, Stuart. 1986. "Variants of Liberalism." *Politics and Ideology.* Eds. J. Donald and S. Hall. Philadelphia: Open University P. 34-69.
————. 1988. "Brave New World." *Marxism Today* Oct.: 24-28.
Hallin, Daniel. 1986. *The Uncensored War: The Media and Vietnam.* New York: Oxford UP.
————. 1991. "TV's Clean Little War." *Bulletin of Atomic Scientists* 47: 17-24.
Hanisch, Carole. 1971. "The Personal Is Political." *The Radical Therapist.* New York: Ballantine. 152-57.
Harman, Chris. 1984. "Women's Liberation and Revolutionary Socialism." *International Socialism* 23: 4-41.
Harris, Thomas. 1969. *I'm OK, You're OK.* New York: Avon.
Hartmann, Heidi. 1981. "The Unhappy Marriage of Marxism and Feminism." *Women and Revolution.* Ed. Lydia Sargent. Boston: South End. 1-42.
Hartz, Louis. 1955. *The Liberal Tradition in America.* New York: Harcourt.
Harvey, David. 1989. *The Condition of Postmodernity.* London: Basil Blackwell.
Herman, Ellen. 1995. *Romance of American Psychology.* Berkeley: U of California P.
Herman, Ellen, and Noam Chomsky. 1988. *Manufacturing Consent.* New York: Pantheon.
Hillman, James, and Michael Ventura. 1992. *We've Had a Hundred Years of Psychotherapy and the World's Just Getting Worse.* San Francisco: Harper.
Hofstadter, Richard. 1955. *The Age of Reform.* New York: Random House.
hooks, bell. 1990. *Yearning: Race, Gender, and Cultural Politics.* Boston: South End.
Howard, Ronald. 1981. *History of Family Sociology: A Social History of American Family Sociology, 1865-1940.* Westport, CT: Greenwood.
Hughes, Harriet M. 1940. *News and the Human Interest Story.* New York: Greenwood.
Hutcheon, Linda. 1989. *The Politics of Postmodernism.* London: Routledge.
"Introduction." 1988. *Rethinking Marxism* 1: 5-13.
Jaggar, Alison. 1983. *Feminist Politics and Human Nature.* Totowa, NJ: Rowman & Littlefield.
Jameson, Fredric. 1979/1980. "Reification and Utopia in Mass Culture." *Social Text* 1: 130-48.

————. 1991. *Postmodernism: Or, the Cultural Logic of Late Capitalism.* Durham, NC: Duke UP.

Jeffrey, Don. 1993. "Joint Project From Jive, New Line Poses Menace II Society." *Billboard* 24 April: 47.

Joeres, R. B., and B. Laslett. 1992. "Psychoanalysis and Feminism: Current Controversies." *Signs: Journal of Women in Culture and Society* 17: 5-6.

Katz, Alfred. 1993. *Self-Help in America: A Social Movement Perspective.* New York: Twayne.

Katzell, Raymond, and James Austin. 1992. "From Then to Now: The Development of Industrial-Organizational Psychology in the United States." *Journal of Applied Psychology* 77: 803-35.

Kauffman, L. A. 1992. "Tofu Politics." *Utne Reader* March/April: 74.

Kellner, Douglas. 1990. *Television and the Crisis of Democracy.* Boulder, CO: Westview.

————. 1992. *The Persian Gulf TV War.* Boulder, CO: Westview.

Kelly, Florence. 1987. "The Women at Hull House." *Women's America.* Eds. Linda Kerber and Jan DeHart-Matthews. New York: Oxford UP.

Kobren, Gerri. 1991. "War on Our Peace of Mind." *Baltimore Sun* 5 Feb.: 1D.

Kolko, Gabriel. 1963. *The Triumph of Conservatism: A Reinterpretation of American History, 1900-1916.* London: Free Press.

Kramer, Peter D. 1993. *Listening to Prozac.* New York: Penguin.

Krupp, C. 1991. "Why Thelma and Louise Scares the Devil out of Men—and Some Women." *Glamour* Aug.: 142.

Laclau, Ernesto, and Chantal Mouffe. 1985. *Hegemony and Socialist Strategy.* Trans. W. Moore and P. Cammack. London: Verso.

————. 1987. "Post-Marxism Without Apologies." *New Left Review* 167: 79-106.

Laing, R. D. 1967. *The Politics of Experience.* New York: Ballantine.

Lasch, Christopher. 1977. *Haven in a Heartless World.* New York: Basic.

————. 1979. *The Culture of Narcissism.* New York: Warner Books.

————. 1984. *The Minimal Self: Psychic Survival in Troubled Times.* New York: Norton.

Laslett, Peter. 1972. *Household and Family in Past Time.* Cambridge, UK: Cambridge UP.

Lazarus, N. 1991. "Doubting the New World Order." *Differences* 3.5: 94-138.

Lears, T. J. Jackson. 1981. *No Place of Grace: Antimodernism and the Transformation of American Culture, 1880-1920.* New York: Pantheon.

————. 1983. "From Salvation to Self-Realization: Advertising and the Therapeutic Roots of Consumer Culture." *The Culture of Consumption.* Eds. T. J. J. Lears and R. Wightman. New York: Pantheon. 1-38.

Leo, John. 1991a. "Community and Personal Duty." *U.S. News & World Report* 28 Jan.: 17.

————. 1991b. "Toxic Feminism on the Big Screen." *U.S. News & World Report* 10 June: 20.

Leonard, Peter. 1984. *Personality and Ideology.* London: Macmillan.

Leto deFrancisco, Victoria, ed. 1995. "Helping Ourselves." *Women's Studies in Communication* 18.2 (Special issue).
Leuchtenburg, William E. 1958. *Perils of Prosperity, 1941-1952*. Chicago: U of Chicago P.
Livingstone, Sonia, and Tamar Liebes. 1995. "Where Have all the Mothers Gone?" *Critical Studies in Mass Communication* 12: 155-75.
Loeb, Paul Rogat. 1994. *Generation at the Crossroads: Apathy and Action on the American Campus*. New Brunswick, NJ: Rutgers UP.
MacIntyre, Alasdair. 1984. *After Virtue*. Notre Dame: U of Notre Dame P.
MacKinnon, Catharine. 1989. *Toward a Feminist Theory of the State*. Cambridge, MA: Harvard UP.
Maio, K. 1991. "Film: Women Who Murder for the Man." *Ms.* Nov./Dec.: 82-4.
Makay, John. 1980. "Psychotherapy as Rhetoric for Secular Grace." *Central States Speech Journal* 31: 184-96.
Mander, A. V., and A. K. Rush. 1974. *Feminism as Therapy*. New York: Random House.
Marx, Karl. 1978a. "Theses on Feuerbach." *The Marx-Engels Reader*. Ed. R. Tucker. 2nd ed. New York: Norton. (Original work published 1888)
———. 1978b. "On the Jewish Question." *The Marx-Engels Reader*. Ed. R. Tucker. 2nd ed. New York: Norton. (Original work published 1843)
"Marxism Now." 1990. *Rethinking Marxism* 3 (Special issue).
Maslin, Janet. 1991. "Lay off Thelma and Louise." *New York Times* 21 July, sec. 2: 11.
Masson, Jeffrey. 1988. *Against Therapy*. Monroe, ME: Common Courage.
Massood, Paula. 1993. "Menace II Society." *Cineaste* 20.4: 44-6.
May, Elaine Tyler. 1988. *Homeward Bound: American Families in the Cold War Era*. New York: Basic Books.
May, Les. 1991. "UI Professor Claims TV Dictates Opinions." *The Daily Iowan* (Iowa City) 7 Feb.: 3A.
Mayo, Elton. 1933. *The Human Problem of an Industrial Civilization*. New York: Macmillan.
McGuire, Ellen. 1992. "I'm Dysfunctional, You're Dysfunctional" (review of Kaminer). *Nation* 255, 28 Dec.: 818-913.
Menace II Society. 1993. Dirs. Allen Hughes and Albert Hughes. Los Angeles: New Line.
Merelman, Richard. 1995. *Representing Black Culture*. New York: Routledge.
Milton S. Eisenhower Foundation. 1993. *Investing in Children and Youth, Reconstructing Our Cities: Doing What Works to Reverse the Betrayal of American Democracy*. Washington, DC: Milton S. Eisenhower Foundation.
Mintz, Steven, and Susan Kellogg. 1988. *Domestic Revolutions: A Social History of American Family Life*. New York: Free Press.
Mirkin, Marsha Pravder, ed. 1990. *The Social and Political Contexts of Family Therapy*. Boston: Allyn.
Mitchell, Juliet. 1974. *Psychoanalysis and Feminism*. New York: Vintage.
Modleski, Tania. 1991. *Feminism Without Women*. New York: Routledge.

Molnar, Alex. 1991. "If My Marine Son Is Killed." *The Gulf War Reader.* Eds. Micha Sifry and Christopher Cerf. New York: Times Books/Random House.

Moore, Steve. 1991. "Psychologist Offers Advice on War Stress." *Berkshire Eagle* 3 Feb.: B1.

Morgan, Robin. 1991. "Digressions." *Ms.* March/April: 1.

Morton, Donald, and Mas'ud Zavarzadeh. 1994. *Theory as Resistance: Politics and Culture After Poststructuralism.* New York: Guilford.

Mouffe, Chantal. 1988a. "Hegemony and New Political Subjects: Toward a New Concept of Democracy." *Marxism and the Interpretation of Culture.* Eds. Cary Nelson and Larry Grossberg. Urbana: U of Illinois P. 89-104.

———. 1988b. "Radical Democracy: Modern or Postmodern?" *Universal Abandon: The Politics of Postmodernism.* Ed. Andrew Ross. Minneapolis: U of Minnesota P. 31-45.

———. 1990. "Radical Democracy or Liberal Democracy?" *Socialist Review* 20: 57-66.

Mouzelis, N. 1988. "Marxism of Post-Marxism." *New Left Review* 167: 107-23.

"Mr. Clinton's Duty on Welfare." 1996. Editorial. *New York Times* 25 July: A22.

Mulhall, Stephen, and Adam Swift. 1992. *Liberals and Communitarians.* Oxford, UK: Blackwell.

Myers, Charles. 1977. *Industrial Psychology.* New York: ArNo. (Original work published 1925)

Neusner, Noam. 1991. "War Support Groups Help Loved Ones Cope." *Baltimore Sun* 6 Feb: G1.

New Age Journal. 1990. Jan./Feb.

New York Radical Feminists. 1973. "Politics of the Ego." *Radical Feminism.* Eds. Anne Koedt et al. New York: Quadrangle.

Nicholson, Linda. 1990. *Feminism/Postmodernism.* New York: Routledge.

O'Connor, John. 1991. "War Takes Toll on TV Viewers." *San Francisco Examiner* 25 Jan.: A1.

"On Transformation Now." 1995. *Transformation* 1: i-iv.

Paglia, Camille. 1992. *Sex, Art, and American Culture.* New York: Vintage.

Palmer, Brian. 1990. *Descent Into Discourse.* Philadelphia: Temple UP.

Pateman, Carole. 1989. *Feminist Critiques of the Public/Private Dichotomy. The Disorder of Women.* Oxford: Blackwell. 118-40.

Payne, Carol. 1973. "Consciousness-Raising: A Dead End?" *Radical Feminism.* Eds. Anne Koedt et al. New York: Quadrangle.

Payne, David. 1989. *Coping With Failure: The Therapeutic Uses of Rhetoric.* Columbia: U of South Carolina P.

Peale, Norman Vincent. 1952. *The Power of Positive Thinking.* New York: Prentice Hall.

Pear, Robert. 1996. "In Les May. Poor May Take the Brunt of Deficit-Cutting This Year." *New York Times* 25 July: A21.

Phelan, Shane. 1989. *Identity Politics: Lesbian Feminism and the Limits of Community.* Philadelphia: Temple UP.

Phillips, Derek. 1993. *Looking Backward: A Critical Appraisal of Communitarian Thought.* Princeton, NJ: Princeton UP.

Phillips, Kevin. 1990. *Politics of Rich and Poor.* New York: Random House.
Piven, Frances Fox, and Richard Cloward. 1993. *Regulating the Poor: The Functions of Public Welfare.* New York: Vintage. (Original work published 1971)
Popenoe, David. 1994. "Fostering the New Familism: A Goal for America." *Responsive Community: Rights and Responsibilities* 2.4.
Poussaint, Alvin. 1996. "Single Parent Families: Implications for American Society." Bernice Milburn Moore Memorial Lecture, Austin, TX, Oct. 8.
Price Pritchett and Associates. 1994. *New Work Habits for a Radically Changing World.* Dallas: Price Pritchett and Associates.
Quayle, Dan. 1991. "American Support for Desert Shield: Address before the U.S. Gulf Forces, Saudi Arabia." U.S. Dept. of State Dispatch, 7 Jan.: 4.
———. 1992a. Speech. Remarks to the Commonwealth Club of California. Federal News Service Wire, Lexis/Nexis database, 18 May.
———. 1992b. "A Great Society Is Based on Values." *St. Louis Post-Dispatch* 24 May: 3B.
Quayle, Dan, and Diane Medved. 1996. *The American Family.* New York: HarperCollins.
Quayle, Marilyn. 1992a. Interview. *Larry King Live.* CNN. 18 Aug.
———. 1992b. Speech. Remarks to the Republican National Convention. Text obtained from Lexis/Nexis database, 19 Aug.
Rapping, Elayne. 1996. *The Culture of Recovery: Making Sense of the Self-Help Movement in Women's Lives.* Boston: Beacon.
Rawls, John. 1971. *A Theory of Justice.* Cambridge, MA: Harvard UP.
Reality Bites. 1994. Dir. Ben Stiller. Los Angeles: Palomar Pictures.
Reinhold, Robert. 1991. "Tensions Crackle as Reality Invades." *New York Times* 17 Jan.: A10.
Religion News Service. 1995. "Focus on the Family: Farrakhan the Latest Voice in a Chorus Calling for Old Fashioned Values." Text obtained from Lexis/Nexis database, 21 Oct.
Rich, Adrienne. 1980. "Compulsory Heterosexuality and Lesbian Existence." *Signs: Journal of Women in Culture and Society* 5: 631-60.
Rieff, Philip. 1966. *The Triumph of the Therapeutic: Uses of Faith After Freud.* New York: Harper.
Roberts, Steven. 1991. "New Generation, Old Lessons." *U.S. News & World Report* 4 March: 11.
Robertson, Pat. 1992. Speech. Remarks to the Republican National Convention. Text obtained from Lexis/Nexis database, 19 Aug.
Roethlisberger, Fritz J., and William Dickson. 1939. *Management and the Worker: An Account of a Research Program Conducted by the Western Electric Company, Hawthorne Works, Chicago.* Cambridge, MA: Harvard UP.
Roethlisberger, F. J., et al. 1954. *Training for Human Relations.* Boston: Harvard UP.
Rohter, L. 1991. "The Third Woman of Thelma and Louise." *New York Times* 5 June: C21.
Roiphe, Katie. 1993. *The Morning After: Sex, Fear, and Feminism on Campus.* Boston: Little, Brown.

Rose, Nikolas. 1990. *Governing the Soul.* New York: Routledge.

Rosenthal, Andrew. 1992. "Quayle's Moment." *New York Times Magazine* 8 July: 32.

Rosenthal, N. B. 1984. "Consciousness-Raising: From Revolution to Re-evaluation." *Psychology of Women Quarterly* 8: 309-26.

Rossman, M. 1979. *New Age Blues: On the Politics of Consciousness.* New York: E. P. Dutton.

Rucinski, Dianne. 1992. "Personalized Bias in the News: The Potency of the Particular." *Communication Research* 19.1: 91-108.

Rustin, M. 1989. "The Politics of Post-Fordism." *New Left Review* 175, May/June: 54-77.

Rybcynski, Witold. 1987. *Home.* New York: Penguin.

Sandel, Michael. 1982. *Liberalism and the Limits of Justice.* Cambridge, UK: Cambridge UP.

Sataline, Suzanne. 1991. "Kids and War: Tempering Reality With Reassurance." *Hartford Courant* 3 Feb.

Satin, Mark. 1978. *New Age Politics.* New York: Dell.

Schor, Juliet. 1991. *The Overworked American.* New York: Basic Books.

Schnickel, R. 1991. "Gender Bender." *Time* 24 June: 52-56.

Schudson, Michael. 1992. "Was There Ever a Public Sphere?" *Habermas and the Public Sphere.* Ed. Craig Calhoun. Cambridge: MIT P. 143-64.

Schwartz, Nancy L. 1979. "The Distinction Between Public and Private Life: Marx on the Zoon Politicon." *Political Theory* 7: 245-66

Scott, Steve. 1991. "Families Favor Blackout." *Dallas Morning-News* 25 Feb.

Selby, Holly. 1991. "24-Hour War Coverage Makes Viewers Anxious." *Baltimore Sun* 23 Jan.: 1D.

Sennett, Richard. 1978. *The Fall of Public Man.* New York: Vintage.

Shapiro, L. 1991. "Women Who Kill too Much." *Newsweek* 17 June: 63.

Shawki, Ahmed. 1990. "Black Liberation and Socialism in the United States." *International Socialism* 47, Summer: 36-40.

Shorter, Edwin. 1975. *The Making of the Modern Family.* New York: Basic Books.

Shreve, Anita. 1989. *Women Together, Women Alone: The Legacy of the Consciousness-Raising Movement.* New York: Viking.

Simon, J. 1991. "Movie of the Moment." *National Review* 8 July: 48-50.

Simonds, Wendy. 1992. *Women and Self-Help Culture.* New Brunswick, NJ: Rutgers UP.

Sklar, Martin J. 1988. *The Corporate Reconstruction of American Capitalism, 1890-1916.* New York: Cambridge UP.

Smith, Page. 1985. *A People's History of the Progressive Era and World War I.* Vol. 7 of *People's History of the United States.* New York: McGraw-Hill.

Smith, Sharon. 1992. "Twilight of the American Dream." *International Socialism* 54: 3-44.

———. 1994. "Mistaken Identity." *International Socialism* 62, Spring: 3-50.

Smith, Vern, and Annetta Miller. 1991. " 'One Big Family' in Crystal Springs." *Newsweek* 28 Jan.: 39-40.

Snitow, Anne. 1989. "Pages From a Gender Diary: Basic Divisions in Feminism." *Dissent* 36, Spring: 205-24.

Solomon, Neil. 1980. *Family Therapy and Social Change.* New York: Irvington.

Sorensen, J., and E. Cudlipp. 1973. *The New Way to Become the Person You'd Like to Be.* New York: Makay.

South Central. 1992. Dir. Steve Andersen. Los Angeles: Warner Brothers.

St. Pierre, Maurice. 1991. "Reaganomics and Its Implications for African-American Family Life." *Journal of Black Studies* 21.3: 325-40.

Stabile, Carol. 1994. "Feminism Without Guarantees." *Rethinking Marxism* 7.

Stacey, Judith. 1994. "The New Family Values Crusaders." *Nation* 25 July/4 Aug.: 120.

Staples, Robert. 1987. "Social Structure and Black Family Life." *Journal of Black Studies* 17.3: 270.

Staples, Robert, and Leanor Boulin Johnson. 1993. *Black Families at the Crossroads: Challenges and Prospects.* San Francisco: Jossey-Bass.

Starker, Steven. 1989. *Oracle at the Supermarket.* New Brunswick, NJ: Transaction.

Statt, David. 1994. *Psychology and the World of Work.* London: Macmillan.

Steinem, Gloria. 1991. "Gross National Self-Esteem." *Ms.* Nov./Dec.: 224.

———. 1992. *Revolution From Within: A Book of Self-Esteem.* Boston: Little, Brown.

Sternhell, Carol. 1992. "Sic Transit Gloria." *Women's Review of Books* 9, June: 3-6.

Swift, Edgar James. 1919. *Psychology and the Day's Work.* New York: Scribner's.

Szasz, Thomas. 1970. *Manufacture of Madness.* New York: Harper.

———. 1984. *The Therapeutic State.* Buffalo, NY: Prometheus.

Terry, Diane. 1995a. "Black March Stirs Passion and Protests." *New York Times* 8 Oct., sec. 1: 24.

———. 1995b. "Family Values: Marching to the Beat of a Million Drummers." *New York Times* 15 Oct., sec. 4: 1.

Tevlin, Jonathan. 1992. "Why Women Are Mad as Hell." *Glamour* March: 206-09ff.

Texas et al. v. Cheryl J. Hopwood. 1996. 5th Circuit Federal Appeals Court, case No. 95-1773.

Thelma & Louise. 1991. Dir. Ridley Scott. Written by Callie Khouri. Culver City, CA: Metro-Goldwyn-Mayer.

Thomas, B. 1991. "The Bad News Bearers at CNN." *Los Angeles Times* 3 March: 16.

Tuchman, Gaye. 1978. *Making News.* New York: Free Press.

Upton, James. 1985. "The Politics of Urban Violence." *Journal of Black Studies* 15: 243-58.

Vanderbilt Television News Archive Index and Abstracts. Nov. 1990-March 1991; Nov. 1991. Nashville, TN: Vanderbilt University. http://tvnews.vanderbilt.edu.

Veroff, J., R. Kulka, and E. Douvan. 1981a. *Mental Health in America: Patterns of Help-Seeking From 1957-1976.* New York: Basic Books.

———. 1981b. *The Inner American.* New York: Basic Books.

Viteles, Morris S. 1932. "Psychology and Industry." *Psychology at Work*. Ed. Paul S. Achilles. New York: McGraw-Hill.

Voss, Randi. 1995. *American Women! Will You Save Your Country?* Diss. U of Texas at Austin.

Wallace, Michelle. 1992. "Boyz N the Hood and Jungle Fever." *Black Popular Culture*. Ed. Gina Dent. Seattle: Bay Press. 125.

Walzer, Michael. 1990. "The Communitarian Critique of Liberalism." *Political Theory* 18, Feb.: 6-23.

Weedon, Chris. 1987. *Feminist Practice and Poststructuralist Theory*. Oxford, UK: Blackwell.

Weiss, Richard. 1969. *American Myth of Success*. New York: Basic Books.

Welter, Barbara. 1966. "The cult of true womanhood." *American Quarterly* 18: 151-74.

Whalen, Jack, and Richard Flacks. 1989. *Beyond the Barricades: The Sixties Generation Grows Up*. Philadelphia: Temple UP.

Whalen, Susan. 1996. "Therapeutic Constitutions of Shop-Floor Speech." Paper presented at the 1996 convention of the Speech Communication Association, San Diego, CA, Nov.

White, Mimi. 1992. *Teleadvising: Therapeutic Discourse in American Television*. Chapel Hill: U of North Carolina P.

Willis, Ellen. 1984. "Radical Feminism and Feminist Radicalism." *The Sixties Without Apology*. Eds. Sonya Sayres, A. Stephanson, Stanley Aronowitz, and Fredric Jameson. Minneapolis: U of Minnesota P.

Wilson, L. 1988. "The Aging of Aquarius." *American Demographics* 10, 7 Sept.: 34-7, 60-1.

"Where We've Been: From Abbie and Jerry to Ben and Jerry's." 1990. *New Age Journal* Jan./Feb.: 39.

Wood, Alice Meiksins. 1986. *The Retreat From Class*. London: Verso.

Wood, Julia. 1993. *Who Cares? Women, Care, and Culture*. Carbondale: U of Southern Illinois P.

Zaretsky, Eli. 1976. *Capitalism, the Family, and Personal Life*. New York: Harper Colophon.

Index

history of, 27
humanistic, 144
industrial, 38-42
language of, 28
self-help movement and, 29-35
Psychotherapy:
  history of, 23-54
  language of, 13
  repressive use of, 2
  See also Therapy
Public apathy, 152, 153
Public sphere, refeudalization of, 164

Quayle, Dan, 61-62, 78, 79
Quayle, Marilyn, 65, 66-67

Race:
  class and, 60-61
  family therapy discourse and, 57
  family values debate and, 53, 57, 59-63
Racial conflict:
  1990s, 53
  therapeutic discourse and, 4
Racism:
  police and, 73
  Reconstruction and, 42
  social crises sparked by, 53
Racist scapegoating, 64, 69
Radical feminism, 105, 109, 110-112, 116-125, 128
Radical Reconstruction, 42
Radical social movements, 151
Radical therapy, 6, 7-10
Rapping, Elayne, 103, 110
Rawls, John, 16
Reagan, Ronald, 73
Reconciliation, 7
Recovery movement, 110
Redemption, 2
Relativism, 161
Repressive use of psychotherapy, 2
Resistance, 14
  feminism and, 104
  to hegemonic ideas, 87
  translated to dis-ease, 4, 24-25, 31
Revolutionary struggle, 158
Revolution From Within (Steinem), 106, 112, 113-116
Rich, A., 122
Rieff, Philip, 15, 17, 31, 49
Robertson, Pat, 65, 80
Roethlisberger, F. J., 23, 38-39

Roiphe, Katie, 124
Rose, Nikolas, 13, 14, 58
Rossman, Michael, 144

Satin, Mark, 133, 140-149, 153
Scapegoating, 2
  family values discourse and, 60-63
  mentally ill, 12
  racist, 64, 69
Schor, J., 67-68
Schwartz, Nancy, 109
Scientific management, 37, 38
Secular grace, 2
Self:
  capitalism and sense of, 26, 161
  saturated, 161
Self-absorption, 2, 8, 25
Self-actualization, 144
  consumption and, 32
  workers and, 4
Self-care, 18
Self-creation, 28
Self-definition, 13
Self-determination, 24
Self-development, obsession with, 36
Self-esteem:
  feminism and, 106, 113-114
  New Age movement and, 148
Self-expression, 8, 24, 28, 32, 48-49, 140
Self-fulfillment, 1960s, 50
Self-help, 2, 24, 29-35
  blacks and, 76
  liberal feminists and, 113-114
  nationalist, 76
  social crises and, 4
  women and, 5-6, 33-34, 43-44
  workers and, 41
Self-reliance, 24, 49
Sennett, R., 162
Separation, culture of, 17
Service economy, 52
Sexual activity, premarital, 63
Sexual identity, 106
Sickness, narratives of, 2
Simon, John, 121-122
Simonds, Wendy, 33-34
Single-parent families, 59, 63
Singleton, John, 69, 76
Slaves, 42
Smith, P., 46
Smith, Sharon, 13, 50
Soap opera narratives, 5

About the Author

Dana L. Cloud, PhD, is a Professor in the department of Speech Communication at the University of Texas at Austin. Her articles critiquing racism and sexism in political and popular culture and defending the materialist tradition of ideology criticism have appeared in the journals *Critical Studies in Mass Communication* and *Western Journal of Communication* and as chapters in a number of books. She is continuing her study of the rhetoric of family values and making progress on a new project about the rhetorical crafting of cross-gender and cross-racial solidarity in the 1930s U.S. labor movement.